British Policy in Aden and the Protectorates 1955–67

This book provides the first detailed account of the confrontation which took place between Britain and President Nasser of Egypt over the Colony of Aden and the surrounding protected states, prior to British withdrawal in 1967. Particular attention is paid to the conflicting goals of Arab nationalism and British imperialism, suggesting that Britain's motivation for this campaign was not solely material but was partly derived from a determination to contain Nasser's influence and to guarantee a continuation of Britain's role in influencing the politics of the Arabian peninsula. Spencer Mawby argues that one of the most significant problems for the British was the decision to undertake a new imperial adventure in Aden at a time when British economic and military power was on the wane, whilst support for the nationalist struggles in the Middle East and the United Nations was increasing. *British Policy in Aden and the Protectorates 1955–67* maintains that the British policy of proscribing the early anti-colonial opposition in Aden and the conduct of military campaigns against tribal insurgents facilitated the emergence of a radical brand of Arab politics in southwest Arabia which ultimately proved more dangerous to the British presence than moderate Arab nationalism.

By demonstrating the manner in which the rise and fall of British imperialism was telescoped into a short period in the late 1950s and early 1960s, this volume offers an important insight into the unique and unacknowledged place of Aden in the history of British decolonisation.

Spencer Mawby is a lecturer in History at the University of Nottingham. He has published work on twentieth century British foreign and colonial policy, and his current research is focused on the relationship between British imperialism and Arab nationalism.

British foreign and colonial policy
Series Editor: Peter Catterall
ISSN: 1467-5013

This series provides insights into both the background influences on and the course of policy making towards Britain's extensive overseas interests during the past 200 years.

Whitehall and the Suez Crisis
Edited by Saul Kelly and Anthony Gorst

Liberals, International Relations and Appeasement
The Liberal Party, 1919–1939
Richard S. Grayson

British Government Policy and Decolonisation, 1945–1963
Scrutinising the official mind
Frank Heinlein

Harold Wilson and European Integration
Britain's second application to join the EEC
Edited by Oliver Daddow

Britain, Israel and the United States, 1955–1958
Beyond Suez
Orna Almog

The British Political Elite and the Soviet Union, 1937–1939
Louise Grace Shaw

Britain, Nasser and the Balance of Power in the Middle East, 1952–1967
From the Egyptian Revolution to the Six Day War
Robert McNamara

British Foreign Secretaries Since 1974
Edited by Kevin Theakston

British Policy in Aden and the Protectorates 1955–67

Last outpost of a Middle East empire

Spencer Mawby

Routledge
Taylor & Francis Group

LONDON AND NEW YORK

First published 2005
by Routledge
2 Park Square, Milton Park, Abingdon, Oxon OX14 4RN

Simultaneously published in the USA and Canada
by Routledge
270 Madison Ave, New York, NY 10016

Routledge is an imprint of the Taylor & Francis Group

© 2005 Spencer Mawby

Typeset in Garamond by Wearset Ltd, Boldon, Tyne and Wear
Printed and bound in Great Britain by MPG Books Ltd, Bodmin

British Library Cataloguing in Publication Data
A catalogue record for this book is available from the British Library

Library of Congress Cataloging in Publication Data
A catalog record for this book has been requested

ISBN 0-714-65459-0

In Memory of Ed Lemons

The last Governor and first High Commissioner of Aden, Charles Johnston, strides out on a visit to the Fadli territory. Among the British and Arab dignitaries following in his wake is Kennedy Trevaskis (third from left).

Contents

Acknowledgements

Numerous people have helped me in various ways during the course of writing this book. The assistance of archivists and librarians at many institutions has been invaluable including the Public Record Office; the Oriental and India Office; the British Library; the American National Archives II at College Park, Maryland; the John Fitzgerald Kennedy Library, Boston; the Lyndon Baines Johnson Library, Austin; the department of Special Collections and Western Manuscripts at the Bodleian Library, University of Oxford; Rhodes House, University of Oxford; St. Antony's College, University of Oxford; Churchill College, University of Cambridge; the Labour Party Archive, University of Manchester; the University of Southampton; the Liddell Hart Centre, King's College, University of London; the British Library of Political and Economic Science; the University of Birmingham, the University of Leicester and the University of Nottingham. The British Academy were most helpful in providing funding for a research trip to the United States. Thanks are also due to the army of unknown workers who have ferried me back and forward to these institutions on public transport, although not, one suspects, to their managers.

Two other institutions, the British-Yemeni Society and the Friends of the Hadhramawt, have been most kind in offering knowledge and advice which a survey of the documents can never provide. In this regard I would particularly like to thank Sultan Ghalib of Qu'ayti, Leila Ingrams, Stephen Day, John Shipman, Julian Paxton, Peter Hinchcliffe, John Ducker and Godfrey Meynell. Their help was particularly generous given that many of them will disagree with some of the conclusions reached in this study. Stephen Day deserves additional mention for his constant support of those undertaking research into the history of Aden and for providing the cover photograph.

I would like to thank Matt Deacon at Wearset and all those at Taylor and Francis who inherited this project and took the time to bring it to completion including, in particular, Terry Clague and Katherine Carpenter. The editor of this book series, Peter Catterall, is responsible for the publication of both this and my previous monograph and deserves whatever share of credit or blame such a decision merits. On both occasions his extremely useful editorial comments have ensured that the final volume was a more presentable product than might have otherwise been the case.

At a more personal level I have been very lucky in my proof readers who were also good friends: Bryan White, Adam Biscoe and John Young provided much needed correction and advice on the manuscript. John Young has also twice acted as my congenial 'line manager' or, more conventionally, Head of School. While the frequently onerous duties of actually researching and writing fall solely upon the author it would have been quite impossible to complete the process without the invaluable advice and inspiration provided by friends who have tolerated Aden while dispensing good advice and good humour. In this regard I would like to thank my compatriots from Hogan's: Tim Stanton, Simon Kear, Paul Trickett and Robin Ryan.

I was fortunate enough to be gainfully employed while working on the book and owe much to colleagues in the Department of Politics at the University of Leicester and the School of History at the University of Nottingham. I would particularly wish to record the professional and personal assistance provided by Geoff Berridge, James Hamill, John Hoffman, Renie Lewis, Jan Melissen and Wyn Rees at Leicester and Karen Adler, Sarah Badcock, Gwilym Dodd, Sue Townsend, Amanda Samuels and Claire Taylor at Nottingham. They and others have made university life tolerable despite the best efforts of those who are currently attempting to destroy the system of Higher Education from which so many of us have benefitted in the past.

My mother, Sheila Mawby, has been a constant source of support and was most generous in believing my constant assertions that the manuscript would eventually be submitted and tolerating my occasional grumbling about the task.

During my trip to the American archives I was treated with wonderful hospitality by Margo Arrowsmith, without whose encouragement to visit I may never have had the opportunity to examine the Anglo-American aspect of the story. This book is dedicated to the memory of another American friend, Ed Lemons. Although we never met, Ed's correspondence served as a reminder when times were hard both that books are valuable and that there are other, more important, things.

Abbreviations

APL	Aden Protectorate Levies
ATUC	Aden Trades Union Congress
EAP	Eastern Aden Protectorate
FLOSY	Front for the Liberation of Occupied South Yemen
FRA	Federal Regular Army
HBL	Hadhrami Bedouin Legion
NLF	National Liberation Front
OLOS	Organisation for the Liberation of the Occupied South
PDRY	People's Democratic Republic of Yemen
PORF	Popular Organisation of Revolutionary Forces
PRSY	People's Republic of South Yemen
PSP	People's Socialist Party
SAA	South Arabian Army
SAL	South Arabian League
UAR	United Arab Republic
UNF	United National Front
UNP	United National Party
WAP	Western Aden Protectorate
YAR	Yemeni Arab Republic

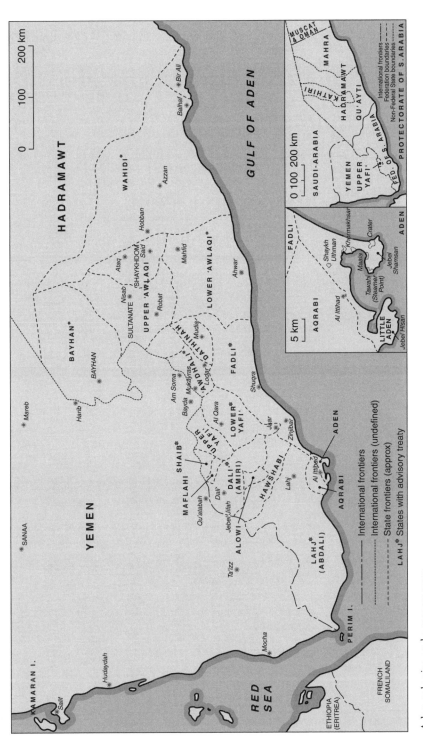

Aden colonies and protectorates.

1 Introduction

British imperialism and Arab nationalism

The aims of this study are to describe the process of imperial expansion and retreat undertaken by the British in southwest Arabia[1] between 1955 and 1967, provide an explanation for why British policy developed in the manner that it did and place the episode in the context of the clash between Arab nationalism and British imperialism in the Middle East. These tasks are closely related to one another and also impose limits upon the scope of the project. Anybody familiar with the modern history of Yemen is aware of how complex the politics of southwest Arabia were for much of the twentieth century. By focusing primarily on the impact of the British in the region it is possible to gain insight into an interesting example of late European imperialism and its effect on the politics of a particular society. Yemen is one of the most fascinating countries in the Arab world and by tracing the relationship between southwest Arabia as a region on the periphery of the British Empire and policy-makers in the metropolis it is hoped that some key developments in the country's history can be clarified and a contribution made to the study of British decolonization. Broader cultural and social developments are given less prominence: significant research has already been conducted into these subjects and they are fruitful fields for further study.[2]

The methods employed during the course of this analysis place it squarely within the field occupied by traditional studies of diplomatic and colonial history based on governmental archives. As far as there is divergence or innovation it is in a greater emphasis upon the ideological underpinnings both of British policy and of the nationalist groups than is common in much writing on decolonization. The recent trend towards writing imperial history from the perspective of the periphery has been a salutary development but one which can only be pursued in an attenuated form here. Arab nationalist texts and pamphlet literature in translation have been utilised but the great majority of the raw primary material from which the narrative and analysis have been constructed come from British governmental archives and the records of the Aden Secretariat. Both of these sources remain, at the time of writing, somewhat under-utilised.[3] In conceptual terms there is also some divergence from current practice. Historians of twentieth century

British foreign and colonial policy frequently fall back on an unsatisfying and narrow notion of national interest to explain developments. The concept is employed so liberally and with such little concern for its content that it explains everything and nothing. An attempt is made here to assess the motivations of the protagonists in a little more detail: in the case of the British, the value placed on a continuing and expansive world role is emphasised and in the case of the nationalist groups the emphasis on freedom and autonomy is noted. Differing British and Arab ideas about the future of southwest Arabia are occasionally juxtaposed in the main body of the text. However, the primary goal of the study is to provide an accurate account of Britain's role in the region based closely on the documentary record.

The history of Yemeni politics may appear tortuous but the basic story of the last 12 years of British rule are straightforward. In the middle of the twentieth century the British embarked on a series of new undertakings in Aden and the Protectorates designed to consolidate their influence. Taken as a whole they constitute what has been termed the forward policy. It was designed as a prophylactic to prevent changing local circumstances and the associated rise of anti-colonial nationalism from undermining the foundations of western influence in the Middle East. Although the British clung on in Aden until 1967, the attempt to prolong British imperialism had unintended consequences, most notably the radicalisation of politics in Aden and the Protectorates. The various expedients employed to contain the rise of nationalist sentiment failed and the old order which the British hoped to preserve crumbled to be replaced by the socialist programme of the National Liberation Front (NLF). After 1967 the new leaders of the People's Republic of South Yemen (PRSY) rejected Cairo's brand of Arab nationalism; the extension of British rule for a sufficient length of time to witness the decline of Nasser's influence provided some consolation for policy-makers in Whitehall.

The structure in which these events are examined is chronological. Chapter 2 outlines the history of neglect of southwest Arabia following Haines's conquest of Aden in 1839 and discusses the changes which began to occur to this policy in the first half of the twentieth century. It also charts the emergence of the Yemeni Imamate as Britain's principal rival for influence in the region. The following chapter describes the apogee of the forward policy in the late 1950s and places events in southwest Arabia in the context of Britain's confrontation with Nasser. Chapter 4 analyses the years between 1959 and 1962 as the watershed period in which nationalist doctrines flooded into the region following their slow seepage into Adenese political discourse during the 1950s. It is suggested that British attempts to consolidate their authority served to accelerate rather than retard this process. The fifth chapter is concerned with the impact of the nationalist revolution in Yemen which led to a proxy war with the Egyptians and explains the rationale behind the eventual decision to offer Aden and the Protectorates independence in the summer of 1964. The election of a Labour government in Britain a few months after this offer had a significant impact on events in southwest Arabia and the sixth chapter examines the extent to which policy changed during Wilson's first 18 months in office. It is suggested that, while the Labour government altered its tactics in order to appease the nationalists, they still hoped to contain Nasser and secure long-term British influence and prestige. The final chapter of the narrative discusses the impact of Labour's controversial decision not to offer the new independent state a defence guarantee and the constant frustrations that accompanied their efforts to create a friendly successor government. The concluding chapter seeks to elaborate upon some of the key questions which arise from these events.

Underpinning the analysis is the notion that British policy-makers were motivated not by a simple calculation of material interests but by a desire to maintain their prestige and influence in the Middle East and a belief that the retention of a role in southwest Arabia was important to achieve this. The British resorted to a wide range of measures to bolster their position including aerial attacks on dissidents in the Protectorates and the effective manipulation of the electoral process in Aden. Given this evidence of British determination to cling on, a strong countervailing force was required to secure their removal: this force was Arab nationalism. The conflict with the nationalists in Aden became increasingly bitter during the decade after 1955 and it was the violence which they encountered on the streets of Aden and in the Protectorates as well as the thinning ranks of collaborators which finally shook British policy-makers out of the belief that they were likely to stay in Aden for decades to come. Although the region was one of the last to experience the full force of Arab nationalism, Nasser's advocacy of pan-Arabism had a profound impact. From the late 1950s the alliance between the British and the old elites of Aden and the Protectorates was ruptured as first the South Arabian League (SAL) and then the National Liberation Front began to challenge the basis of both British imperialism and the traditional forms of government within southwest Arabia. The clash between the British desire to retain a presence in the Middle East and the increasing disenchantment of the peoples of southwest Arabia with Britain's role in the region led to the transfer of the conflict between Nasser and the British government from the banks of the Suez Canal to the streets of Aden. In the aftermath of the 1962 Yemeni revolution there was effectively a proxy war in southwest Arabia between Egypt, represented by the Republican government in the north, and Britain, represented by the South Arabian federation, in the south. The success of the nationalists in acquiring Egyptian support and then challenging the imperial presence was the key to securing Britain's final exit in 1967. It is one of the principal contentions of what follows that it was these changes in the periphery, rather than a loss of will or the draining away of material capability in the metropolis, which best accounts for the British withdrawal from what might be regarded as their last outpost in the Middle East.

British imperialism and the forward policy

It is not difficult to construct a plausible economic rationale for Britain's decision to cling on to Aden Colony while other parts of the empire slipped towards independence. During the 1950s oil production in Arabia increased to meet the energy demands of Britain and western Europe. The expansion of the world economy during that decade would have been impossible without access to cheap fuel from the Middle East. Furthermore, the British sterling area greatly benefited from the export earnings generated by British Petroleum and Shell investments in the oil-producing states. Policy-makers in Whitehall and Aden believed that radical nationalism was a latent menace to these economic interests. This thesis was corroborated when the Iranian government nationalised its oil industry in 1951 and it appeared conclusively proven when the post-revolutionary government in Iraq issued threats to annex Kuwait a decade later. In this latter case the British responded by deploying troops from the base in Aden to the Gulf.[4] Kuwait could not be defended *in situ* because the rulers of the Gulf states, unlike their peers in the Aden Protectorates, were loath to admit their dependence on Britain.[5] Thus, although southwest Arabia lacked natural resources of its own, it came to be seen as the key to the defence of British oil interests. The status of Aden as a British Colony, the perception of the town as a sleepy backwater insulated from wider trends and the co-operation of the rulers of the Protectorates appeared to guarantee the base a long-term place in British strategic planning. As the British Chiefs of Staff noted just prior to the outbreak of the Suez crisis: 'The need to deploy forces in the Colony of Aden and the Aden Protectorates will continue for as long as we can foresee.'[6]

The geographical position of southwest Arabia made a continued role there a convenient solution to the absence of facilities in the Gulf and the British base in Aden became a significant asset for this reason. In social and political terms its distance from the sources of nationalist fervour made it appear as an ideal outpost from which to defend the oil wells of the Middle East and in 1960 the Headquarters of British Forces in the Middle East was transferred to Aden. The continuing British presence may therefore be accounted for by the imperative importance of Persian Gulf oil to the British economy and the belief that the military facilities necessary to contain the latent nationalist threat to Europe's fuel supplies could be found in Aden. There is plentiful evidence in favour of an economic interpretation of British motives.[7] On 16 March 1956 Anthony Eden wrote to Minister of Defence, Walter Monckton, to record his concerns about the situation in the Persian Gulf. He stated forthrightly: 'We cannot allow the oil to be endangered.'[8] From the late 1950s a number of Conservative ministers, including Harold Watkinson, Duncan Sandys and Julian Amery, expended much energy considering which portions of Aden could be amputated to form a sovereign base area in which the British would retain access to military facilities in perpetuity.[9] One Aden High Commissioner, Kennedy Trevaskis, recalled that during a trip back to London he discovered that the Minister of Defence, Duncan Sandys, spent 'hours poring over maps, saying "could we have a sovereign base here and there" and corridors linking them.'[10]

There was, however, more to British policy than oil and bases. The ideological drive is rather less tangible but still significant and is evident in the view taken of the threat from Arab nationalism. Across much of the empire the British believed they would be able to work with the new post-colonial elites under the auspices of the Commonwealth. However, two factors worked against this kind of compromise arrangement with Arab nationalism. The first was that after the loss of India, the Middle East was seen as the last and crucial bastion of British power overseas and the second was the emphasis placed by Arab nationalists on the need to free themselves entirely of imperial influence. In the former case, the importance of the Middle East commitment to what might be called Britain's vision of world order was demonstrated when Bevin and his advisers howled down Attlee's pragmatic advocacy of withdrawal to sub-Saharan Africa after 1945.[11] It was perfectly feasible to argue, as Attlee did, that it was not in Britain's national interest to maintain a presence in the region and to rely, like other powers, upon commercial pressure to maintain the supply of cheap fuel. The great difference in the British position was the feeling that this was an area that was tied up with Britain's broader ambitions to retain an influence on global affairs.

The Conservative governments which conducted British colonial policy for 13 years after Attlee's electoral defeat in 1951 regarded the Middle East as essential to the retention of Britain's global role which was, in turn, a prerequisite to the maintenance of British prestige. There were, however, different schools of thought about the best method of achieving this. A number of prominent figures in the Conservative party argued that Britain should pursue a firm policy to retain what Britain held and eschew withdrawal or 'scuttle'. In the early 1950s the Suez group applied these arguments to the negotiations over the sprawling Egyptian base and after 1956 they reiterated it in debates over the defence facilities in Aden. Lord Salisbury, Duncan Sandys and Julian Amery represented these views within government. Others, most notably, Macmillan's Colonial Secretary between 1959 and 1961, Iain Macleod, were opposed to this line and insisted that the continuation of the world role actually required the co-operation of local nationalists which necessitated concessions from Britain. In the case of Aden those within government arguing for the acceleration of independence to appease local opinion had the support of the men on the spot who were adamant that Britain could retain influence after independence through the establishment of surrogates in positions of influence.

Although disagreements over colonial policy within the party were frequently heated, in the Middle East at least it was always possible to achieve consensus among Conservatives that Nasser's ambitions were as dangerous as those of Hitler and Mussolini a generation earlier. A prominent historian of Anglo-Egyptian relations has noted: 'most British officials and statesmen, from fairly lowly levels in Whitehall to the Prime Minister, shared the idea of Nasser as a latter-day dictator of 1930s vintage.'[12] Distaste for Nasser was also common within the Labour party but their election in 1964 altered the terms of the debate about colonial policy. Bevin's influence was still evident from the determination of the Wilson governments to pursue a world role and, although a faction within the party did wish to circumscribe this, they had little influence with the Prime Minister. However, by this stage advocates of formal empire had been marginalised by the disappearance of most of Britain's overseas possessions during the previous five years. The key issue was how much influence Britain could retain within the limits imposed by financial restraints and the rise of nationalism. Wilson and his ministers were initially optimistic that they could cling on to the defence facilities in Aden. They believed that British influence and the interests of local nationalism could be reconciled. A series of failed initiatives rapidly disillusioned them and years of debate about the precise nature of Britain's future role in the region gave way to the practical discussion of how Britain could secure a safe withdrawal.

The view from Aden was rather different from that in Whitehall. The authorities there were committed to a forward policy. Some regarded this as a buttress to uphold continuing British rule, while others saw it as necessary to the achievement of independence. The continuing hold of imperial ideas and responsibilities on officials working in southwest Arabia was evident from frequent allusions to Britain's role as a teacher, policeman or referee; it was made concrete by the increasing presence of British advisers across the Aden Protectorates in the 1940s and 1950s and by the retention of British sovereignty in Aden until November 1967. The lack of sympathy between Arab aspirations and British attitudes was most starkly expressed in the memoirs of the governor of Aden in 1955, Tom Hickinbotham: he was quite happy to portray the rulers of the Protectorate states as children and to compare their discontented subjects to 'Teddy Boys'. He opined that 'there are times when even the most amiable child must be coerced in its own interest and I have never faltered in my opinion that an ash plant properly applied, is one of the few things that is effective in dealing with thugs in this or any other country.'[13] In retrospect this looks like an overly frank, if revealing, account of British thinking. Subsequent Governors were less obviously reactionary but it remained true that the British did require discipline from subject populations and adopted a punitive approach which was unlikely to be acceptable to an Arab population aspiring to establish their autonomy. Hickinbotham's views are significant because the forward policy in southwest Arabia was generated by the men on the spot rather than by the British government in Whitehall. The motivations behind the policy were various but its key architects, Bernard Reilly and Kennedy Trevaskis, saw it as a prelude to an attenuated form of self-government. On their account the region required a period of formal British tutelage prior to independence. After the demission of authority, Britain's imprint would still be evident in the form of the institutions and ideology which had been implanted. Many policy-makers in Whitehall preferred the continuation of British rule more or less in perpetuity. There was no support in Whitehall or Aden for relinquishing Britain's role in southwest Arabia prior to 1965; their ambitions were either to continue with direct control of the colony or to exercise lasting influence after independence.

Arab nationalism and British imperialism

Britain's tutorial role was anathema to the mass of the Arab population and the explanation of the sudden retraction of British influence may be found in the incompatibility between these two visions of the future. In the early years of the twentieth century Arab nationalism was the province of a small elite who dreamed of a greater Arab role within the Ottoman empire. The Turks were developing a national consciousness of their own and Arab nationalism has been interpreted as a reaction to this development. The revolt in the Hijaz during the First World War provided apparent evidence of the consonance between British and Arab interests and their opposition to Turkish nationalism.[14] However, the British reordering of the Middle East after the Ottoman defeat brought them into conflict with new trends in the Arab world. The precise origins and nature of early Arab nationalism are keenly disputed but it is clear that by the early 1920s urban elites were exercising an increased influence and taking up new doctrines.[15] The ideology propagated by this second generation of nationalist thinkers differed markedly from those of the traditional elites with whom the British had worked previously. The first evidence of this incompatibility was provided by the ejection of Britain's confederate Faysal from Syria in 1920. Subsequently, this opposition to western imperialism took on a more organised form: at a pan-Islamic congress in Jerusalem in 1931 Arab delegates drew up a covenant rejecting the artificial division of the Arab world by the western powers. The Arab Independence Party and the League of Nationalist Action, which became influential during the 1930s, were transient organisations but they did co-ordinate opposition to British and French rule across the artificial frontiers which had been drawn by the occupying powers at San Remo in 1920.[16] As Michael Barnett has noted in his analysis of Arab nationalist doctrine: 'the first concrete and politically consequential meaning associated with Arab nationalism was anti-colonialism and political independence . . . the fight for independence in the name of Arabism helped to deepen and legitimate Arabism.'[17] Although at this stage the British and the French could always find collaborators within the mandated territories, the balance of thinking in the Arab world was beginning to swing against them and the later Nasserite era may be seen as a continuation of this trend. At the very end of the period of British influence in the 1960s there was almost nobody willing to co-operate with British rule as the case of Aden visibly demonstrated. The primary reason for this dwindling of support was a perception that the British were engaged in a policy of divide and rule and the most incriminating example of this was the emergence of a Zionist state in Palestine.

No issue was more significant in accelerating the rise of Arab nationalism than Jewish immigration to Palestine. The Balfour Declaration promising a homeland to the Jews in Palestine and the appointment of the Jewish Herbert Samuel as first High Commissioner for Palestine were interpreted as an affront to the Arab world. The rapid increase in Jewish immigration in the inter-war years caused a further deterioration in Anglo-Arab relations. Probably the most significant watershed was the outbreak of the Arab revolt in Palestine in 1936. The British responded to the outbreak of inter-communal violence between Jews and Arabs with a vigorous counter-insurgency campaign. This was far from the first time that the British had used force against Arabs living in the mandated territories but, whereas on previous occasions they had been implicated in intra-Arab squabbles, in Palestine it appeared that British military power was being deployed in the interests of the Zionist immigrants. At a meeting in Syria in 1937 Haj Amin al-Husayn, who co-ordinated the revolt, brought together nationalist delegates to denounce British policy.[18] The British-sponsored 1939 London conference on Palestine witnessed co-operation between the Arab states in an attempt to resist Zionist proposals.[19] The Arab revolt was also significant in reviving interest in Arab nationalism in Egypt which, as the most powerful of the Arabic-speaking countries, had a special significance for nationalist thinkers.

Since the occupation of the country by the British in 1882 a vigorous local patriotism or, as it was sometimes called Pharoahism, was inculcated amongst the Egyptian population. Like their Arab counterparts Egyptian nationalists stressed the problems caused to their country by British impe-rialism but initially did not link their struggle to wider developments in the Middle East. It was the issue of Palestine which 'put an end to Egypt-ian isolationism.'[20] Nasser's innovation was to demonstrate that Egyptian national interests were consonant with the promotion of pan-Arabism. On his account, Israel was a product of western imperialism that threatened to undermine the security of all her neighbours.[21] After the Free Officers' coup of 1952 Nasser moulded simmering Arab resentment against British imperialism into a nationalist doctrine which had an even sharper anti-British edge than that of Nehru in India or Nkrumah in Africa. In particular, by linking the western presence to the disaster in Palestine, the Egyptian leader lent an unmatched fervour to the Arab struggle for freedom from colonial control. Although the move towards independence in India was accompanied by more bloodshed, it was possible for India to remain in the Commonwealth, while it was unthinkable that an Arab state should do so.

Arab nationalism began to have an impact in Aden and the Protectorates at the moment when the repercussions of the forward policy pursued by the British were beginning to be felt. One of the assumptions behind the forward policy was that Aden could be isolated from nationalist currents. Damascus, Beirut and Baghdad were the cities in which the anti-western brand of Arab nationalism was first generated and it was its adoption by the new military leadership in Cairo which gave it great political significance; Aden by contrast appeared as a provincial backwater. Just at the moment when the British were beginning to stress the value of their only Middle Eastern colony as a territory from which Britain could continue to exercise its global responsibilities, a doctrine virulently hostile to British imperialism began to flourish. Quite clearly the forward policy did much to stimulate nationalism but, had it not been for the regional context and in particular the existence of a charismatic leader of this movement in the form of Nasser, then the British path would have been a good deal smoother. The late application of the forward policy and the sudden upsurge of Arab nationalist feeling had the effect of abridging the imperial episode in Aden and the Protectorates. The Yemeni migrants who flooded into Aden and many of the tribes of the interior were the first and last generations to have any contact with British imperialism. For example, a significant British expedition to the Upper 'Awlaqi Sultanate was first undertaken in 1953. British political officers soon followed and the next decade was one of conflict between local tribes, made indignant by British interference, and the government in Aden which was determined to bring order to an unruly region. Following a period of greater calm in the mid-1960s Upper 'Awlaqi fell under National Liberation Front control in 1967 and the tribesmen became citizens of the renamed People's Republic of South Yemen. After the country became a Democratic Republic three years later they were required to submit to the novel and alien ideology prescribed by the Marxist government. The remainder of the book will be concerned with describing how such an unlikely outcome emerged from the clash between two very different ideas about the future of southwest Arabia.

Notes

1 There are problems with the designations chosen to signify particular geographical areas: a constant risk of lapsing either into anachronism or obscurity. References to southwest Arabia are to the region covered by the reunited, modern state of Yemen, which in the 1950s consisted of the colony of Aden, the Western and Eastern Aden Protectorates and the Imamate of Yemen. The term Yemen has been reserved for the northern territory belonging to the Imam and which later comprised the Yemeni Arab Republic. Rather than employing the term South Yemen, which became shorthand for the People's Republic of South Yemen from 1967 and then People's Democratic Republic of Yemen from 1970, when a reference to this region is required the term Aden and the Protectorates is used.

2 See for example, S. Carapico, *Civil Society in Yemen* (Cambridge, Cambridge University Press, 1998) and P. Dresch, *Tribes, Government and History in Yemen* (Oxford, Oxford University Press, 1989).

3 There are some notable exceptions. See S. Smith, 'Rulers and Residents: British Relations with the Aden Protectorate' *Middle Eastern Studies*, 31 (1995), pp. 509–23; P. Dresch, *A History of Modern Yemen* (Cambridge, Cambridge University Press, 2000); G. Balfour-Paul, *The End of Empire in the Middle East* (Cambridge, Cambridge University Press, 1991), ch. 3. For an excellent published collection of many of the most significant documents see D. Ingrams and L. Ingrams, *Records of Yemen* (Slough, Archive Editions, 1993).

4 M. Snell-Mendoza, 'In Defence of Oil: Britain's Response to the Iraqi Threat Towards Kuwait' *Contemporary Record*, 10 (1996), pp. 39–61.

5 S. Smith, *Kuwait 1950–65: Britain, the al-Sabah and Oil* (Oxford, Oxford University Press 1999), chs 3–5.

6 J. Kent (ed.), *Egypt and the Defence of the Middle East, pt. 3 1953–56*, (London, HMSO, 1998), document 643, p. 521; Public Record Office [Henceforward PRO]: CAB 131/17, DC(56)17, 3 July 1956.

7 Cabinet and Defence memoranda of the late 1950s and 1960s are replete with references to strategic significance of the Aden base. See for example, PRO: CAB 134/1551, CP(O)(57)5, 30 May 1957, CAB 134/2344, OME(60)16, 26 September 1960, CAB 148/3, DOP(O)(63)4, DO(O)63 1st mtg., 23 October 1963.

8 Avon Papers, AP/20/21/40, Prime Minister to Minister of Defence, 16 March 1956.

9 See for example Sandys's presentation to the Cabinet in August 1962 in PRO: CAB 128/36, CC(62)52nd mtg., 1 August 1962. For further details see chapter 4.

10 K. Pieragostini, *Britain, Aden and South Arabia* (London, Macmillan, 1990), p. 40.

11 R. Hyam (ed.), *The Labour Governments and the End of Empire 1945–51, pt. 1 1945*, 'Introduction' (London, HMSO, 1992), pp. xxviii, lv; R. Smith and J. Zametica, 'The Cold Warrior Clement Attlee Reconsidered', *International Affairs*, 61 (1985), pp. 237–52.

12 Wm. R. Louis, 'Britain and the Crisis of 1958' in Wm. R. Louis and R. Owen (eds), *A Revolutionary Year: The Middle East in 1958* (London, I.B. Tauris, 2002), p. 20. For a similar assessment see also R. McNamara, *Britain, Nasser and the Balance of Power in the Middle East 1952–1967* (London, Frank Cass, 2003), p. 3.

13 T. Hickinbotham, *Aden* (London, Constable, 1958), p. 111.

14 The most famous exposition of the compatibility of Arab nationalism and British imperialism was written long before the Suez crisis. See George Antonius, *The Arab Awakening* (London, Hamish Hamilton, 1945) and for a commentary W. L. Cleveland, 'The Arab Nationalism of George Antonius Reconsidered' in J. Jankowski and I. Gershoni (eds), *Rethinking Arab Nationalism in the Middle East* (New York, Columbia University Press, 1997), pp. 65–86.

15 I. Gershoni, 'Rethinking the Formation of Arab Nationalism in the Middle East 1920–1945' in J. Jankowski and I. Gershoni (eds), *Rethinking*, pp. 3–25; E. Chalala, 'Arab Nationalism: A Bibliographical Essay' in T. E. Farah (ed.), *Pan-Arabism and Arab Nationalism* (London, Westview Press, 1987), pp. 18–45.

16 Y. M. Choueiri, *Arab Nationalism: A History* (Oxford, Blackwell, 2000), pp. 92–4.

17 M. N. Barnett, *Dialogues in Arab Politics*, (New York, Columbia University Press, 1998), p. 68.

18 Y. M. Choueiri, *Nationalism*, pp. 97–8.

19 A. Dawisha, *Arab Nationalism in the Twentieth Century* (Oxford, Princeton University Press, 2003), pp. 108–9.

20 A. Rahman, *Egyptian Policy in the Arab World* (Washington, University Press of America, 1983), p. 15.

21 J. Jankowski, *Nasser's Egypt, Arab Nationalism and the United Arab Republic* (London, Lynne Rienner, 2002), pp. 30–2; A. Dawisha, *Twentieth Century*, p. 139.

2 History and politics of southwest Arabia to 1955

Aden and the Protectorates do not fit at all neatly into the twentieth century history of the British Empire. Much of southwest Arabia had only a brief brush with British authority and this telescoping of the imperial experience lends the history of the region some of its uniqueness. During the 1950s the British Empire was on the retreat in Africa and east Asia but in this region it was engaged in a process of expansion. This interventionist policy was evident in the Protectorates where the British attempted to transform the minimally governed principalities of the region into a federal state. In contrast to the fleeting contact with western imperialism experienced by many of the inhabitants of the interior, the citizens of Aden had been subject to British or, more properly, Anglo-Indian control since Captain Stafford Haines seized control of the town from the Sultan of Lahj in January 1839. During the century which followed this successful military action Aden remained a backwater of empire. In tracing the development of British policy across this first century it is noticeable that, despite an apparent lack of enthusiasm for widening their sphere of control, the British displayed a determination not to relinquish what they held when either local or regional actors challenged their presence. Years of neglect were often followed by a flurry of activity when other actors impinged into the region and threatened to damage British prestige. The conflict with Nasser's Egypt in the 1950s and 1960s was the last and most explosive instance of this tendency.

The British in southwest Arabia

The coastline of southwest Arabia, or modern Yemen, is situated astride the most significant trade route between the Mediterranean Sea and the Indian Ocean. Its position at the mouth of the Red Sea on the eastern coast of the Bab-al-Mandab has granted it a strategic and historical significance out of proportion to its human or natural resources. A succession of imperial powers, including Rome, Persia, Ethiopia, Fatimid Egypt and Ottoman Turkey came to regard control of the territory as a significant economic asset and as a means of controlling the prosperous trade between the east Indies and the Mediterranean. The first Europeans to follow this precedent were the

Portuguese who launched an unsuccessful attack on Aden in 1517. They subsequently established a small presence on the offshore islands of Perim and Kamaran.[1] It was not until the eighteenth century that British strategists recognised the region's potential for facilitating trade with India and only at its very end did the conflict with France prompt action. In 1799 the British briefly occupied Perim as a precaution following Napoleon's invasion of Egypt.[2] The subsequent French withdrawal from Egypt removed the immediate threat to communications with India but the British remained concerned that developments in the Arabian peninsula might disrupt trade through the Red Sea. Their concerns were reignited by the success of the Pasha of Egypt, Muhammad 'Ali, in establishing his own sphere of influence in Arabia. The fear that a renascent Egypt would be capable of challenging Britain in the Mediterranean and Middle East intensified after 1831 when Muhammad 'Ali declared Egypt independent of Ottoman control.[3]

During the nineteenth century technological change increased the significance of southwest Arabia to the British. From the 1830s the gradual replacement of sail by steam ships required the East India Company to find a suitable coaling station on the route between India and Suez. Initial attempts to establish a base on the offshore island of Socotra foundered after the troops sent to occupy it were stricken with fever. An alternative was required and the looting of a merchant ship off the coast of Aden provided the pretext for the first British venture onto the mainland. In 1836 the Governor of Bombay, Sir Robert Grant, dispatched Captain Stafford Haines of the Indian Navy to seek an agreement on the use of Aden with the local ruler, Sultan Muhsin of Lahj, who belonged to the 'Abdali clan. This was the beginning of a long and tempestuous relationship between the two men and between the British and the 'Abdalis. Negotiations went badly and Haines fled the town following threats by the Sultan to imprison him. He returned in 1838 with a mandate to establish a coaling station. The Sultan again proved recalcitrant and Haines requested reinforcements from India. In January 1839 he stormed the town with the assistance of gunfire from two Indian Navy frigates.[4] The brief occupation of Perim in 1799 and the capture of Aden 40 years later established a pattern in which the affairs of the region impinged on the consciousness of policy-makers in Bombay or London only when an external actor threatened to establish a rival sphere of influence. Similar kinds of imperative were to be evident a century later when Nasser's ambitions in Arabia were interpreted by British policy-makers as a threat to Britain's post-war role east of Suez.

Haines took over the administration of Aden from the Sultans of Lahj on behalf of the Indian government but it soon became evident that neither Bombay nor London had a great interest in developing this distant branch of the empire.[5] Muhammad 'Ali's influence in Arabia receded during the 1840s and there was therefore no strategic or economic reason why the authorities in India or Britain should undertake any adventures in Aden's hinterland. The next challengers to the British were the Turks. During the 1870s they conducted a number of military expeditions to the northern highlands of Yemen. The British responded by forming alliances with tribal leaders outside Aden in order to insulate the Colony against any potential Turkish infringements. Haines and his immediate successors had taken very little interest in administering the tribal territories surrounding Aden; there could be no economic incentive for entering a region with few natural resources and whose economy was dominated by subsistence agriculture. The tribes who occupied the barren, sparsely populated highlands were, in any case, fiercely resistant to outside interference. However, the strategic threat posed by the Ottomans could not be ignored and in 1873 the British laid claim to a dominant role in nine tribal regions around Aden. The Ottoman Sultan was reluctant to acknowledge a British sphere of influence, as this could presage a permanent division of southwest Arabia between a Turkish dominated north and a British dominated south. It was only after a war scare between the two powers that the Turks agreed to withdraw from those areas which the British claimed fell under the jurisdiction of the nine tribes.[6] The truce proved temporary; Anglo-Ottoman differences in southwest Arabia remained unresolved. A number of further war scares occurred, most notably during the attempted delineation of the frontier by a joint Anglo-Turkish border commission between 1902 and 1904. The Sultan initially refused to accept the existence of separate spheres of influence but in 1914 an Anglo-Ottoman convention was finally signed which provided the basis for the future frontier between the Aden Protectorates in the south and the Yemeni Imamate in the north.[7]

While the hinterland remained largely untouched by colonialism during the century after Haines's assault on Aden, the town itself was transformed. The Arabs abandoned the town during the 30 years after its incorporation into the Anglo-Indian empire and the settlement came to be dominated by the Anglo-Indian soldiery and the Indian merchant community. Coal bunkering became the principal commercial business of the port and the increasing numbers of steamships using the Red Sea route after the opening of the Suez canal in 1869 produced a period of dramatic economic expansion. This in turn brought an influx of Arabs back into the town, a number of whom made Aden their permanent residence. The descendants of these immigrants were later acknowledged as the 'old families' of Aden and the British looked to them for support against later waves of Arab migrants from Yemen. The administration of the town was in Anglo-Indian hands and the Residency was under the control of the Presidency of Bombay. Aden was a peculiar offshoot of the British Empire in India rather than a British Crown Colony. The Bombay Presidency took little interest in economic or political developments on the other side of the Indian Ocean and these matters were left in the hands of the Resident. The neglect of Aden by the upper echelons of policy-makers ensured that the Resident had a fair measure of licence provided his actions did not entail additional expenditure.[8] Until a late stage, therefore, the government of Aden remained in the hands of parsimonious British Residents and Indian civil servants. Even after their return in substantial numbers, the Arabs were excluded from positions of authority. Amongst this group there was much relief when political authority was transferred from Bombay to the Colonial Office in London in 1937.[9]

Two significant events in the history of southwest Arabia preceded the establishment of Aden as a British rather than an Anglo-Indian colony: the consolidation of an independent Imamate in the north and the assumption by the RAF of defence responsibilities in the south. The Imams had played a role in the politics of the region for nearly a millennium and the latest incumbent, Yahya, had fought a long campaign against the Turks. He reaped the rewards of the collapse of the Ottoman empire in 1918 which led to their evacuation of Yemen. After the Turks departed Yahya established a successor state and it rapidly became evident that he wished to extend his authority from the northern highlands across the whole of southwest Arabia including the coastal Tihamah in the west and the British sphere of influence in the south. In pursuit of these ambitions he launched incursions across the old Anglo-Ottoman frontier into those areas which the British regarded as belonging to the nine tribes. After a period of inaction, in 1927 the authorities in Aden eventually responded to Yahya's provocations by bombing the Yemeni frontier town of Qa'tabah. Once it became evident that aerial attacks of this kind were the most efficient means of compelling the Imam to withdraw from the British sphere, the Air Ministry was given formal responsibility for the defence of the interior.[10] Yahya's influence receded and in 1934 he recognised the status quo along the frontier by signing the treaty of Sanaa with the British. The treaty was later to be interpreted differently by the two parties but its immediate effect was to secure the Imam's evacuation of those regions to the south of the old Anglo-Ottoman frontier, with the exception of a small chunk of territory around Bayda.[11]

As well as punitive action against the Imam, the British also employed air power against unruly tribes within their own sphere of influence. Many of the inhabitants of the interior first came into contact with the British through the medium of RAF attacks. Two political officers, Hamilton in the west and Ingrams in the east, were given the formidable task of bringing order to the tribal regions of the interior. They employed both negotiation and punitive action and achieved mixed results. As their own accounts illustrate Hamilton tended to emphasise the utility of military force while Ingrams usually adopted a mediatory role. In his memoirs Hamilton documented the success of his policy of 'fire and slaughter' in subduing the tribes of the interior. Aerial attacks were designed to provide lasting evidence of British authority. In launching bombing raids against the dissident Hawshabi tribes Hamilton ignored the pleas of the local Sultan to refrain from action, recording that 'it was necessary that the villages and their neighbours must understand that their disaster stemmed from me.'[12] Punitive air raids of this kind remained a feature of British policy as late as the 1960s. The frequency with which they had to return to this tactic, very often in the same regions, casts doubt on its effectiveness as a long-term solution to the problem of disorder in the interior. At the same time, Ingrams demonstrated in the east that negotiations could be a successful prelude to pacification and a limited degree of economic development.[13] It was unfortunate that once the local conflicts in southwest Arabia became linked to the wider international struggle to maintain British influence in the Middle East, diplomacy and development were to take second place to military action.

The first century of British rule indicated that Aden had a useful function in safeguarding communications with southern and eastern Asia but that only a threat to those communications from an external power could galvanise imperial governments in Bombay or London into action. The commercial fortunes of Aden waxed and waned, while in the interior the British were for a long period unwilling to take up the burden of development in a hostile environment. Whether the British were benign in their intentions or not, Aden and the Protectorates certainly suffered neglect during the first century of British rule. One catalyst for change was a shift in administrative responsibility for Aden from Bombay to London. The establishment of Aden as a British Crown Colony and the signing of advisory treaties with tribal rulers were to form the basis of a more forward policy after 1937. This new interventionist approach was initially pursued with a degree of caution but the emergence of challenges to British authority in the form of the irredentism of the Yemeni Imams and, later, the Arab nationalism of Nasser, were to give the forward policy a different character in the three decades after 1937. To the outside world British policies appeared anachronistic in an era of decolonization but to those on the ground they seemed a natural response to local difficulties and external interference. By the mid-1950s both the Imam in Yemen and Nasser in Cairo were campaigning for the expulsion of the British from Arabia. At a local level public order problems began to emerge in Aden, while in the Protected states of the interior parochial tribal squabbles began to take on a larger significance.

Aden Colony

Viewed from the centre of British administration at Steamer Point, Aden in the mid-1950s had the appearance of a bustling city port more interested in commerce than politics. The town had retained its historic role as an entrepôt for East–West trade and was visited by all the major shipping lines operating in the western half of the Indian Ocean. During the course of 1955 5,239 vessels called at the harbour making Aden the second busiest port in the world after New York.[14] The other major economic enterprise was the new £45m oil refinery which the Anglo-Iranian Oil Company built in the Colony after losing its facilities at Abadan.[15] By the middle of the 1950s a new urban centre had sprung up around the site of the refinery at

Little Aden. The population of this township, which lay across the bay from the main residential districts of Crater, Maala and Shaykh Uthman, grew to nearly 10,000. A £2m works programme was begun in Little Aden to provide the mushrooming settlement with the requisite infrastructure. This was part of a wider boom in construction which employed an additional 10,000 workers across the Colony.[16] The other major source of employment was government service. This became more significant as the British civil and military presence expanded. The Governors of Aden during this period required additional personnel, first to implement the forward policy and then to subdue resistance to British plans. By 1961 the British civil and military administrations employed over 11,000 local people.[17]

All of this activity provided numerous opportunities for clerks, artisans and unskilled labourers and the demand for the latter was largely filled by immigrant Yemenis. The increased taxation imposed by the Imams produced economic stagnation in Yemen which could not have contrasted more sharply with the booming of the Colony. The economic problems of Yemen affected both the merchant class and the much larger body of farmers and rural labourers; representatives of both classes sought new economic and political freedoms by migrating to Egypt, the Gulf or Aden. The consequence of economic expansion in the Colony and the crude, unsuccessful mercantilism of the Imams was therefore to place the resident population of Aden in a minority amongst a tide of migrant workers from the north. It is estimated that the population of the town grew from 51,500 in 1931 to 225,000 in 1963.[18] Migrant Yemenis formed the largest single element in this expansion and became the Nasserite vanguard in Aden. It is a moot point as to whether the British authorities grew to despise the immigrant population prior to their wholesale adoption of Egyptian revolutionary slogans or as a consequence of it, but from an early stage they came to regard them as dangerous fifth columnists. The traditional old Aden families and the rulers of the interior were seen as natural allies against these essential but untrustworthy *arrivistes*. For their part the Yemeni migrants did not greatly benefit from Aden's construction boom. As late as 1962 the journalist, Peter Somerville-Large, noted that their conditions were 'not altogether happy, for most of them lived in crowded shanty-towns . . . rubble covered hillsides filled with shacks nailed together from pieces of wood and beaten out paraffin tins.'[19] These were the recruiting grounds for nationalist and other radical organisations.

The intra-Arab clash between Yemenis and old Adenis tended to marginalise the Colony's other communities which were shrinking in reaction to developments elsewhere. The decision to hand over the defence of southwest Arabia to the RAF during the 1920s had a significant impact on the Colony's demography. The Indian battalion stationed in Aden was withdrawn and was followed shortly afterwards by the British battalion, leaving policing in the hands of British officered Arab units. The Aden Protectorate Levies (APL) were formed in 1928 and recruited from the Arab tribes of the interior. It was not until the 1950s that British troops began to pour back into the Colony to deal with escalating disturbances across the region. In the interim Aden became a less international and more an Arab town. As Indian independence approached many of the small army of clerks and administrators from the subcontinent returned to their homeland thus reducing still further the size of the non-Arab population.[20] Britain's decision to terminate the Palestine mandate a year after the declaration of Indian independence also had an impact. The creation of an Israeli state provoked anti-Jewish riots in Aden and the Jewish population of the town left *en masse* for Palestine. The once substantial Jewish community shrank to less than a thousand.[21] Although the town retained substantial Somali and Indian minorities at mid-century it was a much less cosmopolitan place than it had ever been since Haines's arrival. Aden was being transformed from an international to an overwhelmingly Arab town at precisely the moment when Arab nationalism was sweeping across the Middle East.

The administration of the Colony did not reflect the increasingly Arab character of the population. As a British Crown Colony since 1937 the population of Aden was subject to a Governor chosen by His Majesty's Government who acted as the direct representative of the British monarch. In practical terms this meant that the Governor took his instructions on key policy issues from the Colonial Office in London and on other issues had almost unrestricted authority. There were few means by which local Arab actors could influence decision-making. A Legislative Council was formed in 1946 but was composed entirely of *ex officio* members and nominees of the Governor. In 1947 the first popular elections were held in Fortress which was one of the two township authorities in Aden. This poll set a precedent for the employment of a very narrow franchise designed to prevent the election of potential dissenters: only 5,000 men were allowed to vote in the election from a total population of approximately 70,000.[22] After 1955 significant reforms were undertaken to this system but two aspects guaranteeing British supremacy were retained: the majority of the Arab population were disenfranchised and the Governor, who from 1963 was restyled High Commissioner, retained powers in the last resort to suspend these constitutional arrangements. In 1965 the administrative reforms of the previous decades unravelled and the High Commissioner resorted once more to direct rule in Aden.

The Western Aden Protectorate

In 1960 the quondam Resident of Aden, Bernard Reilly, estimated that there were no fewer than 90 treaties in force between the British government and the various potentates who had fallen into the British sphere of influence in southwest Arabia.[23] These included treaties of protection which granted Britain exclusive access to an area in return for which the local ruler received a guarantee of protection from external attack and advisory treaties, which made British advice mandatory on all matters except those concerning the Islamic faith. Treaties of protection had first been signed with rulers of the western regions in 1888 and the system expanded thereafter until in 1937 the whole of the interior was granted Protectorate status, including those few remaining areas which had no treaty relations at all with the British. The advisory treaties were of more recent origin and were regarded as a means of achieving constitutional and economic development as well as political control. They included clauses allowing for the removal of rulers should they fail to follow British advice and thus constituted further evidence of increased British willingness to manipulate the politics of the Protectorates. This was the system of indirect rule which the British had employed in territories such as Malaya and Nigeria but it is significant that it was adopted at a much later stage in southwest Arabia than elsewhere. Whereas the first advisory treaties had been signed in Malaya in 1874 it was not for another 70 years that the first ruler of a Western Aden Protectorate (WAP) state agreed to accept mandatory British advice.[24] During this interval notions of princely sovereignty and a tutorial role for western empires were under question and they came under closer scrutiny still after 1945. Nevertheless, the advisory relationship remained the foundation of British authority in the WAP until the overthrow of the rulers in 1967.

The territories that constituted the WAP varied greatly in character as a brief survey of Dali', Lahj and Upper 'Awlaqi illustrates.

The region marked on British maps as the Amirate of Dali' was one of the most unruly in the WAP. The main trade route connecting Aden with the principal Yemeni cities of Ta'izz and Sanaa ran directly through the territory and it was one of the first areas outside Aden in which the British became involved. A long-serving British officer summarised the history of this relationship: 'Since the first treaty with the British in 1880, Dhala's history has throbbed monotonously, like an incurable ulcer, with Turkish intrigue, Yemeni intrigue, trouble with the Qutaibis, the Shairis, the Azraqis, customs rows with Haushabi and Lahej. Frequently the authority of the ruler extends scarcely further than the town of Dhala itself, and many whom the British ... have regarded as owing allegiance to the rulers of Dhala strongly repudiate the suggestion.'[25] Tribal resentment at outside interference remained constant in Dali' and conflicted with the tidying instincts of Colonial Office officials who made repeated but fruitless efforts to force its inhabitants to submit to the rule of their nominal sovereign. Unlike many other rulers, the Amir of Dali' was usually willing to accept British assistance in order to bolster his insubstantial authority. Though some short-term successes were achieved in the area, over the longer term actors external to the Amirate were able to turn the pugnacity of the population of Dali' to their own purpose. During the 1950s the tribes were frequently in alliance with the Imam of Yemen against the British and in 1963 the NLF chose to begin their liberation campaign by sponsoring a tribal revolt in the Radfan which the British regarded as a part of Dali'.

In contrast to Dali‘, Lahj was one of the more settled and prosperous areas of the WAP. This was largely a consequence of geography: the Sultanate covered a low-lying region that could sustain commercial agriculture. Following the success of the Abyan cotton schemes in Fadli and Lower Yafi‘, a similar scheme was introduced in Lahj. It had one of only two intermediary schools in the WAP and the road between Aden and Lahj was one of the few reliable communication links in southwest Arabia. Additionally, Lahj had its own state council and tribal guard. The British estimated its annual income at over £75,000 in 1954–55 which may have been paltry compared to the revenues generated in Aden but contrasted markedly with the funds available to the Amir of Dali‘ who subsisted on approximately £10,000 a year. This comparative economic success formed a base from which the ‘Abdali Sultans could reassert their historic claim to leadership over the south. ‘Abdali assertiveness was unwelcome to the British whose mistrust of Lahj's ruling family dated back to the Haines era. During the 1950s they intervened twice to depose an ‘Abdali incumbent: the reactionary rule of Sultan Fadhl was terminated in 1952 on the grounds of his mental instability and his successor Sultan ‘Ali was removed in 1958 because of his association with Arab nationalism.[26] ‘Ali's adoption of a nationalist programme was facilitated by the more advanced social and political conditions of the country which made it a breeding ground for radical opinion. Lahj was the first state to fall to the nationalist parties in 1967.

Upper ‘Awlaqi, like Dali‘, was a mountainous region racked by inter-tribal feuding. For reasons which remain unclear, the same quarrelsomeness which was regarded by the British with contempt in the case of the tribes of Dali‘ was interpreted as evidence of proud martial spirit in the ‘Awlaqis.[27] As so often in the history of British imperialism a particular people were singled out to take on the responsibility of imperial surrogates. Governor Tom Hickinbotham regarded the inhabitant of Dali‘ as ‘mean’ while bemoaning the decline of the ‘Awlaqis who, on his account, constituted one of the ‘great nations’ of Arabia.[28] The British officered levies were filled with ‘Awlaqis and the Upper ‘Awlaqi Shaykhs were sponsored as potential leaders of southwest Arabia despite the fact that many other rulers in the region regarded them as parvenus. Their territory had been carved out from that of the Sultanate with British connivance. Aside from this loss of territory to and rivalry with the Shaykh, the Upper ‘Awlaqi Sultan had domestic problems: the tribes in the Wadi Hatib resisted British and Sultanic attempts to open them up to government. Matters were further complicated by rivalry between the two rulers: in these disputes the British favoured the Shaykh who, unlike the Sultan, had the confidence of the Aden authorities. The mountainous, sparsely populated territory over which the Shaykh and the Sultan quarrelled was desperately poor. After the cancellation of a British stipend in 1949 the Sultan retreated inside his residence in a fruitless attempt to hide his obvious impecunity. Although British patronage made the conditions of the Ahl Farid Shaykhs somewhat more comfortable, they had problems of their own, most notably the presence of outraged rivalled claimants to the Shaykhdom from the Ahl Bubakr clan.[29]

In sum, the Western Aden Protectorate was an area of the empire which was peculiarly resistant to British notions of good government. Those regions, such as Lahj, which had achieved a modicum of development saw this as a platform for independence. The tiny middle class of the Protectorates who had been schooled by the British were the first to see them as an obstacle to the fulfilment of nationalist notions of freedom and equality. The small towns of the WAP would be a fertile recruiting ground for opponents of British rule. At the same time the tribal population, which could be temporarily pacified either by financial inducements or military coercion, proved intractable in the longer term and remained wedded to autarky. Furthermore, the British began the task of extending their control into the interior at precisely the moment when regional and international conditions were at their least propitious.

The Eastern Aden Protectorate

The Eastern Aden Protectorate (EAP) was a British administrative fiction which extended across a number of contrasting regions to the east of the 'Awlaqi territories. By far the most significant of these was the valley of the Hadhramawt which snakes in a wide arc from west to east before entering the Indian Ocean near the town of Sayhut. The culture and history of the Hadhramawt made it unique in Arabia and its defining characteristic was the extent of migration. Approximately 110,000 Hadhramis were living outside southwest Arabia in the mid-1930s and there were significant communities in British east Africa, the Dutch east Indies, Malaya and India.[30] The financial successes of the migrants contributed significantly to the economic development of the Hadhramawt through the repatriation of profits made overseas. The loss of such remittances during the Second World War inflicted significant damage on the economy of the region. The facts of the Hadhrami diaspora are even more remarkable when contrasted with the lack of penetration into the Hadhramawt by Europeans. Harold and Doreen Ingrams were the first westerners to make their home in the Hadhramawt valley in the late 1930s during which time they negotiated a series of peace treaties with the tribes.

The politics of the Hadhramawt were dominated by two families: the Qu'ayti and the Kathiri. The Kathiri rose to prominence in the fifteenth century when they conquered much of the region which became the EAP but subsequently they sank into insignificance. The Qu'aytis were a branch of the Yafi'i clan who had amassed a sizeable fortune in India and who were invited to return to the region to assist in the process of economic development.[31] In the mid-nineteenth century Umar bin Awadh al Qu'ayti sought to establish his influence in the coastal regions formerly governed by the Kathiris by utilising the wealth his family had accumulated in Hyderabad.

The resulting multilateral struggle for power became entangled with Anglo-Ottoman antagonisms following the dispatch of a Turkish vessel to al-Shihr in support of the Kathiris. The Qu'aytis sought external assistance in the ongoing struggle and in 1882 signed a treaty of friendship with the British. This alliance formed the basis for a series of conquests which established Qu'ayti control of most of the coast and the Hadhramawt valley. The Kathiris were effectively penned into the interior.[32] The rivalry persisted and during the First World War the Kathiris again aligned themselves with the Ottomans and the Qu'aytis with the British. In 1918 a settlement was reached based on mutual recognition by the two rulers, a frontier agreement defining Qu'ayti and Kathiri territory and acknowledgement of their status as a constituent element of the British Empire.[33]

During the late 1930s Harold Ingrams, with the assistance of the Qu'ayti rulers and funds provided by the local al-Kaf family, pacified much of the EAP. Administrative reforms were regarded by the British as a necessary corollary to military pacification and Ingrams prompted Sultan Saleh of Qu'ayti to sign the first Protectorate treaty in southwest Arabia in 1937.[34] Saleh's descendant, Sultan Ghalib, provides the background: 'Sultan Saleh wanted a reliable lieutenant – a Prime Minister – in Ingrams after the fashion of rulers who would employ Europeans directly or on a secondment basis such as the Khedive of Egypt ... However British political thinking regarding the region had changed much and in favour of greater direct involvement and the Protectorate formula based on the Indian and primarily the Malay states was placed before him and he had to agree.' Ingrams became Resident Adviser and southwest Arabia was split for administrative purposes between an Eastern and a Western Aden Protectorate. Two years later the Kathiri Sultan also signed an advisory treaty. Over the next decade a new bureaucracy sprang up in the Kathiri capital, Sayyun, while in the Qu'ayti capital, Mukalla, the EAP Residency instituted a series of administrative reforms. By 1955 the Qu'ayti state was by far the most powerful and advanced in southwest Arabia. The environment in the EAP was more amenable to development than in the WAP. The British were able to engage with a people entirely familiar with modernity from their engagement in trade with the rest of the Indian Ocean and beyond. There was an effective administration on which to build, including health and education services and the economy provided a local source of income which made development and pacification efforts less dependent on Whitehall largesse. Qu'ayti revenues for 1954–55 amounted to £277,474 according to Colonial Office estimates.[35]

Some problems, such as the intractability of the tribes, were shared by the EAP and the WAP. The most inveterate opponents of the new dispensation in the Hadhramawt were the Hamumi tribal confederation who, with encouragement from the Bin Abdat family, began attacking road traffic in 1938. The British responded with RAF bombing raids which temporarily quelled the disturbances without reconciling dissident tribes to the British presence. More significant for the long term than the recalcitrance of the Hadhrami tribes was the emergence of a nascent nationalist movement. It was not coincidental that the EAP was both the first region in southwest Arabia to experience British administrative reform and the impact of nationalist anti-imperialism. Nationalist agitation eventually transferred westwards as the forward policy increasingly obtruded into the lives of those living in the WAP but it was in the EAP that the first glimmerings of a nationalist opposition to British rule began to emerge. Although the rebellion was subdued there was widespread resentment at British interference amongst Islamic modernisers who took as their model the various Islamic reform movements of the east Indies.[36]

The Hadhramawt overshadowed but did not encompass the EAP. To the west, north and east of the valley lay territories which, in contrast to Qu'ayti and Kathiri lands, were almost completely isolated from the outside world. By the start of the 1950s the British had still barely established contact with the tribes of the Wahidi, the northern desert and the Mahra territory. The Wahidi country to the west was stricken by feuding between local potentates and conflicts with the 'Awlaqis on their frontier. Fear of domination by the Hadhramis tended to make the Wahidi rulers look westwards and it was the only region in the EAP to join the South Arabian federation. In the north of the EAP lay a region in which any notion of clearly demarcated frontiers collapsed utterly: the northern desert was the subject of overlapping territorial claims by the Qu'aytis, the Kathiris, the Sultans of Qishn and Socotra and the Saudis. The motive behind British interest in the region and the pretensions of local dynasties was unambiguous: it was believed that an oil discovery was imminent. To the east lay the arid, thinly populated territory of the Mahra which was nominally under the lax administration of the Sultan of Qishn and Socotra but which was actually under no authority but that of the local tribes who were reputedly even more wild and uncontrollable than their counterparts in the WAP. While the tribes dominated the Mahra territory on the mainland, the Sultan remained isolated on the island of Socotra. Although both his mainland and offshore domains were British protected territory he had minimal contact with the British authorities in Mukalla and Aden until the Resident in the EAP, Hugh Boustead, sent a political officer to visit Socotra in 1953 to press upon him the need for reform.[37] The vigorous manner in which the British extended their influence into these regions during the 1950s marked it as an area in which European imperialism was able to flourish in a purported era of decolonization.

The Yemeni Imamate

The most populous region of southwest Arabia was Yemen, which lay to the north of the British sphere of influence marked out as the Western Aden Protectorate. It had been governed by the Hamid al-Din Imams since the collapse of the Ottoman empire. The boundary which the British and the

Ottomans had drawn between the WAP and Yemen was an entirely arbitrary one and events on one side of the frontier resonated across to the other. The unstable politics of the country made it a constant threat to British attempts to impose order in the south and its history is therefore worth examination. The common western view of Yemen under the Imams was that it was making slow progress advancing from the late ninth century, in which it was founded, into the comparative modernity of the tenth century.[38] In fact the period after the withdrawal of the Turks in 1919 was one of dramatic political and social change in Yemen. The innovations of the Hamid al-Din did not amount to modernisation on the western pattern but they were novelties in the history of the Imamate.

Al-Hadi, the first Imam, was a scholar from Medina who was invited to the northern highlands of Yemen in 893 to act as a mediator and spiritual adviser during a period of tribal anarchy. He adhered to the Shi'a doctrine that the leader of the Muslim community should be chosen from among the descendants of the Prophet's son-in-law, 'Ali. In contrast to many Shi'a groups, however, the Zaydi principles espoused by al-Hadi narrowed the field of candidates further to those who could trace their ancestry to Zayd, the son of the fourth Imam. The Zaydis also eschewed the notion of a divinely ordered succession which, in some Shi'a interpretations of Islam, could produce hidden or occluded Imams. Instead Zaydism prescribed that the leaders of the Muslim community should be chosen from those of Zayd's descendants who had demonstrated their spiritual, scholarly and martial qualities. During the long history of foreign invasions of Yemen the Zaydi Imams retained an often tenuous grip on the loyalty of the northern tribes while continuing to assert their broader claim to spiritual authority across the whole of southwest Arabia. In their isolation they advocated an ascetic, scriptural interpretation of Islam which disregarded the philosophical embellishments of Muslim scholars elsewhere in the Arab world.[39] Despite the frequent conflicts between rival claimants, which were a consequence of the flexible criteria applied to the succession, the Imamate proved durable. For a period in the seventeenth century the Qasimi Imams were able to enforce their authority across much of southwest Arabia.[40]

After a further period of ill fortune following the secession of the southern state of Lahj in 1728, in the late nineteenth century the ambitious first Hamid al-Din Imam, Muhammad al-Mansur, initiated a revival in the fortunes of the Imamate. He launched a long and bloody war against the occupying Turks which culminated in 1911 with the signing of the treaty of Da'an by his son, Yahya. Under its terms the Ottoman empire recognised Imamic authority in the northern mountains of Yemen. After 1918 the Turks withdrew and Yahya made plans to extend his domains and it was at this point that he ran into the British. The authorities in Aden insisted that Yahya should respect the spheres of influence embodied in the Anglo-Turkish Convention of 1914. Yahya, who had acquired the sobriquet 'The Butcher' during his campaigns against the Turks, believed that the southern area had been a province of the Imamate *de jure*, since its conquest by the Qasimi Imams. During the 1920s he made a series of incursions southwards which left him in control of much of the British protected states of Dali' and 'Awdhali. The British bombed the Imam's forces out of Dali' in 1928 but it was another six years before Yahya recognised the status quo by signing the treaty of Sanaa. This amounted to something less than an acknowledgement of the frontier and the belligerent Yahya appears to have regarded the treaty as no more than a temporary expedient which would facilitate the stabilisation of his northern front where he was in conflict with Ibn Saud.[41] This war had ended with the routing of Yahya's forces and led to the permanent loss to the Imamate and Yemen of the province of Asir which became a province of Saudi Arabia.[42]

As well as acquiring external enemies with alarming regularity Yahya had numerous domestic opponents. In the newly conquered west and south, which had not experienced Imamic rule for centuries, Yahya and his son Ahmad were regarded with fear and suspicion. Furthermore, the changed character of the Imamate under the Hamid al-Din alienated their traditional Zaydi adherents. The attempt to transform the Imamate into a hereditary monarchy in which the ruler could draw upon significant military and economic resources alarmed both progressive and conservative opinion. Traditionally, Imams were not chosen on the basis of their paternity. In 1927 Yahya broke with established practice and appointed his son Ahmad, Crown Prince. No such position existed in Zaydism. The announcement offended the conservative *ulama* and distressed other *sayyid* families, who feared permanent exclusion from the succession. The most significant of the latter group were the al-Wazir clan who made their own bid for the Imamate when Yahya was assassinated in 1948.[43] Ahmad rapidly defeated the al-Wazir rebellion and reclaimed the Imamate within weeks of the assassination. He subsequently followed the precedent set by his father and nominated his son Badr as his successor. In appointing Badr to the regency in 1959, just prior to receiving medical treatment in Italy, Ahmad took another unprecedented step. The traditionalists were again appalled, particularly as Badr was known to admire Nasser's brand of secular nationalism and was regarded as a much less suitable candidate than his uncle Hasan, who espoused conventional Zaydi values.[44]

Prior to the twentieth century the Imams had relied on the allegiance of tribesmen to supply them with the manpower required for their military campaigns. Yahya's decision to establish a standing army was a novelty which brought in its train unfortunate consequences for the Hamid al-Din. It created a new class of professional soldiers with little loyalty to the institutions of the Imamate and alienated the tribes. The army's officers required instruction and to meet this need a treaty of friendship was signed with Iraq in 1931 which allowed Yemenis to train at the military academy in Baghdad.[45] Yahya reconsidered once he became aware that this cadre was being contaminated with the revolutionary ideas which flourished in the

Fertile Crescent at this time and he curtailed the programme. Nevertheless, contacts with the Iraqi and Egyptian armies continued and the revolution of 1962 was conducted by the new officer class, many of whom had been students in Baghdad. By that time the loyalty of the tribes to the Imamate was also less secure. Yahya utilised his new regular army as a means of asserting his independence from the two great tribal confederations of the north, the Hashid and the Bakil. They were suspicious of this latest novelty for precisely that reason. In 1959 the estrangement with the Hashid was made permanent when Ahmad executed their paramount Shaykh in retaliation for his involvement in tribal disturbances during Badr's regency.[46] The Hashid were among the most significant supporters of the early republic.[47]

A further source of dissension within the Imamate was the determination of Yahya and Ahmad to increase their revenues. Yahya appointed members of his own family to act as governors in the provinces. One of their primary tasks was to ensure that the system of Islamic taxation was strictly enforced. However, there was a tendency for these regional governors to seek additional sources of income and Ahmad, who governed the great southern city of Ta'izz, was particularly assiduous in formulating new tariffs and imposts upon the merchant community. On assuming the Imamate his exploitative financial measures spread across a wider geographical area and brought with it a collapse in trade. The cupidity of the Hamid al-Din was at odds with the asceticism of many of their predecessors but, more significantly, it generated hostility to the institution of the Imamate among the merchant community and the nascent class of professionals.[48] This was exacerbated by the fact that the majority of those involved in trade and the professions were Shafi'i Sunnis who approached Zaydi doctrines and very frequently the Zaydis themselves with distrust. The result of these political and economic grievances was widespread migration of the commercial and peasant classes from Yemen. Many Yemenis established themselves in Aden, which became a hotbed of anti-Imamic opinion in the 1940s and early 1950s.[49]

Conclusions

The problems of the Imams and the British mirrored one another: whatever the differences in the form of administration which they were trying to impose both were engaged in bringing 'government' much more directly into the lives of the people of southwest Arabia. The Zaydi revivalism of the Hamid al-Din confronted the same obstacles as the British imperial project. Times had changed and the climate in which the British in the south and the Imams in the north undertook their conflicting political programmes was not congenial either to western imperialism or eastern theocracy. Reciprocal British and Imamic attempts to hinder one another added further difficulties to these apparently atavistic enterprises. Outside the urban areas the Governors of Aden and the Imams persistently ran up against the independence and bellicosity of the tribes. In the towns and cities new classes were emerging to which Arab nationalism had a strong appeal. Nasser was a most effective spokesman for impoverished Arab urbanites but his appeal to the emerging professional class was just as significant. Exiled Yemenis in Aden, employees of the new administrations being established by the British in the Protectorates and disgruntled opponents of the Imam in provincial Yemeni towns such as Hudaydah and Ta'izz began to look to Cairo for leadership during the 1950s. Imam Ahmad attempted to ride the nationalist tide, while the British sought to contain it but in the 1960s both were swept out of southwest Arabia. The immediate origins of these events can be traced to developments in the previous decade and these will be considered next.

Notes

1 E. Macro, *Yemen and the Western World* (London, Hurst, 1968), p. 1; R. Bidwell, *The Two Yemens* (Harlow, Longman, 1983), pp. 16–17.
2 R. J. Gavin, *Aden Under British Rule 1839–1967* (London, Hurst, 1975), p. 22; R. Bidwell, *Yemens*, pp. 28–9.
3 R. W. Stookey, *Yemen: The Politics of the Yemen Arab Republic* (Boulder, West-view, 1978), pp. 156–7.
4 E. Macro, *Western World*, pp. 28–9.
5 The classic text dealing with Haines's conquest and the early government of Aden was written by Gordon Waterfield. It was originally published by John Murray in 1968 and has recently been republished with an envoi by Stephen Day. See G. Waterfield, *Sultans of Aden* (London, Stacey International, 2002).
6 R. G. Gavin, *British Rule*, pp. 135–46.
7 J. C. Wilkinson, *Arabia's Frontiers: The Story of Britain's Boundary Drawing in the Desert* (London, I. B. Tauris, 1991), pp. 102–5.
8 R. G. Gavin, *British Rule*, ch. 7.
9 T. Hickinbotham, *Aden* (London, Constable, 1958), pp. 23–4.
10 R. G. Gavin, *British Rule*, pp. 280–3; Karl Pieragostini, *Britain, Aden and South Arabia: Abandoning Empire* (London, Macmillan, 1991), pp. 22–3.
11 J. C. Wilkinson, *Frontiers*, pp. 162–4.
12 Lord Belhaven, *Uneven Road* (London, John Murray, 1955), pp. 129–33.
13 Ingrams's own account of his time in the Hadhramawt, which was originally published by John Murray in 1942, has appeared in a 4th edition. See H. Ingrams, *Arabia and the Isles* (London, Kegan Paul International, 1998), chs 23–30.
14 *Colonial Office List 1958* (London, HMSO, 1958), p. 49.
15 R. Bidwell, *Yemens*, p. 81.
16 *Colonial Office List 1956* (London, HMSO, 1956), p. 50.
17 R. Bidwell, *Yemens*, p. 83.
18 R. G. Gavin, *British Rule*, p. 320.
19 P. Somerville-Large, *Tribes and Tribulations* (London, Robert Hale, 1967), p. 15.
20 J. E. Peterson, *Defending Arabia* (London, Macmillan, 1986), p. 34.
21 R. G. Gavin, *British Rule*, p. 323.
22 R. Bidwell, *Yemens*, p. 76.
23 B. Reilly, *Aden and the Yemen* (London, HMSO, 1960), p. 15.
24 S. Smith, 'Rulers and Resident: British Relations with the Aden Protectorate', *Middle Eastern Studies* 31 (1995) pp. 511–12.
25 D. Foster, *Landscape with Arabs* (London, Clifton, 1969), p. 94.

26 For the removal of Fadhl see Smith, 'Rulers', p. 516; for the removal of 'Ali see chapter 3.
27 Belhaven, *Road*, p. 78.
28 T. Hickinbotham, *Aden*, pp. 114, 116–17.
29 Interview with Sultan Ghalib of Mukalla.
30 W. G. Clarence-Smith, 'Hadhramaut and the Hadhrami Diaspora in the Modern Colonial Era' in U. Freitag and W. Clarence-Smith (eds), *Hadhrami Traders, Scholars and Statesmen in the Indian Ocean* (Leiden, Brill, 1997), p. 5.
31 H. Ingrams, *Arabia* pp. 143–4.
32 U. Freitag, 'Hadhramis in International Politics 1750–1967' in U. Freitag and W. G. Clarence-Smith (eds), *Hadhrami Traders*, pp. 116–21.
33 C. Lekon, *The British and Hadhramaut 1863–1967* (PhD, London, 2000).
34 H. Ingrams, *Arabia*.
35 *Colonial Office List 1956* (London, HMSO, 1956), p. 53.
36 J. Kostiner, *The Struggle for South Yemen* (Croom Helm, London, 1984), pp. 25–6; R. G. Gavin, *British Rule*, pp. 305–7.
37 IOR: R/20/B/2124, Boustead to Chief Secretary, 25 January 1954.
38 E. O'Ballance, *The War in the Yemen* (London, Faber, 1971), p. 7.
39 R. W. Stookey, *Yemen*, ch. 4.
40 R. Bidwell, *Yemens*, p. 22.
41 R. G. Gavin, *British Rule*, pp. 295–6.
42 J. E. Peterson, *Yemen: The Search for a Modern State* (London, Croom Helm, 1982), p. 59.
43 R. Stookey, *Yemen*, p. 192.
44 H. Ingrams, *The Yemen: Imams, Rulers and Revolutionaries* (London, John Murray, 1963), pp. 108–15.
45 J. Leigh Douglas, *The Free Yemeni Movement* (Beirut, American University of Beirut, 1987), pp. 24–5.
46 J. E. Peterson, *Modern State*, pp. 49–53.
47 R. W. Stookey, *Yemen*, p. 229.
48 Ibid, pp. 193–6.
49 J. Leigh Douglas, *Free Yemeni*, ch. 3.

3 Zenith of the forward policy 1955–1959

Between 1955 and 1959 the British pursued an ambitious programme in southwest Arabia designed to consolidate their long-term influence in the region. This forward policy emerged piecemeal rather than as part of a grand design. It was an outcome of the accordance between the natural inclination of the men on the spot to pursue a policy of imperial pacification and the instincts of Whitehall policy-makers which were to maintain a significant role in Middle East politics. Aden was a useful military base and became the headquarters of British Forces in the Middle East in 1960. Its hinterland provided a *cordon sanitaire* but the base itself could have been safeguarded with a less activist policy had there not been an overwhelming concern with the expansionist ambitions of the Yemeni Imams and the regional aspirations of Nasser. The latter in particular struck at widely held conceptions of Britain's role as a significant world power. It is worth first considering the clash between the British desire to play an influential role in Middle East politics and Nasser's commitment to Arab nationalism in order to put the conflicts in southwest Arabia in context. Subsequently the manner in which the low intensity warfare in the Aden Protectorates became a part of the Anglo-Egyptian struggle is examined. Events in the EAP, Lahj, Upper 'Awlaqi and Dali' are interpreted as instances of this trend. Britain's long-term plans for southwest Arabia will then be considered as will the opposition to them that emerged from Yemen and the colony of Aden. The ascent of nationalist feeling in Yemen and Aden Colony during the late 1950s illustrates the pervasiveness of Nasser's influence at this time.

The Arab challenge to Britain's informal empire

During the course of 1955 Nasser laid successful claim to the leadership of the Arab world. For the next decade he became a cynosure guiding politicians and people from Algeria to Yemen in their struggle to recreate a dignified role for the Arabs following the perceived humiliations of European rule and the establishment of a Zionist state in Palestine. Alongside his personal charisma Nasser offered the Arab world an ideology: his straightforward brand of nationalism, which on occasions spilt over into paranoia and xenophobia, was adopted across the region as a panacea for the long-standing malaise of the Arab peoples. His own conversion to the Arab nationalist cause was a relatively late one but he was hugely successful in propagating the ideas of key nationalist thinkers. During the mandatory period a number of influential Arab writers began to argue that culturally, historically and linguistically the Arabs were a single people for whom unity must be a priority. The writings of the Iraqi educationalist, Sati' al-Husri were particularly significant because of his suggestion that, as the most populous country in the Arab world, Egypt should take the lead in pursuing unification.[1] The problem for men such as al-Husri was that many Egyptians believed the culture of the Nile valley was distinct from that of the Arabs of the Fertile Crescent and the Arabian peninsula. This led to the view that the country had its own distinct national interest to pursue. Nasser resolved the problem of Egyptian particularism by arguing that Arab nationalism could be a useful instrument in combating the threat which Israel and the western imperial powers posed to Egypt. There was regional opposition to Nasser's programme, first from the old elites of the Arab world, alarmed by the levelling trends on view in Cairo, and subsequently from leftists and nationalist particularists in the Fertile Crescent, but his demotic appeal remained largely undamaged until the disaster of the war with Israel in June 1967.[2]

In his public pronouncements Nasser repeatedly identified western imperialism as the principal obstacle to Arab unity.[3] Although this had not been at the forefront of his thinking at the time of the overthrow of King Faruq in 1952, his concern with the deleterious impact of European influence upon Egyptian politics and culture was evident from the retrospective defence of the coup which he published as 'The Philosophy of the Revolution'. This short tract argued that the European powers had perpetuated divisions between the Arabs and provided a potent insight into the terms of nationalist debate in Egypt at this time. Nasser suggests that it was necessary for Egypt to play a role in the African, Muslim and Arab worlds but he gives priority to the Arab circle. The primary problem for the Arabs was the disunity which was evident from their failure to prevent the establishment of a Jewish state in Palestine. Nasser stressed the role of British imperialism in precipitating the catastrophic 1948 war with Israel. On his account a cultural and political revival was essential to prevent a repetition of this disaster and, in achieving this, Egypt confronted precisely the same problems as the other Arab states: 'One region, the same factors and circumstances, even the same forces opposing them all. It was clear that imperialism was the most prominent of these forces; even Israel itself was but one of the outcomes of imperialism. If it had not fallen under British mandate, Zionism could not have found the necessary support to realise the idea of a national home in Palestine.'[4] Egyptian resentment of British imperialism was evident during the Anglo-Egyptian talks on the future of Britain's Suez base. Egyptian negotiators proved extremely sensitive to any evidence that British influence might linger after formal withdrawal. One manifestation of this was their insistence that any technicians who remained behind to maintain the base should not be allowed to wear uniforms.[5]

The Anglo-Egyptian conflict of the 1950s and 1960s was predicated not on a clash of interests but on an incompatibility between two different visions of Middle East order and formed the backdrop to events in southwest Arabia. Since the 1870s the British had been constructing an informal empire in the Middle East and after 1945 British policy-makers steadfastly resisted the loss of a special role in the world. Consequently, for the British, as well as the Egyptians, the negotiations over the Suez base were painful. Like Nasser, Churchill conceptualised British foreign policy as operating within three circles: the Atlantic, continental Europe and the overseas empire.[6] Many Conservative politicians continued to regard the third circle as the most significant. Unfortunately, this circle impinged upon Nasser's conception of Muslim, African and Arab roles for Egypt. The overlap was most obvious in places where Britain retained a military presence, including Egypt, Iraq, Jordan and Aden. From this perspective the loss of the enormous Suez base constituted a potential danger to Britain's continuing global role.

In challenging Britain's role in the Middle East Nasser threatened British determination not to accept a destiny in which it was relegated to the position of a small, over-populated, second-tier industrial nation. It is difficult to uncover the implicit assumptions of British policy-makers; because they were shared there was little reason to state them in policy debates. The memoirs of British politicians are very different from 'The Philosophy of the Revolution' and are, in general, less illuminating. Decisions are customarily couched in terms of an inexactly defined national interest. Explicit statements of the values which policy-makers aim to uphold are rarer. In the case of the Middle East the valedictory dispatch of Charles Johnston provides a valuable exception. Johnston was a diplomat who had first encountered Nasser's influence as ambassador to Jordan. At the end of his term as last Governor and first High Commissioner of Aden he wrote to the Colonial Secretary, Duncan Sandys, that the British tradition of involvement overseas 'has brought out an adventurous swashbuckling strain which might otherwise too easily have become recessive. Unless somehow or other she can continue to look outwards Britain might too easily find herself becoming a very dull place – a sort of poor man's Sweden. Unfortunately however suitable targets for our natural extroversion are becoming rather thin on the ground ... All the more reason in my submission, for keeping up our traditional links with areas which like South Arabia, are of traditional British concern.' The Prime Minister, Harold Macmillan and his foreign secretary, Alec Doublas-Home gave this analysis their personal approval and it was distributed to the Cabinet.[7]

Despite the evident contradictions between Britain's desire to play a predominant role in Middle East politics and Nasser's determination to secure Arab autonomy, an Anglo-Egyptian agreement was completed in October

1954 after nine years of intermittent but fraught negotiations. For long periods the British had insisted on maintaining a military presence inside the Canal Zone. However, the final agreement included stipulations for a full military withdrawal from the Suez base. From a strategic perspective Egypt was becoming less important to the British as the Chiefs of Staff moved away from the so-called 'outer ring' strategy which focussed on Egypt towards an inner ring strategy designed to contain the Soviet Union on its frontiers and which centred on the so-called Northern Tier states Iraq and Turkey. The signing of the treaty therefore appeared to augur well for Anglo-Egyptian relations by removing one of the key sources of tension between the two countries.[8] Such auguries were misleading: the British vision of the Arab world's future was in dramatic contrast to the prescriptions of Arab nationalism. Rather than diffusing tension, the increasing significance of the alliance with Iraq to Britain's new Northern Tier strategy implicated them in the ongoing and increasingly bitter rivalry between Baghdad and Cairo.[9] In the same month that the Anglo-Egyptian base agreement was finalised the Prime Minister of Iraq, Nuri al-Said, visited Turkey to discuss an alliance between the two countries. In February 1955 a defence pact between Turkey and Iraq was signed. The reactions of the British and Egyptian governments to this event provided a definitive demonstration of the irreconcilability of British imperialism and Arab nationalism. Faysal I, the grandfather of the Iraqi King, Faysal II, had been placed on his throne 25 years earlier by the British Prime Minister, Winston Churchill. Turkey was the first and only Middle Eastern power aligned to Britain through the North Atlantic Treaty. The alliance between these two pro-western Middle Eastern states provided British policy-makers with an opportunity to revive British fortunes. In April they joined with Pakistan and Britain to form the Baghdad Pact. The Pact offered the possibility of perpetuating British influence in the region at a time when formal colonialism was increasingly problematic. Subsequently, the British encouraged Iran and Jordan to accede.[10]

To Nasser the attempt to bind Iraq and Jordan to a coalition of non-Arab western oriented powers was a threat to Egypt's regional ambitions. In his view the interests of Egypt were linked inextricably to those of the wider Arab world. Nasser responded to the actions of Turkey and Iraq by drawing closer to Syria and negotiating an arms deal with the Soviet Union. His argument that the Baghdad Pact was a cover for western imperialism was forcefully presented by radio Cairo and in the Arab press.[11] The key battleground in the Anglo-Egyptian confrontation was Jordan. When Eden dispatched the Chief of the Imperial General Staff, Gerald Templer, to negotiate Jordan's entry into the Baghdad Pact in December 1955, Cairo launched a propaganda offensive which accused the young Hashemite ruler, King Husayn, of acting as an imperialist dupe. Riots broke out in the Jordanian capital, Amman, and it is likely that Husayn only retained his throne by abjuring any intention of joining the Pact. As a sop to nationalist opinion he subsequently dismissed the British commander of the Jordanian Arab Legion, John Glubb. These events were viewed in Whitehall as merely the latest move by Nasser to expel British influence from the Middle East.[12]

The disturbances in Jordan illustrated the contrary aims of the British and Egyptians. British efforts to revive their influence appeared to damage Egyptian security by undermining the united Arab front against Israel; Nasser's reinterpretation of Arab nationalism was, in turn, a threat to Britain's great power status. Just as the manoeuvres behind the Baghdad Pact undermined plans to unite the Arab world, Nasser's violent reaction compromised British ambitions to remain a global actor. It was not merely because he challenged British interests or because he upset the Cold War balance of power in the Middle East that Nasser was regarded as such a rebarbative figure by a generation of British statesmen. British hostility to Nasser predated the dramatic events at Suez and lingered long afterwards. During the winter of 1955–56 Eden habitually referred to Nasser as a new Mussolini; the latter had been an earlier *bête noire* of the Prime Minister. In a conversation with his former Private Secretary, Evelyn Shuckburgh, on 29 January 1956 Eden 'compared Nasser with Mussolini and said his object was to be a Caesar from the Gulf to the Atlantic, and to kick us out of it all.'[13] Should Nasser succeed in doing so then Britain's Middle Eastern front in the Cold War would collapse and oil supplies from the region would become vulnerable to the Soviets. Increasingly, British policy-makers believed the only means by which such a disastrous scenario could be avoided was to weaken or overthrow the Egyptian leader. Macmillan confided to his diary on 3 October 1955 that the government intended 'to make Nasser uncomfortable and build up the Northern States.'[14] The idea of discomforting Nasser took substantive form a few months later with the development of the new doctrine on Egypt. By March 1956 Nasser's year-long campaign of subversion against Britain's Hashemite allies, his successful courting of the Soviet Union as an arms supplier and finally the collapse of the Anglo-American Alpha initiative to resolve the Arab-Israeli conflict caused British ministers to translate their feelings of antipathy towards the Egyptian leader into a policy of outright opposition. Macmillan's replacement as Foreign Secretary, Selwyn Lloyd, produced a programme of actions designed to isolate and weaken Nasser. Much against the wishes of Humphrey Trevelyan, the British ambassador in Cairo, Eden authorised Lloyd's plan to co-operate with the American administration in implementing measures to destabilise the Egyptian government.[15] Although there were some differences between British and American attitudes to Nasser, joint operations to undermine his position went ahead under the codename Omega. The primary aim of the Omega operations was to discredit Nasser as an Arab leader by weakening his domestic position and building up his rivals abroad.[16]

This hostility to Nasser was not merely personal; he was the representative of a generation of nationalist thinkers who saw their future not in terms of continued co-operation with the imperial metropolis but with the complete overthrow of British influence. After India was granted independence in 1947 the Middle East became the focus of British imperial ambitions. Since the collapse of the Ottoman Empire the British had steadily built an informal empire in the region and even after the abandonment of the Suez base Britain had an extensive network of formal and informal ties to Cyprus, Aden and the Protectorates, Oman, the Gulf principalities, Iraq, Jordan and Libya. These guaranteed continuing British economic and strategic interests in the Middle East but also gave her an independent role in the increasingly bipolar system of global politics. An earlier generation of nationalist leaders, drawn from the old elites of the Arab world had co-operated with Britain's Middle East ventures. The most notable of these were the Hashemites. They had identified the Turks as the principal obstacle to Arab unity and viewed the British as potential allies in constructing an Arab nation under their control. By striking out at the two Hashemite kings, Faysal II in Iraq and Husayn in Jordan, Nasser endangered this congenial vision of an orderly Middle East constructed according to British designs.

The attempt to sustain British predominance in an era of nationalism was viewed sceptically in Washington. It is noticeable that despite his flirting with the Communist bloc countries American administrations were consistently more willing than the British to contemplate rapprochement with Nasser. Once they understood the extent of Nasser's hostility to British plans, the Eisenhower administration attempted to dissuade the British from encouraging new Arab members to join the Baghdad Pact. Anglo-American differences on the matter of how to deal with Arab nationalism diverged still further after Nasser nationalised the Suez Canal. The motivation behind Eisenhower's opposition to the British invasion of Egypt is the subject of some debate but it reflected at least in part the greater priority which the United States gave to the Cold War confrontation in comparison with the increasing British obsession with the threat from Arab nationalism.[17]

Events in southwest Arabia are often omitted when describing the rise in Anglo-Arab tensions during the two crucial years of 1955 and 1956. Clearly, Aden and the Protectorates lagged some way behind Iraq or Jordan in both British and Egyptian priorities. Nevertheless, prior to the Anglo-French attack on Egypt in November 1956 southwest Arabia was the only region of the Middle East where Arabs were in direct armed conflict with the British; it was also the one area of the Middle East where the British were on the advance. The remainder of this chapter will outline nature of the forward policy in the 1950s and the emergence of a nascent Arab nationalist opposition in Aden and the surrounding Protectorates.

The forward policy in the Protectorates

The 1950s are sometimes portrayed as an era of British imperial recession illustrated most vividly by the Suez debacle. In the case of the Arabian peninsula, however, British influence markedly increased during the decade and there is no evidence that Suez generated new reflections. Both in the Gulf, where the British were vigorous in pressing the claims of their allies to the Buraymi oasis while strengthening their ties with local rulers, and in South Arabia, where the forward policy appeared to be accelerating, the British continued to exercise a predominant influence. During the mid-1950s the Western and Eastern Aden Protectorates still appeared isolated from events elsewhere in the Middle East. The forward policy conducted in this region was a response to local exigencies and the opposition to it came from local actors. Subsequently, southwest Arabia became a key front in the wider Middle East struggle between Nasser and the British. By the end of the decade policy-makers in Cairo and London were paying increasingly close attention to events there and, while local conflicts continued to generate their own tensions, they did so in the context of a proxy war between British and Egyptian surrogates.

Governors and later High Commissioners of Aden demonstrated a significant degree of freedom from Whitehall control when it came to the quotidian exercise of their powers. Matters of larger policy, such as plans for federation or for the merger of Aden with the protected states, were also usually generated by the men on the spot rather than the British government. However, when wider issues of colonial policy were at stake the Colonial Office, the Foreign Office and very often the Prime Minister participated in the debate. British ministers were keen to retain defence facilities and more generally were concerned that British actions in southwest Arabia should not damage British prestige in the Middle East. In practical policy terms this meant that they wished to retain and consolidate British authority as part of a wider effort to retain a role in the Middle East rather than begin the process of handing over power to local actors. Similarly, those who took up arms against the extension of British control initially did so in response to the byzantine parochial intrigues which accompanied the forward policy. Only gradually did these disputes become attached to the wider struggle in the Middle East; nevertheless, by 1959 these connections were becoming increasingly evident.

Tom Hickinbotham, the Governor, Kennedy Trevaskis, the WAP Resident Adviser and Hugh Boustead, the EAP Resident Adviser, were united in their determination to uphold British responsibilities at a local level and this was the motor behind the forward policy. Indeed each was so consumed by the quagmire of local politics that it makes little sense to view the forward policy as part of a grand strategy for securing Britain's material interests. For Hickinbotham its essence was the imposition of order upon anarchy. Despite some differences over tactics, Aden and Whitehall shared the goal of attempting to consolidate British control. Hickinbotham's policies were implemented with the tacit consent of the Conservative government. This initially meant combating the parochial challenge posed by the Saudis and the Hamid al-Din but increasingly it required the insulation of the region against Nasser's rising influence in the Middle East. In retrospect it is evident that the pursuit of the forward policy had the reverse effect to that intended: it strengthened ties between opponents of British actions in the Protectorates and external actors such as Egypt, Saudi Arabia and Yemen who had their own disputes with the British. This trend is best illustrated through a brief examination of the impact of British policy in some key regions of the Protectorates.

a. The Eastern Aden Protectorate

Amidst the general increase in Anglo-Egyptian tension across the wider region developments in the Eastern Aden Protectorate went unnoticed in London and Cairo. It is very doubtful whether most Conservative ministers of the time would have had even the vaguest notion of where, amongst the remains of the British Empire, the Hadhramawt or the British residency at Mukalla, were situated. A British official who worked in the northern desert on the frontiers of the EAP recalled: 'Such catfights as I had so far refereed seemed ... to be pregnant with earth-shattering consequences; but in the rarefied atmosphere of Mukalla they were like so many rooks quarrelling in a tree.'[18] If this was the view from the administrative centre of the EAP it should be acknowledged that to observers in Whitehall the tribal politics of the region were all but invisible. Nevertheless, events across the EAP in the 1950s provide some of the most vivid illustrations of British determination to restructure the politics of southwest Arabia. The impulse to move forward was felt in this region as strongly as elsewhere and took the most literal form of an advance into previously uncharted regions.

The prospect of oil discoveries was the only potential point of interest for authorities in London but to the British who administered the EAP from Mukalla there were other motives for pursuing a forward policy. Outside of the main towns the region was scarred by dreadful poverty and a concerted effort at development was a priority for British officials in the region. In general, conditions were more propitious for such an enterprise in Qu'ayti and Kathiri than in the WAP. The most important British initiatives were in the fields of drought relief, irrigation and road building. Two roads were built from the EAP coast into the heart of the Hadhramawt valley. However, these constructions were not welcomed by those local people whose livelihoods were threatened by British interference. The bedouin who had traditionally transported men and material inland on their camels attacked vehicles that made use of the new roads. Cars and trucks constituted unfair competition in their eyes and their passengers were regarded as intruders. The insurgent camel-drivers were supplied with arms by the Saudis and in June 1955 they trapped units of the British officered Hadhrami Bedouin Legion (HBL), on the more westerly of the two new roads. It was only reopened and the rebellion temporarily quelled as a result of RAF attacks upon the rebels.[19]

Through the suppression of such uprisings the British consolidated their control in the central regions of the Hadhramawt, while in the northern desert the British extended their influence into uncharted regions in an effort to stake out the territory for their favoured concessionary, Petroleum Concessions Limited. This process culminated with the building of a fort at Habarut in 1956; an act which was 'eyed as an outrageous intrusion by the inhabitants of the area.' By this stage the British were close to the ill-defined northern frontier between the EAP and Saudi Arabia where they ran into the agents of the American oil consortium ARAMCO who had armed support from their Saudi patrons. As in the case of 'the battle of the roads' in the previous year the authorities in Mukalla responded forcibly. The HBL were ordered to the far corner of the EAP and successfully ejected the Saudi-American intruders.[20]

Those who opposed the forward policy in the EAP, including recalcitrant local rulers, were punished if they failed to co-operate with the forward policy. To the south of the northern desert the British pressed forward into the desolate Mahra territory which stretched along the coast between the domains of the Qu'ayti and Omani Sultans. The nominal ruler of this area, Sultan Isa, lived in splendid isolation on the offshore island of Socotra. Like so many other such dignitaries he was regarded as neglectful by the British. He rarely visited the mainland and his obstruction of British efforts to enter the area nearly brought about his downfall. The British suspected that there might be oil in Mahra and were determined that Sultan Isa, or any other EAP ruler, should not be allowed to monopolise the profits from a putative oil boom. With their minds turned to the long-term future of the region, the authorities in Mukalla drafted plans for an EAP federation which was intended to provide political stability and a framework for economic development, both of which were regarded as essential should oil be discovered. The rulers of the EAP states in general, and Isa in particular, were distrustful of British intentions and of each other and the federal scheme foundered in late 1954 following a series of fruitless negotiations. Subsequently, the British made plans for a less ambitious solution: an oil agreement prescribing how the profits from any oil find might be shared. However, the EAP rulers remained unable to overcome their suspicions of one another and this scheme too had to be abandoned. The Resident in the EAP, Hugh Boustead, singled out Sultan Isa as the most significant obstacle to progress in these negotiations. During the first months of 1956 Boustead drew up plans to depose Isa but the British eventually contented themselves with marginalising him through the appointment of a new representative on the mainland. The Mahra country became subject to regular visits by the HBL for the first time.[21] The history of relations between the British residency in Mukalla and Isa demonstrate that by the 1950s the forward policy was reaching into the most secluded regions of the EAP. The same trend is evident in the WAP.

b. Lahj

If events in the EAP have both contemporary and posthumous obscurity, developments in Lahj were sufficiently significant for Macmillan to leave a tendentious account of them in his memoirs.[22] The more advanced state of the economy and the historic claims of the 'Abdali Sultan of Lahj, who had lost Aden to the British a century earlier, made this territory vulnerable to Nasserism. Ever since Haines had seized Aden from the 'Abdali Sultans their relations with the British had been uneasy and this continued into the 1950s. The Aden authorities concluded, with some justification, that the latest 'Abdali incumbent, Sultan Fadhl, was unlikely to supervise the creation of an effective administration and he was deposed in 1952 in favour of his brother 'Ali whose efficiency and modernising instincts led Trevaskis to regard him as 'an ideal choice.'[23] 'Ali made a good impression on the British as a dashing and competent ruler. He was however also representative of a new breed of ruler whose progressive views constituted a potential threat to continued British control. In particular his adoption of a 'modernist' nationalist agenda was crucial in bringing Nasserism to the Protectorates. Ruth Knox-Mawer, a journalist for the Daily Express who knew 'Ali well, recorded the differences between him and the more orthodox, Sultan Saleh of 'Awdhali: 'Seen side by side like this, Ali's expensive silk shirt and immaculate trousers next to Saleh's tribal khaki, the contrast between them was striking: the contrast between the old and the new type of ruler, between the would-be modern and the necessarily feudal, and made even more striking by the fact that they were both young men of about the same age, and both very handsome. Saleh's face was the more determined of the two, almost ruthless the face of a man of action, while Ali had the look of a dreamer.' 'Ali himself explained the difference in political terms: 'I suppose you might sum it up like this. Quite soon there will be no such thing as a Sultan here. We shall all be swept away and my comment would be a very good thing too. Because you see to be a nationalist is to be a republican. But for Sultan Saleh such an outlook would be impossible. His is the old way, ours is the new.'[24]

Matters were not quite as straightforward as this implies: 'Ali clearly believed that he could secure the continued influence of his family even in a republican system. His ambitions were to combine the reassertion of 'Abdali supremacy in southwest Arabia with a programme of modernisation based on the Egyptian model. In order to achieve this he tied his fortunes to those of the nationalists. Thus, whereas Sultan Isa of Qishn and Socotra ran into problems for his backward looking approach, 'Ali was to fall foul of the British for attaching himself to the latest trends in the Arab world. In fact, 'Ali was precisely the kind of moderate nationalist with whom the British had been forced to compromise elsewhere in the empire and towards the end of British rule a belated attempt at rapprochement was made.

The benefits of 'Ali's administrative competence were rapidly offset by his attachment to nationalism. William Luce, who replaced Hickinbotham as Governor in 1956, regarded 'Ali as an Egyptian surrogate. Luce and Trevaskis interpreted his alliance with the South Arabian League (SAL) as a threat to Britain's role in the region. The League had been founded in 1951 and was led by Muhammad al-Jifri. Its goal was an independent southwest Arabia. On the grounds that he was 'trafficking with Colonel Nasser in Cairo', al-Jifri was excluded from Aden Colony in August 1956. By this time Britain was planning war with Egypt to regain control of the Suez canal. In the midst of the Suez crisis, the Prime Minister, Anthony Eden, took a moment to declare he wished to see the SAL leader 'laid by the heels'.[25] 'Ali's subsequent decision to allow Muhammad al-Jifri and his two brothers to operate from Lahj and his increasing reliance on their advice seemed to the WAP Resident Adviser, Kennedy Trevaskis, to imperil Britain's forward policy. In particular, the support which Lahj gave to dissident groups elsewhere in the Protectorates had the potential to undermine Trevaskis's plans to create a pro-British federation amongst the WAP states.[26] When rumours spread during the first months of 1958 that 'Ali would enter into some form of confederation with Egypt the case for regarding 'Ali and the SAL as Nasser's proxies, and by extension for his removal, appeared proven.

The process of ousting 'Ali was accompanied by a degree of intrigue involving all parties, remarkable even by the exacting standards of southwest Arabia. Although the evidence on the Arab side is filtered through jaundiced British perceptions, 'Ali's aim at this time was evidently to re-establish 'Abdali influence throughout southern Arabia. In order to achieve this he consorted with the SAL, the Imam of Yemen and the newly formed United Arab Republic (UAR) of Syria and Egypt. Luce's aims and methods are more transparent: he wished to remove nationalist influence from Lahj by ridding the territory of both the SAL leadership and the Egyptian teachers employed by 'Ali. The latter were regarded as Nasser's vanguard in the territory. On 7 April 1958 Luce recommended an armed intervention into Lahj to arrest Muhammad al-Jifri and his brothers. He hoped this would provoke 'Ali into abdicating.[27] Apparently convinced that the Jifris were negotiating Lahj's entry into the UAR, on 18 April Luce authorised their arrest in an operation codenamed POUCH. The attempted snatch proved unsuccessful; Muhammad al-Jifri escaped to Ta'izz in Yemen and his brother 'Alawi fled to Upper 'Awlaqi.[28]

The Jifris' escape and 'Ali's refusal to abdicate left Luce with the dilemma of how to eliminate SAL influence permanently without stirring up further nationalist feeling. His solution was to engage in a series of provocations designed to pressure the sensitive 'Ali into rash actions which could provide the basis for his removal. 'Ali described the tactics employed by Luce during the course of POUCH in a letter of protest delivered to the Governor on 29 April: 'a number of tanks and guns surrounded my palace at Lahj, a large convoy of trucks the length of which was about two miles had occupied Lahj

... They occupied my police station and attacked the officer in charge of the police station and his officers, cut the telephone cables, disrupted the communications and prevented the people from leaving their houses. Some of your soldiers performed acts of robbery in the country.'[29] Luce took the opportunity of the visit of a number of Protectorate rulers to London in May to increase the pressure on 'Ali. British officials in Whitehall were instructed to snub 'Ali, while in Lahj itself Luce banned the flying of Egyptian flags and prevented the Egyptian teachers from returning to work. He explained that these actions were designed to 'so injure the Sultan's personal prestige as to deter him from returning to the State.'[30] 'Ali duly responded by delaying his return from London in order to visit Milan, while encouraging his officials back in Lahj to defect over the border into Yemen. These events and the rumour that 'Ali's next stop was Cairo provided the pretext for Luce to order the Sultan to London to explain his actions. 'Ali was 'visibly shaken' when presented with this summons and opted to fly to Egypt instead. This was the opportunity Luce had sought. He withdrew the British government's recognition of 'Ali and installed the more pliant Fadhl ibn 'Ali as Sultan. This had long been his preferred outcome.[31] 'Ali's removal temporarily undermined SAL influence in Lahj but less than a decade later the British were forced to reopen negotiations with 'Ali in order to seek his assistance against the more radical groups who emerged in the early 1960s.

c. *Upper 'Awlaqi*

Nowhere better illustrates the unforeseen long-term problems which emerged as a consequence of the forward policy than the Upper 'Awlaqi region. Prior to the 1950s the British had known the area as a source of recruits for the local security forces but it was not until 1951 that the decision was taken to pacify the area. Over the course of the next decade a series of minor conflicts were fought in the region as local tribes resisted increased British control. Opposition to the British was not restricted to tribal factions but extended to the rulers. Although the Ahl Farid, who controlled the Shaykhdom in the east of the region, had levered themselves into power with British assistance and remained committed to this alliance, the Sultan, who ruled the western regions, was reluctant to make contact with the Aden authorities. Suspecting that he was consorting with Imam Ahmad, Hickinbotham ordered the occupation of the Sultanate in early 1953. This was the starting point for the arduous process of pacification.

Until the British entry the Upper 'Awlaqi region was governed by tribal law or, as the British would have it, anarchy. Following the outbreak of a commonplace but violent local feud in the Wadi Hatib the Aden Protectorate Levies entered the valley in November 1953. There was every expectation that the local tribe, the Rabiz, would resent the intrusion and in response the APL were instructed to seize hostages, requisition grain and seize the tribe's animal stock.[32] As predicted the Rabiz resisted these incursions into their territory. Rather than risk a permanent commitment of troops the local political officer attempted to mediate a truce with the insurgents. However, in the midst of the negotiations a small APL force continued to pursue the punitive measures outlined in their original instructions. They attacked a house in which the elderly aunt of one of the key Rabiz tribal leaders, 'Ali Mawar, lived and killed her. This farcical but tragic incident had serious consequences given that it constituted a blatant slur upon tribal honour. The killing precipitated a renewal of the conflict, with the Ahl Shams sub-section of the Rabiz, to whom 'Ali Mawar belonged, taking the lead.[33] The British could not ignore the rebellion because it jeopardised their plans to build a road through the Wadi Hatib. Furthermore, once the Imam of Yemen began supplying the insurgents with arms the Upper 'Awlaqi region became a significant front in the Anglo-Yemeni conflict. In order to deal with the insurrection a small fort was built at Robat from which it was hoped punitive expeditions could be launched against the Ahl Shams.

The decision to construct a fort in the midst of Rabizi territory proved disastrous. Robat was isolated in the midst of a mountainous and hostile territory and resupplying the garrison was onerous and costly. The Government Guards, who had been responsible for maintaining day-to-day order in the WAP since 1938, were given the task of convoying supplies back and forth to Robat. They were repeatedly fired upon by the Ahl Shams and in early February 1955 one guard was killed and seven wounded by insurgent tribesmen. In June a much larger attack on a convoy of Government Guards and Aden Protectorate Levies returning from Robat resulted in the deaths of six Arab soldiers and two British officers.[34] The local commander reported, 'Shamsi are pure Bedouin gangsters ... Robat is the worst wicket in the Protectorate and it is unwise to go on playing the Yemen on such ground.'[35] Eden was furious at this debacle, which constituted an embarrassing blow to British prestige at a time when his government was attempting to consolidate their influence in the Middle East through the expansion of the Baghdad Pact. The insistence of the military authorities that the Robat commitment was unsustainable was most unwelcome. The Aden authorities were informed: 'Ministers are concerned at the loss of prestige which may follow the evacuation ... any action, such as abandonment of the Fort, should be followed quickly by action which would clearly demonstrate our determination to restore and maintain control over the area as a whole.'[36] This proved quite impossible. The garrison locked the doors of Robat fort behind them on leaving and a small expeditionary force was dispatched which was unable to find the Ahl Shams. Subsequently, the RAF launched desultory air strikes from Aden into the Wadi Hatib but it remained outside British administrative control for the rest of the decade.[37]

d. Dali'

Although events in Dali' during this period were less dramatic than those in the previous two cases they nevertheless provide instructive examples of the relentless, quotidian problems of implementing the forward policy. Once again the British struggled to find local leaders willing both to co-operate in reform and forgo the opportunity of attaching themselves to the Arab nationalist cause. In 1947 the British removed Sultan Haidera from power on the grounds that he failed the first test: he was incorrigibly committed to tyranny rather than enlightened reform. Haidera fled to Yemen where he engaged in various plots to destabilise his former patrimony with the connivance of Imam Ahmad. By mid-1956 Dali' was, along with Upper 'Awlaqi, the most troublesome region of the WAP. The Sha'iri and Radfani confederations, which were inside Dali' on British maps, if not in any other meaningful sense, were amongst the most inveterate defenders of tribal autonomy. They were implicated in a plot to assassinate the British political officer sent out to negotiate with them in 1951. Their dissent provided an opportunity to Haidera who, in co-operation with his host, Imam Ahmad, supplied arms to dissident tribesmen. In August 1956 Sha'iri tribesmen murdered a prominent *sayyid* who the British had used as a mediator.[38] During the next six months there were continuous attacks on roads and settlements until Luce secured some abatement by raiding the dissidents' arms source at Qa'tabah inside Yemen. The problem of long-term pacification of Dali' proved irresolvable and in April 1958 a new crisis arose when Radfani tribesmen shot at the British adviser and an accompanying force of Government Guards during a tour of the area. The officer and the Guards were for a time besieged by approximately 300 insurgents and the RAF were required to resupply them from the air. In a spirit reminiscent of many earlier imperial adventures a British relief column was organised but on this occasion they were able to take advantage of support from Venom and Shackleton aircraft.[39] The siege was lifted but the Radfan remained unadministered and would be the base from which the NLF launched their own rebellion against the British five years later.

There is a clear trend evident in Dali' and the previous cases: in the EAP opponents of the British entered into a tacit alliance with the Saudi authorities to oppose Britain's advance; when the British challenged Sultan 'Ali's policies in Lahj he turned to Egypt for succour; in Dali' and Upper 'Awlaqi the Radfanis and the Shamsi welcomed assistance from the Imam of Yemen. The role of actors external to Aden and the Protectorates became increasingly significant in subsequent years and this development undoubtedly had its origins in the forward policy. However, the British authorities in Aden believed they had an effective strategy to counter their opponents: they hoped to create a cohesive federation from the Protectorate states which would effectively contain nationalism both prior to and after the grant of independence to the region.

Founding the federation

The forward policy acquired momentum because of the actions of policy-makers in Aden rather than in Whitehall. It was nevertheless underpinned by the determination of Conservative ministers to cling on to Aden Colony for as long as possible. While there was unanimity that Britain must continue to exercise influence in southwest Arabia, a divide opened in British policy-making circles between those, mainly in Aden, who believed a continued presence in the region could be guaranteed by a political settlement with an independent but pro-British Arab government and those, mainly in London, who wished to retain sovereignty over Britain's last imperial possession in the Middle East indefinitely. The idea of switching to a system of informal control in Aden met with scepticism from Conservative ministers.[40]

The principal advocate of such a change in policy was the British Resident Adviser in the Western Aden Protectorate, Kennedy Trevaskis. What Trevaskis appreciated more acutely than any other British minister or official was the requirement to build effective institutions which could guarantee continuing British influence in southwest Arabia. He had come to the region in 1951 following service in Africa and over the following 15 years developed an extensive knowledge of tribal affairs. Most of those working under him in the WAP respected his abilities. Others found him domineering and bullying. He had a natural capacity for command but was a difficult subordinate. This was partly a consequence of his singleness of purpose. Trevaskis was convinced that the best means both of protecting British influence and securing political stability was to create an independent federal state dominated by Britain's allies among the tribal rulers. This set him against the nationalists in Aden, who could not imagine a worse fate than subordination to the pro-British rulers; Yemeni modernisers, who wanted a union between the territories governed by the Imam and those under British control in the south; and the tribes of the WAP, to whom the notion of loyalty to some broader South Arabian federation was alien. His plans also caused some consternation in Whitehall where a number of policy-makers wished to retain direct British control and did not trust the rulers as guarantors of British influence.

Trevaskis was relentless in his pursuit of a federation amongst the states of the interior as a first step towards the creation of a united state encompassing Aden and the Protectorates. In 1952 he and Boustead drew up schemes for separate federations in the WAP and the EAP but these foundered on opposition from the rulers. After a second attempt to secure a federal agreement during the course of 1954 failed, Trevaskis returned to the fray for a third time in 1955. In August he submitted new proposals to the British government. Macmillan and Eden, who could have had only the haziest idea of what the implications of Trevaskis's plan were, felt instinctively that federation might lead to independence which they opposed. The problem for Trevaskis was that the Conservative government was not yet ready to relinquish formal control of southwest Arabia. Aden was still regarded as a significant asset in terms of both British strategy and prestige. Neither the Churchill nor Eden governments were prepared for a wide scale demission of power to the imperial periphery in the mid-1950s. In 1954 a Whitehall analysis of the future of the colonies concluded that as many as twenty colonies would require some measure of continued British control in perpetuity.[41] When Trevaskis's federation proposals were presented to the Cabinet sub-committee dealing with colonial affairs Lord Salisbury, who was an inveterate opponent of decolonization, warned of 'the dangers of giving the rulers an exaggerated idea of the independence they were likely to achieve.' It was this view which prevailed and the section of Trevaskis's scheme promising early independence was excised and replaced with a vague promise of self-government.[42] In order to establish the decoupling of federation and independence, the Colonial Office Under-Secretary, Lord Lloyd, visited Aden in May 1956 and announced that the Colony could never progress beyond 'a considerable degree of internal self-government.' This blunt rejection of an independent future for southwest Arabia horrified both British officials in Aden and the local rulers, many of whom were beginning to chafe at British interference. As Robin Bidwell has described, 'British officials on the spot were aghast at this curt refusal of further discussions which, they felt, would only provoke hostile feeling.'[43] Lloyd was sufficiently sharp to recognise some of this negative reaction. He reported on his return to London that Sultan 'Ali of Lahj responded to the proposal for federation without independence by reminding the Governor that the protected states, although bound to the United Kingdom by treaty, were already independent. In this atmosphere the talks on federation collapsed.

The audit of British imperial commitments ordered by Macmillan at the outset of his premiership in January 1957 confirmed the importance of Aden to Britain's Middle East strategy.[44] The base was singled out as a vital asset in the defence of British Middle East interests. In addition the Defence White Paper produced just a few months after the end of the Suez crisis affirmed that Aden should be retained as a key element of Britain's new defence policy. It stated: 'Britain must at all times be ready to defend Aden Colony and Protectorates and the territories on the Persian Gulf for whose defence she is responsible. For this task land, air and sea forces have to be maintained in that area.'[45] With the failure of federation a new political strategy was required for maintaining this control at a time when Arab nationalism was gaining new adherents. Hickinbotham's replacement, William Luce, was not initially inclined to pursue Trevaskis's plans for constitutional advance. He accepted the British government's argument that continual discussion of federation was in danger of hastening the spread of nationalism and for a time this remained the official view. The alternative to political advance was seen as economic development. The government's Middle East committee concluded: 'proposals for further development arise fundamentally from the defence and diplomatic requirements of the United Kingdom and the Middle East. For strategic, commercial and diplomatic reasons Great Britain needs to retain the Colony; the retention of the Colony is greatly facilitated by retention of control of the Protectorate.'[46] The Colonial Secretary, Alan Lennox-Boyd, told the Colonial Policy committee in January 1958 that his department 'had concluded that we had a strong interest in maintaining control of Aden Colony for an indefinite future period.' They in turn endorsed the analysis of the Middle East committee.[47]

While these discussions continued in London, Trevaskis was planning to revive the federation idea. On 20 February 1958 he met representatives of Bayhan, Fadli and 'Awdhali and the rulers of those states subsequently wrote to Luce indicating a desire to federate.[48] This request and the rapid advance of Nasser's cause, represented most immediately by Egypt's sudden union with Syria in February 1958, caused Luce to reconsider his previous opposition to the Trevaskis programme of federation, merger and independence. At the end of March 1958 he sent 'important, long and rather shattering letters' to the Colonial Office. Luce declared that British policy in Aden was swimming against four tides: the spread of decolonization, the rise of Arab nationalism, the decline of British power and the expansion of Russian influence. If the government in London chose to resist these forces 'in the process of holding on to the bitter end we should have given Russia and Egypt the opportunity to strengthen their hold on the Middle East and would have done untold harm to our interests in other parts of the Arab world.' As early withdrawal was unthinkable, Luce concluded that the only the viable option was a return to Trevaskis's principles: 'to embark on a policy of gradual disengagement from our position in south-west Arabia with the object of strengthening our friends in both Colony and Protectorate.' He therefore proposed a ten-year strategy for British disengagement. The revival of the federation idea was to be the first step in this process.[49]

Luce was injudicious in attaching the notion of federation to that of independence. The authorities in Whitehall remained sceptical of the idea of independence within ten years.[50] This latest scheme for constitutional change was eventually supported by the Foreign Secretary, Selwyn Lloyd, Colonial Secretary, Alan Lennox-Boyd and Minister of Defence, Duncan Sandys, but solely on the basis that it would 'eventually lead to a strengthening of our whole position in the Aden area.' In June 1958 the Cabinet formally endorsed Luce's federation proposals and representatives of five states visited London for a discussion of the financial implication of federation in July.[51] Subsequently, Luce abandoned the ten-year timetable and instead pressed ahead with the two crucial pre-requisites of his scheme: federation in the Protectorates followed by a merger with the Colony. This, he hoped would lay the basis for a stable state in which anti-British elements would be subdued by Britain's friends among the Aden elite and the rulers of the Protectorates.[52]

Another element of Luce's ten-year disengagement plan proved contro-versial: the proposal for a merger between Aden and the Protectorate states caused some alarm amongst Conservative ministers. Lennox-Boyd supported the Governor's suggestion that Aden should be incorporated into the puta-tive federation and told the Colonial Policy committee in December 1958 that the union of Aden with the shaykhdoms 'would subject the extreme political elements in the Colony to the moderating influence of the more Conservative Rulers in the Protectorates.' However, Sandys was reluctant to take any step which might jeopardise British control of the base. He did not believe that handing over authority in Aden to the tribal leaders could provide as effective a guarantee of access to British defence facilities as the maintenance of British sovereignty.[53] Fortunately for Luce, a final resolution of the merger issue was not required to reach agreement on federation and the issue was left pending while detailed constitutional arrangements were finalised. On 11 February 1959 Bayhan, 'Awdhali, Fadli, Lower Yafi', Dali' and the Upper 'Awlaqi Shaykhdom united to form a federation. The new state remained largely dependent on British advice and finance. The Gover-nor in Aden was the federation's head of state and had powers to declare a state of emergency. He retained control of foreign affairs, budgetary matters and security, while the federal authorities had responsibility for issues such as health, education and transport. The Supreme Council of the new federa-tion consisted of the Protectorate rulers or their nominees. The system was predicated on a continued identity of interests between the rulers and the British and on the same day as the federal agreement came into force a treaty of friendship between Britain and the new federation was signed.[54] Given that western liberal democracy was entirely alien to the tribal culture of the Protectorates, the domination of the system by tribal chiefs was in a sense natural but it is worth noting that it also suited British interests. A Foreign Office official explained Selwyn Lloyd's view 'that recent experience in the Middle East had shown the instability of democratic systems of government . . . he would, therefore, hope that in the administration of the Federation the democratic element would be kept to the minimum. If extremist elements from the Colony were to gain control of the Federation it might well result in the whole of South West Arabia joining the anti-British camp.'[55]

Lloyd's concerns partly reflected the fact that Aden was one of the few remaining imperial possessions that could be justified on material grounds. The conclusion that Aden must be retained as a colony rested on the premises that the base was vital to British interests and that it could not be guaranteed by a treaty relationship with a friendly government. The author-ities in Aden contested the validity of this latter proposition and towards the end of the 1950s the balance began to swing towards this point of view. However, underlying all of this was the perception, which was confirmed rather than falsified by the Suez crisis, that Nasser was a threat to Britain's continuing role in the world. In February 1958 Macmillan had a conversation with his predecessor about the lessons of the Suez crisis. He concluded: 'If the Americans had helped us the history of the Middle East w[oul]d have changed. Now, I fear, Nasser, (like Mussolini) will achieve his Arab empire & it may take a war to dislodge him. Yet (in these nuclear days) limited war is difficult and dangerous.'[56] It was from the Aden base that this counter-attack was conducted and it was in Yemen that the proxy war against Egypt was fought. The intensity of this confrontation suggests that it was about something more than a profit and loss account of empire.

Anti-imperialism in Aden

It was in Aden that the impact of Arab nationalism in southwest Arabia was most evident, particularly amongst the substantial Yemeni labour force. The rise of Nasser's fortunes provided the context for a nationalist campaign in the town which exploited local discontent over labour conditions and British manipulation of electoral politics. When serious disturbances began in 1956 they took many British officials by surprise. The hub of British administration at Steamer Point was not far distant from the crowded residential district of Crater but the contrast between the decorum of the former and the fervid atmosphere of the latter was symbolic of a gulf in attitudes. The journalist David Holden recalled his first visit to Crater during the Suez crisis in 1956: 'Crater is always alive, a world removed from the colonial gentility of the British at Steamer Point . . . I could see in room after dark room, in shop after cramped shop, the familiar face of President Nasser . . . and from somewhere in every street there came the sound of a harsh and crudely amplified Arabic voice in whose words and timbre even the novice could identify *Voice of the Arabs* on Cairo Radio attacking British imperialism . . . the Arabs were plainly conscious that they had found a new leader, a new Saladin, as their press and radio had christened him and they were jubilant. "Gamal Abdul Nasser!" shouted a small boy one morning as I went by . . . he kept up the chant the length of a street, with many a silently approving glance from the Arabs we passed on the way.'[57]

Despite the view from Whitehall that Aden was a backwater in which British imperialism could safely continue into the foreseeable future, by the time of the Suez crisis the town was sucking in the anti-imperial sentiments which were a crucial aspect of Nasser's transformed Arab nationalism. One of the two main parties in Aden, the United National Front (UNF) wholeheartedly adopted nationalist slogans and consequently drew support from discontented Yemeni migrant workers; the other, the Aden Association, represented the interests of the old Aden families and was thoroughly opposed to Nasserism. Both organisations were riven by factionalism and neither proved enduring. It was the impotence of these local actors that led some British policy-makers to conclude that Aden could be isolated from developments elsewhere in the Arab world. Few were aware of the emergence of small underground groups with a radical anti-imperialist programme. To this day it remains difficult to trace their origins. It appears that a small group of educated middle class Adenis were responsible for importing radical ideas into Aden. During the 1950s, from its base in Beirut George Habash's *al-Urwa* group mobilised students across the Arab world in support of their campaign against Israel. *Al-Urwa* was self-consciously pan-Arabic in its ideology and membership; it gained new members from across the Arab world including Yemen, Aden and the Protectorates. The future President of the PRSY, Qahtan al-Sha'bi, was a member. From 1958 *al-Urwa* tied itself explicitly to Nasser's programme as the Arab Nationalist Movement and the cell established in Aden was the progenitor of the National Liberation Front.[58] Additionally, a Marxist party called the Democratic National Union was established in Aden in 1953 and Ba'thist cells were operating there from 1956.[59]

The significance of the emergence of these radical groups is more evident in retrospect than it could have been at the time. It was the existence of an effective trade union movement with an explicitly political agenda which had the more immediate impact. The serious industrial relations problems in Aden were impossible to ignore and British mishandling of these opened the way for the radicals to assume centre stage. Under the leadership of Abdullah al-Asnaj, the Aden Trades Union Congress (ATUC) became the most effective vehicle for Arab discontent in Aden. Al-Asnaj was born in Sanaa but educated in Aden and worked as a clerk for Aden Airways. His youth and energy made him vulnerable to British charges of callowness but an examination of his career reveals a sophisticated and independent thinker. He was committed to the notion of a united, republican Yemen free of the influence of both the Imams in the north and the British in the south. In achieving this goal he attempted to steer a course between those pan-Arabists willing to follow Nasser whatever course he set, Marxist influenced radicals committed to a campaign of violent insurrection, and the British who, as we have seen, were determined to retain a predominant role in the region. His relations with the latter were tainted by al-Asnaj's willingness to utilise industrial unrest to further his political programme. Nevertheless, he was one of the last of the Arab nationalist leaders in the south to condone the use of violence and, as with Sultan 'Ali and the Jifris, the British re-entered negotiations with him amidst the chaos which accompanied their attempts to withdraw.

The connections between the Aden terror campaign of the mid-1960s and the industrial unrest of the previous decade are still insufficiently acknowledged. In early 1956 a series of strikes broke out at the port and the oil refinery. The main grievance concerned the living conditions of the workers. Even Hickinbotham acknowledged that 'the root cause of these industrial disturbances is that in some cases the standard of living of the lower grade workers is definitely lower than it should be and in other cases the standard of living has been raised by various means without an adequate salary increase being granted to enable the worker to support his new standard.'[60] On 20 March rioting broke out at Little Aden. British troops opened fire injuring four of the workers, one fatally. The strikes in the port continued until the middle of April and further stoppages occurred during the course of the summer.[61] Eventually ATUC negotiated a deal to end the strike based on an increase of a shilling a day for refinery workers.[62] Although industrial relations were less obviously problematic during the following two years, the conditions of Yemeni immigrant labourers continued to generate tension. Open conflict remained a latent possibility and eventually found expression over the issue of the franchise.

In November 1955 Hickinbotham introduced a new constitution for the Colony which for the first time made provision for elected representatives to join the Aden Legislative Council. The UNF denounced the measure as an ill-disguised attempt to consolidate British control. The subsequent elections were conducted on the basis of a narrow franchise restricted to British subjects or protected persons. Consequently, the majority of the population, who had been born outside the Colony and Protectorate, were disenfranchised. The UNF called for a boycott and less than half of those eligible actually voted.[63] On taking over from Hickinbotham a few months later, Luce recognised the nature of the problem: 'Here we have a town of 138,000 inhabitants, of whom 48,000 are Yemenis with no political rights, 15,000 are Indians, 10,000 are Somalis and 4,000 are Europeans; we are left with about 60,000 Colony and Protectorate Arabs and a total electorate under the present constitution of about 10,000. On this very narrow foundation we are proposing to set up the superstructure of a state ... it is quite obvious that we can't go back but I fear the whole operation will inevitably be accompanied by a feeling of unreality.'[64] Despite this shrewd analysis, Luce made little attempt to reconcile the large immigrant community in Aden to British rule and instead pursued a policy of confrontation with them. The failure to address the political grievances of the bulk of Aden's population would narrow British support to the extent that the numbers of those willing to co-operate with them became vanishingly small.

While recognising the difficulties posed by the industrial situation, Luce did not regard attempts to propitiate the Yemeni immigrants as feasible. Any extension of the franchise or an increase in popular representation inside the Aden Legislative Council risked giving the nationalists sufficient influence to undermine Britain's continued domination of the political life of the Colony. Luce was willing to be rather more flexible on the second than the first point and in December 1956 proposed that the number of elected members on the Legislative Council be increased to 12. They would sit alongside 11 nominated and *ex officio* members. To ensure that the immigrant population remained unrepresented he suggested a further lengthening of the residential qualification.[65] Even though Luce proposed a compensatory reduction in the income qualification, the Colonial Office regarded his submission as 'a little conservative' and noted that the proposed new residential qualification was more restrictive than in other colonial territories. In the light of these reservations, Luce abandoned the planned change to the residential qualification. The primary guarantee of continued British control was to be the retention of substantial reserved powers, including the right to veto sensitive legislation and to resort to rule by decree.[66] Various technical issues delayed a final decision on the franchise until April 1958.[67] The final agreement satisfied Britain's allies in the Legislative Council because it expanded the role of the small Colony elite of old Aden, which they represented, while firmly excluding *arrivistes*. Furthermore, the British were to retain control of the key matters of defence, foreign affairs and internal security. Donald Foster, who served 15 years in southwest Arabia, judged that the new electoral arrangements were 'rather like giving a child a gramophone record but insisting that only father's choice of records should be played.'[68] Outside the small circles of old Aden there was fury at the proposals.

The continued restrictions on the franchise, unresolved industrial relations problems and the influence of Egyptian propaganda led in March 1958 to the outbreak of a campaign of violence directed against the British and local collaborators.[69] This was a small-scale precursor to the NLF terror campaign of the mid-1960s. ATUC held a successful general strike on 26 April 1958 in protest at working conditions.[70] Confronted with the dual threats of industrial action and violent intimidation of the electorate Luce declared a state of emergency in May. The deterioration in the security situation led Lennox-Boyd to consider the abandonment of the new franchise proposals but he decided, 'Cairo would be able to make far better propaganda use of its withdrawal.' Luce was instructed to use force to deal with demonstrations and to employ his reserved powers should the nationalists opt to contest the election.[71] When rioting broke out in Crater at the end of October Luce acted vigorously. British regular troops were deployed to control the disturbances and 250 'Yemeni unemployed hooligans' were deported from the Colony. Luce instructed his officials to 'seize the present post-riot opportunity to defeat all Yemeni bad-hats that we can lay our hands on.' The police were set a target of deporting 15 to 20 Yemenis a day. They were unable to meet this figure but deportations did become increasingly indiscriminate.[72] The poll of January 1959 took place in an atmosphere of growing suspicion between the British and the Aden nationalists. No opposition figure agreed to stand and only 6,000 people, or a third of the small proportion of those eligible, voted in the election.[73]

In the absence of any political representation inside government, ATUC presented their complaints to the Colonial Secretary on 14 February 1959. The occasion was Lennox-Boyd's inauguration of the federation, which the trade union movement took as an opportunity to rehearse the grievances of the Adeni workers and to contrast these with the pretensions of the federal rulers. Their most immediate criticism was that Yemeni workers 'suffer ill treatment, for the police from time to time, get hold of a number of building labourers and throw them over the borders ... thereby creating unrest and panic among the remaining Trade Union labourers.' However, ATUC had a much broader agenda and they made explicit their commitment to the Arab nationalist cause: 'The dream of Arab unity around which the feelings of the Arab people everywhere accumulate is transformed always into a fearful one when its realisation is coupled with strange hands new to the position which come to our land as capturers and we get nothing from them except oppression ... We believe in the unity of the Arab people in the whole of the Yemen territory.'[74] It was views such as these which led Luce to conclude that ATUC leaders were implacable in their opposition to British influence.

Anti-imperialism in Yemen

Imam Ahmad, who continued to pursue his own claim to Aden and the Protectorates in this period, did not regard the pan-Arab dreams of the urban radicals of Aden with any sympathy. His claim to spiritual leadership over a community of the faithful derived from Zaydi traditions which were entirely at variance with those outlined in Nasser's 'Philosophy of the Revolution.' Ahmad's thorough rejection of all aspects of modernism made an impression on the handful of British journalists and officials who visited Yemen. To one he was 'the last medieval tyrant of this world', while another compared him to Shakespeare's Richard III.[75] His greatest priority was the conflict with the British on his southern frontier. The Aden authorities were well aware of Ahmad's enmity and fully reciprocated. Hickinbotham described him as 'completely untrustworthy'.[76] Even before he began to consort with the agents of Cairo and Moscow, Ahmad's attempts to undermine Britain's allies in the Protectorates could provoke indignation from British officials. Seager, Trevaskis's predecessor in the WAP, penned a furious indictment of the Imam in 1952: 'Like Hitler he is trying to pick off our people in rotation ... He poisons the minds of our comparatively simple-minded tribesmen ... he will loom more and more as a grave threat to our supremacy in South-West Arabia.'[77] Over the course of the next decade the British engaged in a series of covert operations designed to undermine Ahmad which contributed to the eventual downfall of the Imamate in 1962.

It is difficult to judge so alien a figure as Ahmad but it appears that his primary goal was to preserve and consolidate his family's control over the Zaydi Imamate and, if possible, extend its authority across southwest Arabia. The British forward policy threatened both these goals. The creation by the Aden authorities of a stable Shafi'i-dominated federal state threatened to attract the non-Zaydi population of the southern portions of the Imam's kingdom, while any hope of extending the Hamid al-Din patrimony beyond the current frontier was stymied by British support for the local rulers. Ahmad concluded that the British advance into the Protectorates imperilled his position to a greater extent than events in Egypt after the Free Officers' coup. Although they shared nothing other than a hostility to

British imperialism, Nasser, Ahmad and King Saʻud signed a tripartite alliance at Jiddah in April 1956.[78] Two years later Ahmad established a nominal attachment to Nasser's newly formed United Arab Republic. More peculiarly still, Ahmad's son Badr was at the forefront of a policy of improved relations with the Soviet bloc which led to the import of Soviet arms to the region. Badr appears as a much less formidable figure than his father and was disliked by the Zaydi *ulama* for his lack of martial qualities and his willingness to toy with republican and even socialist ideas. His relations with the British went through a major transformation: prior to the 1962 Republican coup, he was viewed as the figure most likely to successfully import Egyptian and Soviet influence; after it, he was regarded as a potential ally in containing Egyptian expansionism in Arabia.

Despite their divergent doctrines the Arab nationalists and the Imam had one thing in common: hostility to the British. Between 1955 and 1959 the frontier conflict between the Protectorate rulers and the Imam became a proxy war between the British and Egyptian governments. From the perspective of the British administration in Aden the essential problem was the Imam's sponsorship of tribal opponents of their allies inside the Protectorates. During the course of 1954 various solutions to this problem had been discussed, including air attacks against the supply bases which Ahmad had established on his side of the frontier and even a land invasion of Yemen. The difficulty was that any such action was likely to unite the international community against what would appear to be a case of late imperial adventurism.[79] The solution to this problem was found in a policy of what was known locally as keeni-meeni: subversion and intrigue whose covert nature prevented scrutiny by opposition politicians in Whitehall, the United Nations or future historians. When the Minister of State at the Colonial Office, Henry Hopkinson, visited Aden in January 1955, Hickinbotham complained that the restrictions on air action across the frontier were undermining British authority in the face of the Imam's assaults. As an alternative he proposed taking 'measures through Rulers and others, to cause internal disturbance in the Yemen.' Two months later he requested £25,000 to conduct a campaign of subversion inside the Imamate. The principal item of expenditure was the supply of arms to friendly rulers in the Protectorates who would have responsibility for implementing the policy.[80] These proposals remained in abeyance for the next six months but the Imam's role in sponsoring the Shamsi insurgency which led to the fall of Robat precipitated a new debate in which Eden made clear his support for a policy of subversion inside Yemen.

The continuation of Yemeni sponsored insurrections in the Protectorates and the increasing prominence of Badr in leading Yemen towards alliances with Egypt and the Soviet Union encouraged the authorities in Aden to develop plans to weaken or possibly remove Ahmad. This policy had strong support from the highest levels of the British government. At the start of September 1955 Eden asked whether 'political work' against the Imam had begun. In the following month Hickinbotham outlined details of his planned special operations inside Yemen. However, there was resistance to his plans from the Foreign Office and agreement on covert action was not reached until December 1955.[81] On 22 March 1956 Hickinbotham was finally authorised to 'give arms, ammunition and money to Yemeni malcontents to encourage them to cause trouble within the Yemen borders.'[82] A month later, Trevaskis had his first meeting with the 'cloak and dagger' men from London. They presented him with a series of ideas for counter-subversion which he regarded as wholly inadequate. During the course of the following week he persuaded them of the need to start arming potential dissident tribes inside the Imamate and of the long-term requirement for friendly Protectorate rulers to organise punitive raids over the frontier.[83]

The first British-sponsored cross-border raids into Yemen took place against the background of a wider crisis for Britain's influence in the Middle East. Although Ahmad was a thoroughgoing reactionary he was allied with Nasser under the Jiddah pact and his son Badr had taken the unprecedented step of touring Cairo, London, Prague, Moscow and Peking. In June 1956 he signed a treaty of friendship in Moscow which led to the opening of a Soviet legation in Ta'izz. In the most unlikely marriage of convenience imaginable, Moscow began shipping T-34 tanks and other military equipment to the Imam. Ahmad had little idea what to do with this military equipment which soon fell into desuetude from lack of maintenance.[84] Nevertheless, excited reports of Soviet arms shipments duly reached policy-makers in London during the summer of 1956.[85] Trevaskis was particularly attentive to the arrival of these 'splendid weapons' and warned that their appearance on the frontier would provoke mass desertions from previously loyal pro-British tribes.[86]

By December 1956 plans were completed for attacks into Yemen from three Protected States: 'Awdhali, Bayhan and Dali'. The subsequent raids marked the beginning of three successive British sponsored winter campaigns along the frontier, which were to escalate annually. The Dali' operation proved the most difficult to organise. Trevaskis recorded: 'There has been very little friction between the Dhala and Yemen frontier tribes in the past and because of this, the weak personality of the Amir and the fact that a large part of the Dhala population has already been suborned . . . the scope for special operations has been limited . . . special operations have mainly been entrusted to a picked commando force which carried out a series of frontier raids on frontier Yemeni villages during January and February causing casualties and damage to property and livestock.' The Aden High Commission distributed 400 rifles and £2,000 in support of cross-border attacks from Dali'. Operations organised from the other two states were on a larger scale: 980 rifles and £3,200 were supplied in Bayhan; 477 rifles and £2,427 were given to the authorities in 'Awdhali for the conduct of attacks into Yemen.[87] The raids were carefully controlled by Luce who was concerned that 'Yemen egged on and perhaps strengthened by Egypt and

Russia, will continue and intensify its efforts to subvert the whole of the Western Protectorate'.[88] He correspondingly increased and decreased activity on the frontier according to the extent of Yemeni subversion inside the Protectorates.[89] Eden and Lennox-Boyd approved of the escalation of British counter-action and were dismissive of Foreign Office objections.[90] In the aftermath of the Suez humiliation Yemen constituted the frontline of the war against radical nationalism in the Middle East. Eden's successor, Harold Macmillan, granted the Aden authorities still wider licence in the covert war with the Imam. During the course of 1957 the Aden High Commission responded to continued subversion of Protectorate tribes with arms shipments to anti-Imamic forces inside Yemen. These were designed to redirect Ahmad's attention from the southern frontier to his own patrimony. Large-scale shipments to Yemeni dissidents within the country's interior appear to have been delivered via the Sharif of Bayhan in October 1957.[91] This marked an escalation of the conflict: British strategy up to this point had been to work through loyal tribes inside the Protectorates and dissident Yemeni tribes close to the frontier.

The Imam refused to be cowed by British actions and ratcheted up his own campaign inside the Protectorates. In December 1957 Luce reported on the 'biggest and most dangerous subversive effort we have yet experienced.' In response to Foreign Office advocacy of a negotiated solution he asserted: 'I cannot therefore be expected to agree that . . . it is wise to sit back even temporarily and allow Yemen to continue its subversion unimpeded.'[92] He requested authority to launch larger scale raids across the frontier and to supply more arms to the Imam's opponents inside Yemen. Lennox-Boyd and Lloyd agreed to this escalation although the latter wished to keep the door to a negotiated solution ajar.[93] The notable difference between British organised frontier operations in this period and those undertaken 12 months earlier was the larger scale involvement of the RAF. Although these 'tit-for-tat' measures were an ostensible response to the Imam's incursions, Luce and Trevaskis found that inducing such provocations was a straightforward matter. The tactics adopted are evident from Trevaskis's description of a frontier battle near Qa'tabah on 30 January 1958: 'The biggest action we've had. More or less according to plan. Armoured car patrols provoke them into opening up on us with their guns. The Venoms rocketed . . . Well over 1,000 Yemenis involved in battle, their casualties must have been pretty bad. We shall have another go tomorrow.'[94] Luce also continued to arm dissident tribes inside Yemen. The 'Awdhali Sultan was authorised to smuggle arms to the Rassassi tribes on the other side of the frontier while the Sharif of Bayhan supplied weapons to the two most powerful tribes in the north of Yemen, the Hashid and the Bakil.[95]

Alongside this extensive campaign of subversion the British began to consider the possibility of a coup to overthrow Ahmad. The problem was that, although they wished to be rid of Ahmad and Badr, they emphatically did not want the Imamate to be replaced by a populist republican government to which the Aden radicals could align themselves. This was a point on which Whitehall and the authorities in Aden could agree. Riches of the Foreign Office explained: 'a revolution would be a pity . . . A more efficient dictatorship or a more democratic government would . . . be more likely to undermine our position in the Protectorate more effectively than the present dispensation.'[96] Nevertheless, the removal of Badr and Ahmad did not necessitate the end of autocratic Hamid al-Din rule; Ahmad's brother Hasan was opposed to Badr's accession and seemed committed to a conservative policy. The first person to suggest offering support to Hasan was the British chargé in Ta'izz, Kemp. He warned on 20 July 1957 that Soviet or Egyptian agents in Yemen might administer a drugs overdose to Ahmad in order to secure Badr's succession and recommended urgent action to bolster Hasan's position. A month later the Permanent Under-Secretary at the Colonial Office suggested: 'the fact that Badr was in the hands of the Russians made it worthwhile thinking about supporting Hassan.'[97] However, when first consulted on this point Luce opposed the idea of a pro-Hasan coup on the grounds that there was 'nothing to choose between the rivals.'[98] It was the failure of the frontier campaign of 1957–58 to subdue Ahmad which caused Luce to reconsider. Kemp returned to the idea of sponsoring a pro-Hasan rebellion in February 1958: 'if this does not take place a consolidation of Egyptian and Soviet influence . . . seems inevitable . . . Badr would be a figurehead to be got rid of as soon as it suited the Egyptians to set up a regime similar to their own.' It was noted in the Colonial Office that Kemp's proposal 'ties in to some extent with the proposals made by Luce.'[99] The nature of Luce's plan is clarified in Trevaskis's diary under the heading 'big proposal': 'We are now convinced that the Imam is in the pockets of the Egyptians and Iron Curtain countries. Their influence will increase unless something is done to change regime and bring in a friendly government which will back away from Eg[yptian]-Russ[ian] influence . . . We feel therefore that we should back Hasan and start the revolt to this end.'[100] This idea acquired the codename INVICTA.

Trevaskis and Luce waited eagerly for a decision on their 'big proposal' while the choice between covert action and UN mediation was debated by a small circle of ministers and officials in Whitehall during the summer of 1958. The alternative to action to destabilise Yemen was to seek a negotiated solution to the frontier problem under UN auspices which was a course advocated by the Foreign Secretary, Selwyn Lloyd.[101] After meetings with Luce at Chequers, ministers rejected the UN option in June 1958 on the grounds that the presence of UN observers along the frontier 'would tend to inhibit the United Kingdom from taking necessary military action.'[102] The scale of military measures which should be adopted remained unresolved but attention focused increasingly on the possibility of an anti-Badr coup. All parties regarded consultation with Washington as an essential prerequisite to any such drastic action and in April 1958 a Colonial Office official recorded: 'the Americans have been induced to consider that the overthrow of the Imam is a possible course, although they would prefer the UN option.'[103] In May British and American officials travelled to Aden to examine the feasibility of overthrowing Ahmad and Badr. Lennox-Boyd briefed Macmillan on the results of this mission which identified Badr as the source of British problems in the region and made clear that Hasan was 'less wedded to the active prosecution of the Yemen's claim to the Aden Protectorate.' The two options canvassed were an 'early revolt' to replace Ahmad with Hasan or the preparation of contingency plans to prevent Badr's succession following the Imam's demise. The balance of opinion within the British government was in favour of the first alternative but the American administration were unconvinced about the practicality of the scheme.[104]

These delays vexed Luce. During the course of 1958 he sent a series of messages to London stressing the need for a coup in order to counter the rise of Soviet and Egyptian influence in Yemen.[105] Given the problems confronting joint Anglo-American action, a range of alternatives were considered in order to forestall Cairo and Moscow. The most radical solution, as proposed by the Minister of Defence, Duncan Sandys, was a British invasion of Yemen. This certainly cut through some of the complexities surrounding covert action but was judged inadvisable given the climate of anti-colonialism in which such an operation would be conducted.[106] Instead Luce was forced to fall back on familiar counter-measures. The RAF made renewed attacks across the frontier, the most significant of which was the bombing of the Yemeni fort at Harib on 8 July 1958.[107] On 21 January 1959 the Aden authorities were licensed to conduct further incursions into Yemen and a third round of intensive winter raiding across the frontier began. From the British perspective the hero of this latest campaign, which was the largest in scale to date, was the brother of the 'Awdhali Sultan, Jaabil bin Husayn. Trevaskis interpreted a raid of 3 February in which Jaabil's tribesmen and a force of Government Guards dynamited the houses of dissidents inside Yemen as 'a little justice' for previous Yemeni subversion. British regular troops played a supporting role in attacks into Yemen.[108] From early in 1959 the British also began laying mines and sabotaging facilities within Yemen.[109]

These events on the frontier added to the sense of crisis within Yemen. Opposition to Ahmad and Badr from the tribes and in the cities was increasing and Ahmad himself was gravely ill. In yet another break with tradition he flew to Italy for medical treatment in April 1959 leaving Badr to run the country. Badr promised reform but disturbances broke out in both Ta'izz and Sanaa and he was forced to request assistance from the northern tribes. Neither the army nor the tribes seemed willing to accept direction from Badr and chaos ensued. Order was restored only when Ahmad returned to the country in August.[110] The documentary record is insufficiently full to give anything other than a speculative account of British involvement in the anti-Badr disturbances during the summer of 1959. The Ministry of Defence discussed the 'training and preparations' necessary to implement a coup in September 1958 but no authority to proceed was given at this stage.[111] It does however seem likely that Badr's assumption of the regency when his father travelled to Italy finally convinced the British and Americans to step up their covert activities inside the country. All planning prior to this occasion had concentrated very closely on the specific danger posed by Badr. The possibility that Ahmad would never return and that Yemen would be led by Badr into the Soviet camp must have been considered. The British had armed the Hashid and Bakil tribes with the assistance of the Sharif of Bayhan prior to 1959 and it was these two tribal factions who Badr found it most difficult to control during the regency. In addition to this circumstantial evidence, there are two substantive pieces of documentary evidence suggesting that the INVICTA operation to replace Badr with Hasan was activated. The first is a briefing document supplied to Luce's successor as Governor of Aden, Charles Johnston in August 1961. This document reviews the history of 'counter-subversive measures' and states that most of the documents relating to these activities have been destroyed. However, it records that in 1959 a plan called INVICTA 'was revived as a measure to be taken if the Imam suddenly died or was otherwise removed and Badr looked like succeeding and was conditionally agreed.'[112] It also contains an opaque reference to a controversy over moving 'operations up to Beihan' in 1959. This was the site from which the Hashid and Bakil would have been supplied. The second piece of evidence is a letter from Julian Amery to the Minister of State at the Foreign Office, John Profumo, dated 26 June 1959 which states clearly: 'With the failure of INVICTA the Governor sees no possibility of bringing down Badr.'[113] The statement that INVICTA operations had failed indicates that prior to June 1959 the British had been engaged in an unsuccessful effort to remove Badr. The reliability of this source is enhanced by the fact that Amery also corresponded with Trevaskis who would have had day-to-day responsibility for such operations.

Perhaps less important than the details of the anti-Badr activities undertaken by the British during the regency is their rationale. They formed part of a broader attempt to exclude Egyptian influence from Arabia which encompassed measures against ATUC in Aden and the SAL in the Protectorates. Al-Asnaj, the Jifri brothers and Badr had varied political agendas of their own but British opposition to each was based on their potential to import radical Arab nationalism to the region from Cairo. This would both threaten Britain's key military base in the region and destroy British pretensions to continuing influence in the Middle East. When Ahmad returned to Yemen he rebuked Badr, reversed his domestic reforms and began the process of severing ties with the Egyptians who he began to recognise as a greater threat to him than the British. While the Yemenis worked to undermine Britain's forward policy in the Protectorates the British conducted a tit-for-tat policy in Yemen. This set a precedent for the Civil War period in which the British were to once again become implicated in intrigue inside Yemen. In retrospect the subversion of the Imamate turned out not to be in Britain's long-term interest.

Conclusions

Although a lack of will to maintain the empire is sometimes cited as one of the reasons for its downfall, this was certainly not the case in southwest Arabia. The political programme undertaken there by Luce and Trevaskis was remarkably ambitious. With Nasser at the peak of his prestige in the aftermath of Suez and international demands for decolonization increasing, they sought to preserve their own interests by creating a haven in southwest Arabia for those traditional rulers who supported a continued connection with Britain. In Whitehall there was no lack of will to support this programme. In some ways policy-makers in London, who had a less clear view of the situation on the ground, made even more optimistic assumptions than their envoys and this was reflected in their doubts about constitutional change. Key figures such as Salisbury, Sandys and Lord Lloyd believed it was feasible to maintain British sovereignty in Aden permanently. In 1959 it appeared that this optimism had, to a degree, been justified. The constitution of the new federation was certainly an odd one but its birth was relatively painless. The border war with the Imam had ended in victory for the British and Ahmad spent the next three years staving off the threat from his erstwhile ally in Cairo. The South Arabian League had been decapitated and Lahj joined the federation later in 1959. These successes were offset by a series of trends which had a damaging long-term effect on British plans. The forward policy was an elaborate policy edifice with insecure foundations. The reverberations which accompanied British institution building spread across southwest Arabia and awakened nationalist sentiment. This was particularly evident in Aden, where the British were ruthless in their efforts to flatten any opposition to their programme from urban radicals but it was also visible in Yemen and the Protectorates, where traditional rulers were willing to make marriages of convenience with actors external to the region in order to oppose British policy. The full implications of these developments did not become apparent until the Yemeni revolution of 1962. In the interim British policy-makers continued to debate the best way in which they could secure their last Arabian outpost against wider developments in the Middle East.

Notes

1 N. Rijwan, *Nasserist Ideology: Its Exponents and Critics* (New York, John Wiley, 1974), p. 54; A. Dawisha, *Arab Nationalism in the Twentieth Century* (Princeton, Princeton University Press, 2003), pp. 104–5.

2 M. Kerr, *The Arab Cold War* (Oxford, Oxford University Press, 1964).

3 A. Dawisha, *Nationalism*, pp. 139–41.

4 G. Nasser, *Philosophy of the Revolution*, (English edition, Buffalo, Economica, 1959) pt. 3.

5 A. Dawisha, *Nationalism*, pp. 136–9. There is a substantial literature dealing with the details of this relationship. See R. Ovendale, 'Egypt and the Suez Base Agreement' in J. W. Young (ed.) (1988), *The Foreign Policy of Churchill's Peace-*

time Administration 1951–1955 (Leicester, Leicester University Press, 1988), pp. 135–55; J. Kent, 'The Egyptian Base and the Defence of the Middle East', *Journal of Imperial and Commonwealth History* 21 (1993), pp. 45–65; Wm. R. Louis, 'The Tragedy of the Anglo-Egyptian Settlement of 1954' in Wm. R. Louis and R. Owen (eds) (1989), *Suez 1956* (Oxford, Clarendon Press, 1989), pp. 43–72.

6 L. J. Butler, *Britain and Empire* (London, I. B. Tauris, 2002), p. 97; D. Reynolds, *Britannia Overruled*, (Harlow, Longman, 1991) p. 202; D. Sanders, *Losing an Empire, Finding a Role*, (Basingstoke, Macmillan, 1990), pp. 6–8.

7 PRO: CO 1055/167, Johnston to Sandys, 16 July 1963, Macmillan to Foreign Secretary, 2 September 1962, Home to Prime Minister, 20 September 1963.

8 Wm. R. Louis, 'Tragedy', pp. 43–72.

9 M. Elliot, *'Independent Iraq': The Monarchy and British Influence 1941–58* (London, I. B. Tauris, 1996), pp. 116–17.

10 M. Persson, *Great Britain, the United States and the Security of the Middle East* (Lund, Lund University Press, 1998); B. Holden Reid, 'The Northern Tier and the Baghdad Pact' in J. W. Young (ed.) *The Foreign Policy of Churchill's Peacetime Administration 1951–1955* (Leicester, Leicester University Press, 1986), pp. 159–80; N. J. Ashton, 'The Hijacking of a Pact: The Formation of the Baghdad Pact and Anglo-American Tensions in the Middle East, 1955–1958' *Review of International Studies* 19 (1993), pp. 123–37.

11 A. Dawisha, *Nationalism*, pp. 164–6; M. Barnett, *Dialogues in Arab Politics* (New York, Columbia University Press, 1989), pp. 116–18.

12 M. B. Oren, 'A Winter of Discontent: Britain's Crisis in Jordan' *International Journal of Middle Eastern Studies* 22 (1990), pp. 171–84.

13 E. Shuckburgh, *Descent to Suez* (London, Weidenfeld and Nicolson, 1986), p. 327.

14 P. Catterall (ed.), *The Macmillan Diaries: The Cabinet Years 1950–1957* (London, Macmillan, 2003), 3 October 1955, p. 490.

15 PRO: FO 371/118852, Watson to Trevelyan, 22 March 1956, 6 April 1956, 13 April 1956, Trevelyan to Kirkpatrick, 26 March 1956.

16 K. Kyle, *Suez: Britain's End of Empire in the Middle East* (2nd ed. London, I. B. Tauris, 2003), p. 101.

17 The most detailed account of Anglo-American relations in the Middle East before and during the Suez crisis remains W. S. Lucas, *Divided We Stand* (London, Hodder and Stoughton, 1991).

18 P. S. Allfree, *The Hawks of the Hadhramaut* (London, Robert Hale, 1967), p. 31.

19 H. Boustead, *The Wind of Morning* (London, Chatto and Windus, 1971), pp. 210–11; PRO: CO 1015/1081, Aden (Acting Governor) to Secretary of State, 21 June 1955, 22 June 1955, 28 June 1955, 14 July 1955.

20 IOR: R/20/B/2455, Governor (Aden) to Secretary of State, 30 September 1955, Chief Secretary (Aden) to Resident Adviser (Mukalla), 30 September 1955, Governor (Aden) to Secretary of State 4 October 1955.

21 S. Mawby, 'Britain's Last Imperial Frontier', *Journal of Imperial and Commonwealth History* 29 (2001), pp. 87–8.

22 H. Macmillan, *Riding the Storm*, 1956–59 (London, Macmillan, 1971), pp. 504–5.

23 K. Trevaskis, *Shades of Amber* (London, Hutchinson, 1968), pp. 21–2.

24 J. Knox-Mawer, *The Sultans Came to Tea* (Gloucester, Alan Sutton, 1984), pp. 79–80.

25 PRO: PREM 11/1461, Lennox-Boyd to Eden, 9 August 1956, Lennox-Boyd to Eden, 16 August 1956, Eden minute, 16 August 1956, PREM 11/2401, Luce to Secretary of State, 21 August 1956,

26 K. Trevaskis, *Shades*, pp. 112–13, 135–7.
27 IOR: R/20/B/3262, Hutton to Governor, 31 March 1958, Governor to Secretary of State 7 April 1958, Governor to Secretary of State, 18 April 1958, Governor to Secretary of State, 19 April 1958; PRO: CAB 128/32, CC(58)30th mtg., minute 2, 14 April.
28 PRO: CAB 128/32, CC(58)43rd mtg., minute 2, 21 April 1958, DEFE 11/256, HQ(BFAP) to Ministry of Defence, 18 April 1958, Aden (Luce) to Secretary of State, 21 April 1958.
29 IOR: R/20/B/3263, Sultan Ali to the Governor, 29 April 1958.
30 PRO: CO 1015/1551, Governor to Secretary of State, 2 June 1958.
31 PRO: PREM 11/2755, Secretary of State to Aden (OAG), 7 July 1958, FO to Milan, 8 July 1958, Secretary of State to Aden (OAG), Aden (Acting Governor) to Secretary of State, 3 July 1958, Aden (OAG) to Secretary of State, 4 July 1958, Aden (OAG) to Secretary of State, 5 July 1958, Milan to FO 9 July 1958, CO 1015/1551, Governor (Aden) to Secretary of State, 21 July 1958.
32 Richard Holmes Papers, Box 1, Trevaskis to PO(NE), 17 November 1953.
33 Ibid., Box 2, Johnson Memo on Political Background to Operation Niggard, 6 December 1960.
34 PRO: CO 1015/836, Aden (Hickinbotham) to Secretary of State 21 February 1955, Aden (Hickinbotham) to Secretary of State, 25 June 1955.
35 PRO: CAB 21/4357, HQ (British Forces, Aden) to HQ (MEAF), 24 June 1955.
36 PRO: CAB 131/16, DC(55)4th mtg., minute 1, 27 June 1955, CO 1015/836, Aden (OAC) to Secretary of State, 23 June 1955, PREM 11/1461, Aden to Secretary of State 16 June 1955 with Aden minute, 17 June 1955, Johnston to de Zulueta, 18 June 1955, Aden (OAG) to Secretary of State, 20 June 1955, Ministry of Defence to GHQ(MELF), 27 June 1955.
37 PRO: CAB 131/16, DC(55)5th mtg., minute 2, 11 July 1955, DC(55)18, 8 July 1955, PREM 11/1461, Aden (OAG) to Secretary of State with Eden minutes, 9 July 1955.
38 PRO: CO 1015/837, Aden (Luce) to Secretary of State, 30 August 1956, Governor to Secretary of State, 1 October 1956 with Dhala/Radfan paper; CO 1015/1315, Aden (Luce) to Secretary of State, 6 December 1956.
39 PRO: DEFE 11/256, HQ(BFAP) to Ministry of Defence, 28 April 1958, CO 1015/1299, Ministry of Defence to Prime Minister, 5 May 1958.
40 These views on empire were not the sole preserve of the Conservatives: at this time the opposition Labour Party had their own reservations about the grant of early independence to small territories and to those which were racially mixed. See P. Catterall, 'Foreign and Commonwealth Policy in Opposition' in W. Kaiser and G. Staerck (eds) *British Foreign Policy 1955–1964: Contracting Options* (Basingstoke, Palgrave/Macmillan, 2000), p. 91.
41 D. G. Boyce, *Decolonisation and the British Empire* (Basingstoke, Palgrave, 2003), p. 117.
42 PRO: CAB 134/1201, CA(56)1st mtg., minute 2, 4 January 1956, CA(56)13th mtg., 12 March 1956; CAB 134/1202, CA(56)1, 2 January 1956, CA(56)12, 8 March 1956, CAB 21/4357, Brook for PM, 12 March 1956.
43 R. Bidwell, *The Two Yemens* (Harlow, Longman, 1983), pp. 78–9.
44 PRO: CAB 134/1551, CP(0)(57), 30 May 1957.
45 *Parliamentary Papers 1956–1957*, Vol. 23, Cmnd. 124.
46 PRO: CAB 134/2340, OME(57)73, 20 December 1957, CAB 134/2341, OME(58)1st mtg., 1 January 1958.
47 PRO: CAB 134/1557, CPC(58)3rd mtg., 30 January 1958.
48 IOR: R/20/B/3259, Amir of Bayhan, Sultan of 'Awdhali and Fadli Naib to Luce 21 February 1958, Trevaskis to Chief Secretary, 21 February 1958.

49 PRO: CO 1015/1911, Luce to Gorell Barnes, 27 March 1958, 28 March 1958, Gorell-Barnes to Secretary of State, 31 March 1958. For a favourable commentary on Luce's proposals see G. Balfour-Paul, *The End of Empire in the Middle East* (Cambridge, Cambridge University Press, 1991), pp. 69–70.

50 PRO: CAB 134/2341, OME(58)6th mtg., minute 3, 10 April 1958, CO 1015/1911, Gorell-Barnes to Luce, 14 April 1958.

51 IOR: R/20/B/3259, Simmonds to Protectorate Secretary, 8 July 1958; PRO: CAB 128/32, CC(58)50th mtg., minute 6, 26 June 1958, CAB 129/93, CP(58)131, CO 1015/1669, Lennox-Boyd to Heathcoat-Amory, 11 June 1958, CO 1015/1667, Notes of Meetings with WAP rulers, 1 July 1958, 15 July 1958.

52 PRO: CO 1015/1911, Aden (Luce) to Secretary of State, 29 November 1958.

53 PRO: CAB 134/1557, CP(58)10th mtg., 19 June 1958, CPC(58)16th mtg., minute 2, 22 December 1958, CPC(58)12, 16 June 1958, CPC(58)16, 20 October 1958, CPC(58)23, 18 December 1958, CO 1015/1910, Kirkman to Reilly, 19 November 1958.

54 J. Kostiner, *The Struggle for South Yemen* (London, Croom Helm, 1984), p. 9.

55 PRO: CAB 134/2341, OME(58)14th mtg., minute 2, 12 December 1958, CAB 134/2342, OME(58)48, 4 December 1958, CO 1015/1910, Riches minute, 12 December 1958.

56 Macmillan Diaries 1957–63, d31, 15 March 1958.

57 D. Holden, *Farewell to Arabia* (London, Faber and Faber 1966), pp. 24–5.

58 W. W. Kazzika, *Revolutionary Transformation in the Arab World* (London, Charles Knight, 1975), ch. 2; H. Lackner, 'The Rise and Fall of the National Liberation Front as a Political Organisation' in B. R. Pridham (ed.), *Contemporary Yemen* (London, Croom Helm 1984), pp. 46–61; J. Kostiner, *Struggle*, pp. 56–7. These accounts differ on the dates and details of a complex story but concur on the existence of Nasserist organisations in the south antecedent to the formation of the NLF in 1963.

59 J. F. Devlin, *The Ba'th Party* (Stanford, Hoover Institution Press, 1976), p. 112; J. Kostiner, 'Arab Radical Politics: Al-Qawmiyyun al-Arab and the Marxists in the Turmoil of South Yemen', *Middle East Studies*, 17 (1981), p. 455.

60 PRO: CO 1015/1240, Aden (Hickinbotham) to Lennox-Boyd, 21 March 1956.

61 PRO: CO 1015/1240, Aden (Hickinbotham) to Secretary of State, 8 March 1956, 19 March 1956, 22 March 1956.

62 PRO: CO 1015/1240, Aden (Hickinbotham) to Secretary of State, 29 March 1956.

63 PRO: CO 1015/1024, Hickinbotham to Lennox-Boyd, 23 November 1955, Aden (Hickinbotham) to Secretary of State, 16 December 1955.

64 PRO: CO 1015/1132, Luce to Secretary of State, 15 September 1956.

65 IOR: R/20/B/2409, Luce to Chief Secretary, 7 November 1956; PRO: CO 1015/1017, Luce to Lennox-Boyd, 11 December 1956, CO 1015/1638, Luce to Gorell Barnes, 4 March 1957.

66 PRO: CO 1015/1638, Morgan to Luce, 28 March 1957, Morgan to Gorell Barnes, 11 March 1957, Gorell Barnes to Morgan, 22 March 1957, Luce to Morgan, 27 April 1957, Pearson minute, 7 May 1957, Watt minute, 8 May 1957, Gorell Barnes minute, 13 May 1957, Gorell Barnes to Luce, 4 June 1957.

67 PRO: CO 1015/1638, Luce to Morgan 12 July 1957, Simmonds to Morgan 1 August 1957, Morgan to Gorell Barnes, 13 August 1957, Morgan to Luce, 22 August 1957, CO 1015/1639, Luce to Morgan, 26 October 1957, Morgan to Chief Secretary, 30 November 1957, Governor to Secretary of State, 7 February 1958, 10 April 1958, Secretary of State to OAG, 18 April 1958.

68 D. Foster, *Landscape with Arabs* (Brighton, Clifton, 1969), p. 32.
69 PRO: CO 1015/2088, Aden (Luce) to Secretary of State, Lennox-Boyd to PM, 2 May 1958, Governor to Secretary of State, 4 June 1958, 12 June 1958, Dutton to Morgan, 7 July 1958.
70 PRO: CO 1015/2013, Governor (Aden) to Secretary of State, 14 February 1958, 30 April 1958.
71 PRO: CO 1015/1639, Morgan to Luce, 22 October 1958.
72 This was a small-scale precursor to the NLF terror campaign of the mid-1960s. For details see PRO: CO 1015/2038, HQ(BFAP) to Ministry of Defence, 31 October 1958, 1 November 1958, 2 November 1958, Aden (Luce) to Secretary of State, 3 November 1958; IOR: R/20/B/2011, Simmonds to Chief Secretary, 7 November 1958, R/20/B/3002, Simmonds to Chief Secretary, 8 November 1958, Luce minute, 15 November 1958, Assistant Chief Secretary to Chief Secretary, 2 January 1959, Simmonds to Assistant Chief Secretary, 16 January 1959.
73 PRO: CO 1015/1387, Aden (Luce) to Secretary of State, 4 January 1959.
74 PRO: CO 1015/2013, ATUC to Secretary of State, 14 February 1959.
75 E. Downton, *Wars Without End* (Toronto, Stoddart, 1987), p. 247; D. Holden, *Farewell*, p. 85.
76 T. Hickinbotham, *Aden* (London, Constable, 1958), pp. 70–1.
77 IOR: R/20/D/2122, Seager to Chief Secretary, 31 January 1952.
78 E. O'Ballance, *The War in the Yemen* (London, Faber and Faber, 1971), p. 54.
79 PRO: PREM 11/1461, RMS Queen Elizabeth to FO (PM for MoD), 3 July 1954, Churchill to Lyttelton, 17 July 1954, Lyttelton to Churchill 1954.
80 IOR: R/20/B/2635, Note of a Discussion at Government House, 11 January 1955, Governor to Secretary of State, 3 March 1955.
81 PRO: PREM 11/1461, de Zulueta to Stacpoole, 5 September 1955, Lennox-Boyd to PM, 9 September 1955 with Eden minutes, DEFE 11/338, Hickinbotham to Gorell Barnes, 13 October 1955, Lloyd to Lennox-Boyd, 27 November 1955, Lennox-Boyd to Lloyd, 10 December 1955.
82 IOR: R/20/B/3265, Phillips memo to Governor, 19 August 1961.
83 Kennedy Trevaskis Papers Part II, Rhodes House, s546, Box 2a, Desk Diary entries, 23, 24, 27 April 1956.
84 E. O'Ballance, *War*, p. 55–6; D. A. Schmidt, *Yemen: The Unknown War* (London, Bodley Head, 1968), pp. 40–1; H. Ingrams, *The Yemen: Rulers and Revolutionaries* (London, John Murray, 1962), p. 99.
85 PRO: FO 371/120699, EM 10338/14, Monteith to Lloyd, 10 July 1956, EM 10338/16, Monteith to Lloyd, 29 October 1956.
86 PRO: DEFE 4/94, COS(57)4th mtg., minute 2, 10 January 1957; IOR: R/20/B/2650, Trevaskis to Phillips, 27 June 1957.
87 Kennedy Trevaskis Papers Pt. 1, Rhodes House, s367, Box 5a, Undated Trevaskis Note on Special Operations in the Western Aden Protectorate.
88 PRO: CO 1015/1259, Luce to Lloyd, 19 January 1957.
89 IOR: R/20/B/2637, Deputy Governor to Secretary of State, 23 January 1957, Governor to Secretary of State, 26 January 1956, Governor to Secretary of State, 28 January 1956.
90 PRO: PREM 11/2401, Lennox-Boyd to Eden, October 1956 with Annex, CO minute to Eden, 3 January 1957, 10 Downing Street to CO, 4 January 1957.
91 PRO: DEFE 4/98, COS(57)55th mtg., minute 1, July 1957, PREM 11/2401, Aden (Luce) to Secretary of State, 4 December 1957.
92 PRO: CO 1015/1304, Aden (Luce) to Secretary of State, 2 December 1957.
93 PRO: PREM 11/2401, Aden (Luce to Secretary of State, 3 December 1957, de Zulueta to PM, 6 December 1957, Lennox-Boyd to Macmillan, 6 December

1957, Lennox-Boyd to Macmillan with Macmillan minute, 9 December 1957, Secretary of State to Luce, 11 December 1957.

94 Kennedy Trevaskis Papers Pt. 2, Rhodes House, s546, Box 2a, Desk Diary entry, 30 January 1958.

95 PRO: PREM 11/2401, Aden (Luce to Secretary of State, 4 December 1957.

96 PRO: CO 1015/1086, Riches to Morgan, 30 October 1956 with Morgan minute, 14 November 1956.

97 PRO: CO 1015/1265, Taiz (Kemp) to FO, 20 July 1957, CO 1015/1259, Fretwell minute, 22 August 1957.

98 PRO: DEFE 4/98, COS(57)61st mtg., minute 1, 26 July 1957, CO 1015/1265, Phillip (Aden) to Reilly (CO), 13 November 1957.

99 PRO: CO 1015/1266, Note by Kemp, February 1958, Hammer minute, 4 March 1958.

100 Kennedy Trevaskis Papers Pt. 2, Rhodes House, s546, Box 2a, Desk Diary entry on 'Big Proposal'.

101 PRO: CO 1015/1321, Lloyd to Prime Minister, 12 April 1958, Morgan minute, 16 April 1958, Secretary of State to Aden (Luce), Bishop to Laskey, 12 May 1958, CAB 128/32, C(58)31st mtg., minute 4, 15 April 1958, CAB 129/92, C(58)81, 14 April 1958.

102 PRO: DEFE 11/257, COS(58)49th mtg., minute 6, 10 June 1958.

103 PRO: CO 1015/1321, Morgan minute, 18 April 1958.

104 PRO: PREM 11/2755, Lennox-Boyd to Macmillan, 19 May 1958, FO to Washington, 8 June 1958, Washington to FO, 10 June 1958.

105 PRO: DEFE 11/256, Aden (Luce) to Secretary of State, 17 April 1958, DEFE 11/258, Aden (Luce) to Secretary of State, 17 July 1958, 23 July 1958, 25 August 1958, 23 September 1958.

106 PRO: DEFE 11/257, Lee minute, 2 July 1958, JP(58)85, Operations Against the Yemen, Sandys to Prime Minister, 9 July 1958, DEFE 11/400, Draft Memo on 'Attacks From Yemen', December 1958.

107 PRO: DEFE 11/258, Aden (Luce) to Secretary of State, 15 July 1958, CAB 131/19, D(58)13th mtg., minute 1, 18 July 1958.

108 IOR: R/20/B/3318, Phillips to Assistant Chief Secretary, 22 January 1959, Chief Intelligence Officer to Chief Secretary, 11 February 1959; Kennedy Trevaskis Papers Part II, Rhodes House, s546, Box 1b, Trevaskis Diary, 21 January 1959, 26 January 1959, 30 January 1959, 4 February 1959, 16 February 1959, 19 February 1959.

109 PRO: DEFE 11/400, McLeod to Minister of Defence, 31 December 1958, Aden (Luce) to Secretary of State, 11 February 1959, Secretary of State to Luce, 13 February 1959, 22 February 1959, DEFE 4/116, COS(59)16th mtg., minute 1, 3 March 1959.

110 P. Dresch, *A History of Modern Yemen* (Cambridge, Cambridge University Press, 2000), pp. 83–4.

111 PRO: DEFE 11/258, McLeod to Minister of Defence, 10 September 1958.

112 IOR: R/20/B/3265, Phillips to Governor, 19 August 1961.

113 PRO: CO 1015/1912, Amery to Profumo, 26 June 1959. A further piece of negative evidence is the absence of messages from Luce demanding action to remove Ahmad and Badr at this time; during the course of 1958 he had persistently advocated such measures and the lack of any documents of this kind in 1959 suggests he must either have abandoned this option or that some such action had been taken.

4 Debating Aden's future 1959–1962

Since its capture by Haines in 1839 the purpose which Aden served within the British imperial system had been ill defined. Its future rarely concerned British imperial strategists. On those rare occasions when it did there was usually a conflict between the men on the spot and those at the centre of metropolitan affairs. During the nineteenth and early twentieth century lines of authority ran from Aden to Bombay to Calcutta and then back to the India Office in London and these administrative arrangements tended to accentuate differences over policy. By 1959 the twisted bureaucratic position of the Colony within the British administrative system had become less tangled. The Governor ran the Colony and offered advice to the rulers of the protected states through political officers *in situ* while liaising with the Colonial Office in London. The latter then reported issues of wider concern to other Whitehall departments. However, the significance of the Aden base to British Middle East strategy gave the issue of its future greater prominence in ministerial thinking during the 1950s and generated a degree of scepticism about the plans being made by the men on the spot. Trevaskis's vision of an independent southwest Arabian state required the merger of Aden with the Protectorates and the suppression of both the urban nationalists and tribal dissidents in the Protectorates. In the longer term he was confident that a set of institutions could be constructed which would tie southwest Arabia into Britain's informal empire after independence. William Luce and his successor as Governor, Charles Johnston, were persuaded of the merits of this approach, as were the Colonial Office. It took rather more time to convince Conservative ministers who were sceptical of the ability of the Aden authorities to construct a state sufficiently robust to resist the rise of Arab nationalism. Conservative imperialists favoured the continuation of formal empire through the permanent retention of British sovereignty as the best means of retaining British influence in Arabia and the Middle East. These attitudes frustrated the Aden authorities, who were anxious to expedite the merger of Aden Colony with the federation while conditions remained propitious. It will be useful to first describe the bureaucratic obstacles to the switch to informal empire before examining the still more formidable local impediments in the way of the forward policy.

The merger controversy

The issue of whether Aden should be incorporated into the federation generated a lengthy, complex dispute. Proponents of merger characterised themselves as liberal advocates of independence and their opponents as fusty imperialists. Certainly the strong opposition of right wing conservatives such as Julian Amery and Duncan Sandys to the idea of merger lends credence to this portrayal of the critics of merger. There was a view within the Macmillan government that the incorporation of Aden into the federation would lead to independence and the loss of British base facilities. This concern expressed itself in hostility to proposals for any form of constitutional advance and, once this cause was lost, in advocacy of sovereign base areas. The latter notion would require the British to retain sovereignty over those portions of the Colony that formed the infrastructure of the base. However, it is possible to exaggerate the extent to which this line differed from that followed by the men on the spot. Advocates of merger only really disputed the means by which Britain could retain predominant influence. In his memoirs Trevaskis provided a sophistic account of this controversy in which he portrayed himself as a far-sighted supporter of self-government for colonial peoples and the opponents of merger as purblind reactionaries.[1] A more dispassionate defender of William Luce's policies has also bemoaned the British government's failure to accept his wise counsel that merger should be regarded as a prelude to independence.[2] What is neglected in these accounts is that the independence envisaged for the region by Trevaskis and Luce was to be heavily circumscribed. Their concern was not with self-determination for the local population but with the installation of Britain's allies as guarantors of British influence. Indeed, in order to achieve a merger of Aden and the federation the notion of consent was abandoned precisely because the policies pursued by British administrators were so unpopular in Aden. Independence was a matter of pragmatic adjustment from formal to informal empire and its rationale was that only the latter could ensure continued British influence and confound the nationalist opposition. A detailed examination of the controversies surrounding merger during the three years after the creation of the federation is required in order to tease out the nuances of these arguments.

In the aftermath of the establishment of the federation in February 1959 Trevaskis and his colleagues had less than four years in which to bring to fruition their vision of southwest Arabia's future. It is worth remembering that policy-makers are not blessed with hindsight in the manner of historians and could not know that September 1962 was to be a watershed in Yemeni history. Nevertheless, they were well aware that at some point events in the wider Middle East would again have an impact on southwest Arabia. Although Trevaskis remained sanguine about progress until the Republican revolution in Yemen, it seems evident that even during a period when the twin threats of Nasserism and Yemeni irredentism were in abeyance, little advance was made in solving the problems of continuing tribal intransigence in the Protectorates and urban discontent in the Colony. For the first two years of the federation the government was unable to develop any coherent strategy for its future because of differences over how best to secure continued access to British military facilities in Aden. It was not until early 1961 that Trevaskis and Johnston gained London's assent for the incorporation of Aden into the federation. Although this marked a step towards building an independent state in southwest Arabia, this enterprise did not have any appeal to either the Arab nationalists in Aden or insurgent tribesmen in the Protectorates. Both groups were aware that the purpose of Trevaskis's plan was to secure the domination of Britain's allies amongst the federal rulers and thus perpetuate British influence. It would do nothing to pacify insurgent tribesmen disturbed by British attempts to regulate their affairs or urban nationalists in the Colony who bitterly opposed interference by the Shaykhs and Sultans of the interior.

Even before the formal inauguration of the federation the Colonial Office were making efforts to enlighten other departments about the potential benefits of uniting the Colony with the putative federation. Lennox-Boyd explained in December 1958 that such a union 'would subject the extreme political elements in the Colony to the moderating influence of the more Conservative rulers in the Protectorates.'[3] He did not conceal the fact that merger would be a step towards independence. Instead he suggested that the alternative policy of clinging on grimly to British sovereignty in Aden, 'would soon jeopardise the practical value of our military base here, and would create a running sore in our relations with the Arab world generally.' This kind of thinking was alarming to those concerned to maintain a British global role such as the Chief of the Imperial General Staff, Francis Festing, and the Parliamentary Under-Secretary at the Colonial Office, Julian Amery. The latter opposed abandoning sovereignty over such a valuable strategic asset 'not on the merits of the case but for our local Aden reasons.'[4] Luce was informed that the issue was causing the government 'much perplexity' and that a resolution of the matter would have to be postponed.[5] Nevertheless, it was evident that the subject of sovereignty over the base was linked to the question of merger in the minds of policy-makers. The debate had an air of unreality about it: although Luce was no doubt correct in arguing that the permanent retention of Aden would make Britain unpopular in the Arab world, the issue which ignited nationalist opposition to the British in the Colony over the next three years was his proposal to subject the Adenis to government by the federal rulers. From the perspective of Luce and Trevaskis, merger made eminent sense as a way of preserving long-term British influence but the majority of the residents in Aden regarded it as an unprecedented threat to their independence.

By contrast, many British policy-makers interpreted the Trevaskis plan as a danger to British imperial prestige. In order to incorporate Aden into the federation it would be necessary to end direct British rule: the town would no longer be a Crown Colony but rather a constituent part of a federation which would have a treaty relationship with Britain. This could damage British attempts to sustain their role in the Middle East. The government began a fresh study of the strategic significance of the Aden base in early 1959. The tenor of these discussions is indicated by Festing's summary that 'if we wished to retain the ability to intervene quickly in the Persian Gulf there was no alternative to the retention of the Aden base.'[6] This opinion was, of course, given with the full knowledge that the government did wish to retain a capability to intervene in Kuwait. Even those more sympathetic to independence for southwest Arabia were forced to admit that finding alternative facilities would be 'a very costly business'.[7] One potential solution for resolving the apparently conflicting requirements of the men on the spot and the military planners was to carve out an enclave or a sovereign base area in Aden over which the British could retain direct control. This would allow the rest of southwest Arabia to proceed towards independence while guaranteeing unconditional access to Aden's defence facilities. Similar ideas had been discussed the previous year and in April 1959 Sandys, with encouragement from Amery, requested a new report on the matter.[8] Luce, who had been frustrated by the opposition to his independence proposals, reacted with some annoyance to its revival. He solicited the view of the commander of British forces in Arabia who warned: 'in India and Egypt we have built up such a fund of ill-will that the Treaty allegedly designed to secure the base has been doomed to failure before the ink on its signatures was dry. Mr Amery proposes to repeat this pattern in Aden.' Alongside this critique, Luce offered reassurance that Britain's allies in the Colony were 'democrats by expediency rather than conviction.' He argued that concessions to the federal rulers would ensure their loyalty, while pursuing the Amery plan for sovereign enclaves would force them to contemplate an alliance with the Nasserists. This failed to convince Conservative ministers, who believed that Aden was too precious an asset to risk if Britain were to remain a world power. Amery himself was looking forward to a renaissance of British imperialism or, as he put it, 'a reversion to more retentive and even acquisitive policies.' Even the cautious head of the Colonial Office, William Gorell Barnes, was unimpressed by Luce's analysis and suggested that some parts of the empire 'either because of their small size or because of their strategic importance to the West cannot be allowed full self-determination.'[9]

The result of this disagreement was another of those incremental compromises which so worried the Conservative imperialists. The Governor's views could be gainsayed but not entirely ignored. He visited London in July 1959 to press his case for merger and independence. Two months later he was authorised to take some initial, cautious steps towards greater co-operation between the Colony and the federation. There was to be no governmental statement in favour of Aden's incorporation into the federation but, should local actors begin to lobby for it, British ministers indicated they would tolerate another review of constitutional issues. Lennox-Boyd envisaged 'many years' passing before an actual merger took place. In return for this moderate concession and the dropping of the enclave proposal, Luce agreed not to promote closer association between the federation and the Colony in the near future.[10] Thus, as late as 1959 the Conservative government was relying on a policy of inertia to secure its hold on Aden at a time when Arab nationalism had established its ascendancy and less strategically significant territories in Africa were moving swiftly towards independence. It is not surprising that this solution proved transitory.

In the absence of any agreed strategy, Luce set about surreptitiously building a local coalition in favour of merger. This was fairly straightforward in the federation, where the rulers were eager to gain access to the resources of the Colony, but much more difficult in Aden itself. Despite Luce's protestations to the contrary, very few Adenis were eager to join the federation and the divisive nature of local politics was not conducive to the creation of a coalition in support of the Governor's policy. ATUC, which represented the views of the vast immigrant population, were excluded from the political process because of their commitment to nationalism. The most conservative of the political parties, the Aden Association had split. The influential Luqman family, who had dominated the Association and were perhaps the most prominent members of the old Adeni elite, established their own party, the People's Congress which campaigned for self-government for Aden outside the federation. Luce responded by cultivating the Luqmans' rival, Hasan Bayumi who had formed the United National Party (UNP). Bayumi had the usual mixed motives for aligning himself with the British: he combined a genuine belief in the merits of a continued British connection with a pragmatic desire to utilise the patronage they could offer in order to eclipse the Luqmans and the nationalists. Towards the end of 1960 Bayumi began tentative discussions with federal ministers about the feasibility of merging the federation and the Colony.[11]

The Trevaskis plan for merger required the British to force a reluctant Aden population into what was later described as a 'shotgun wedding' with the federation.[12] There were probably only a handful of people within the Colony in favour of merger and it required much ingenuity to manoeuvre them into a position of authority from which the proposals could be implemented, in spite of the protests of the majority of Adenis. Utilising Bayumi's isolated support for membership of the federation, on 3 September 1960 Luce reported that the idea of merger had become 'a very live issue here.' He suggested that the allegiance of Britain's 'friends' in the Colony and her allies among the Protectorate rulers could only be maintained by offering the former internal self-government within two years and the latter a greater say in the affairs of Aden. The grant of concessions to these groups would cement their friendship and guarantee access to the base. Luce identified Britain's enemies as ATUC and Nasser's United Arab Republic. He advocated a three-step solution to the problem: the transformation of Aden from a Colony into a protected state, the incorporation of this new Aden

Protectorate into the federation and then, eventually, independence for the whole. These proposals were criticised on the grounds that it would be more difficult to sustain Britain's allies in an Aden Protectorate than it would be if its colonial status were maintained. The new Colonial Secretary, Iain Macleod, informed his colleagues the following month that there were 'distinct signs of public interest in a further stage of constitutional development' but did not present Luce's plan for transforming Aden from a Crown Colony into a Protectorate. From the perspective of Whitehall the matter still did not appear urgent. Macmillan merely offered the comment 'we should take special care, in promoting the constitutional development of Aden, to safeguard our defence requirements.'[13]

The appointment of a new Governor, Charles Johnston, necessitated further delays while he reviewed the situation. Macleod gave him permission to 'brood on the subject for a few months before tending advice.'[14] The requirement for Johnston to familiarise himself with the situation was partly a consequence of his lack of experience in dealing with colonial issues. Prior to his arrival in Aden, he had been a Foreign Office employee and those who had been in the Colonial Service for much longer came to believe that the austerity and patrician values, which Johnston had imbibed from the British diplomatic corps, made him an inappropriate choice. He had a particularly uneasy relationship with the bullish Trevaskis. On one occasion Johnston rebuked Trevaskis for making inappropriate jokes about his decision to study at Oxford rather than at his father's *alma mater*, Cambridge. Trevaskis tendered his resignation and the Colonial Office was forced to step in to smooth matters over.[15] The Political Officers who worked for Johnston never felt that he had the necessary charisma to develop an effective relationship with the Arabs or even his own subordinates. Nevertheless, Johnston was an intelligent man and his wonderfully lucid dispatches are reflective of the fact that he was also a published poet.

Johnston's appointment spurred Trevaskis into action. He took the opportunity of the new Governor's 'brooding period' to explicate the case for the incorporation of Aden into an independent federation as the best means of guaranteeing British influence. What this required was a careful process of state building which placed the federal rulers in a dominant position. They could be relied upon for the compelling reason that 'they are anxious as ourselves to prevent Aden coming under Nasserite control.' The best guarantee against this eventuality would therefore 'lie in a form of union which would ensure that the bulk of the essential authority and above all control of the armed forces rested with the present federal leaders.' The Colonial Office provided a different perspective by reminding Johnston that the base was the primary British interest and that the retention of sovereignty over the defence facilities 'as of right and not by treaty' was an interesting possibility. In a long dispatch of 3 March 1961 Johnston finally declared his support for Trevaskis's approach of merger followed by independence. He thus broke the bureaucratic stalemate which had marked

British policy for the two years since the establishment of the federation. Johnston was concerned that the Aden nationalists would garner widespread support in the Colony for a campaign of opposition to merger. He therefore suggested that, prior to merger, Aden should be granted internal self-government. It was essential that measures were taken to ensure the pro-merger Bayumi rather than the Arab nationalists would exercise these new powers. The whole project therefore turned on the likely success of levering Bayumi into power in Aden prior to the attainment of self-government and his ability to manoeuvre Aden into the federation. Johnston's general strategy was to 'use the conflicting fears and aspirations of Colony and Federation to produce a balance of forces giving us the position we require.' He admitted that this sounded, 'cynical, Machiavellian and generally in line with the worst traditions of European diplomacy.' Such distasteful measures were necessary to achieve the laudatory goal of establishing an 'independent and prosperous Arab state in relations of friendly partnership with ourselves.'[16]

The first question the Colonial Office asked was 'whether end justifies these means.' One official summed up the dilemma neatly: 'Alternative to such jiggery-pokery (which means putting moderates in power and trusting largely to their own wits to keep them there) is to allow the popular voice in the Colony to say what kind of future it wants. Danger is that Colony workers would be dragooned easily by [ATUC] Union leaders who are unashamedly Arab nationalist.' The tactics that Johnston intended to employ to avert such an eventuality made the scheme more attractive to policy-makers in Whitehall than Luce's earlier overtures.[17] Macleod visited Aden for discussions on the matter and in May 1961 presented proposals to the Cabinet which closely resembled those of the Governor. The goal of this new policy was to be the establishment of self-government in Aden. However, British interests were to be guaranteed by the retention of reserved powers in the fields of defence, foreign affairs and internal security and by the inclusion of Aden in the federation, which was dominated by Britain's allies. This still did not satisfy those who believed that Britain's continuing role in the Middle East required the unconditional retention of the Aden base. Amery warned that the state that Johnston was planning to construct would be vulnerable to Arab nationalism and reiterated his support for the indefinite retention of the Colony. Sandys's replacement as Minister of Defence, Harold Watkinson, expressed a preference to 'leave matters in Aden as they now were'. Despite widespread support for the preservation of the status quo, Macleod secured Cabinet approval for both constitutional advance in Aden and its merger with the federation.[18]

In June 1961 detailed work began on the practicalities of the merger scheme. The federal rulers rather than the Legislative Council in Aden were the first to be consulted. They had been adamant since the first tentative discussions of merger that Aden should be assimilated into the federation and that the views of the local population regarding this matter were of little account. Their opinion was that the incorporation of Aden into the federation was merely a matter of returning what had been taken by force from the Sultan Muhsin of Lahj in 1839. As usual Sharif Husayn of Bayhan put this in the bluntest terms: 'we are the Adenis. Her Majesty's Government knows from whom it took Aden and with whom it made treaties. Our hope is that Her Majesty's Government will now return what it has been holding in trust.'[19] The rulers made clear their outright opposition to plans to grant self-government to Aden prior to its entry into the federation. After a series of intemperate meetings at the Colonial Office they were eventually induced to accept some form of constitutional advance in the Colony provided that absolute guarantees were given that Aden would join the federation at a later date. In early July a number of Adeni politicians, including Bayumi, conducted preparatory discussions with the rulers in London.[20] These merger talks resumed in Aden at the start of August. Bayumi was receptive to the rulers' overtures but few of those regarded as Aden moderates were eager to accept what was widely interpreted as a take-over of the town by the federal rulers. Both the Luqmans' faction and ATUC attempted to impede progress towards a deal. Bayumi was recorded as 'all out for an agreement with a Federation' but the other representatives of the Aden Legislative Council set stiff conditions for a merger which they knew would be unacceptable to the federal rulers.[21]

The most difficult issue in the negotiations was the question of whether to consult the Adeni population who were known to be hostile to merger and the matter of elections would remain controversial for years to come. On 20 September 1961 following six weeks of frustrating negotiations Bayumi completed a unilateral deal with the federal rulers which would place him in power and obviated the need for any further consultation with the Adeni electorate. Under its provisions, the federal rulers would request that Aden be granted a greater measure of self-government with Bayumi as Chief Minister. In return, Bayumi promised that Aden would join the federation within four to six months. To the authorities in Aden this arrangement could 'at least offer us a reasonable prospect of eventual success.'[22] The problem was, as British officials acknowledged, the 'amount of present support for Bayumi is probably very small.' The Colonial Office were much less content than the authorities in Aden to abandon plans to seek the consent of the Aden electorate prior to their incorporation into the federation. At the start of October Johnston explained that the only alternatives to the Bayumi deal were to abandon the talks and allow popular elections in Aden or to put the merger talks in 'cold storage' and switch attention to the negotiation of a new franchise for Aden. He favoured the Bayumi option of merging Aden and the federation and postponing elections. This would take advantage of the disarray in nationalist circles in the aftermath of Syria's secession from the United Arab Republic.[23] Thus, the Aden authorities, who favoured rapid constitutional advance, were required to manipulate local politics and to pursue a far more interventionist policy in order to build a sturdy constitution for their favoured political order. By contrast, those who envisaged clinging to Aden in perpetuity were content with a much less activist policy which amounted to a kind of passive clinging on to what Britain held.

Johnston visited London in November 1961 and persuaded the new Secretary of State for the Colonies, Reginald Maudling, of the requirement to postpone any election in Aden until after it had joined the federation. Maudling explained to his colleagues that Britain's 'loyal friends' among the federal rulers were opposed to elections in Aden and that, in any event, 'the moderate leaders in the Colony might well be defeated in elections held before merger, despite the proposed alteration of the franchise in their favour.' He therefore recommended that Bayumi should be authorised to proceed with his plans to organise a pro-merger majority in the current Aden Legislative Council. Ministers approved this plan and Johnston publicly declared British support for merger in January 1962.[24] The government had thus effectively endorsed the peculiar deal which Bayumi had made with the rulers in September 1961: Adeni consent for merger would only be sought after Aden had joined the federation. Two difficulties were unresolved: in Whitehall there was renewed debate over the possibility of sovereign base areas, while in Aden the precise form of consent which the Colony ought eventually to give remained a source of tension.

The public endorsement of merger by the British government was far from resolving the political problems confronting the British. No means had yet been found by which rising nationalism in Aden could be reconciled to either formal or informal British control over the politics of southwest Arabia. The key source of uncertainty was whether the nationalists could be prevented from blocking British access to the Aden base. During 1961 the nature of these dilemmas was illustrated when President Qassim of Iraq indicated his desire to revive long-standing Iraqi claims to sovereignty over Kuwait. A small British force was sent to the Gulf and the less minatory tone employed by Iraq in the aftermath of this deployment appeared to vindicate this swift action. Many policy-makers regarded the use made of the facilities at Aden during this operation as demonstrable proof of the utility of the base. After the crisis abated, Macmillan, who was eager for Britain to have an independent role in Middle East politics, suggested that the Aden base should be retained for at least a decade. Given the imminence of the planned merger it was doubtful whether the whole of Aden could be kept under British imperial control for ten years and this led the government to reconsider the potential for carving out sovereign base areas inside Aden. These would remain British controlled territory even after Aden had achieved independence as part of the federation. Unfortunately for advocates of this approach, it was practically impossible to disentangle those military facilities required by the British armed forces from the civilian areas of the town which were to achieve self-government inside an expanded federal south Arabian state. The Chiefs of Staff were convinced of the impracticality of sovereign base areas and felt obliged to reiterate their negative conclusions regarding this matter time after time.

In the midst of the 1961 Kuwait crisis the Chiefs restated their belief that sovereign base areas were not a feasible proposition.[25] In its aftermath they argued that the success of the operation proved the requirement for military facilities in Aden.[26] This seemed to narrow down the options of policy-makers to either the retention of direct control or the negotiation of a defence treaty guaranteeing British access. Such calculations neglected widespread suspicions within the British government about the feasibility of continued colonial rule and the reliability of defence treaties. In January 1962 Watkinson returned to the fray and insisted that there should be a 'close examination of the possibilities of sovereign enclaves.' He had support among ministers but was opposed by the Chief of Defence Staff, Mountbatten, who noted that the Chiefs had repeatedly rejected this option, most recently in August 1961. They were nevertheless obliged to rehearse once more the reasons why sovereign base areas were not 'a practicable solution' to the problem of retaining defence facilities. This did not deter Macmillan from stressing the requirement for a base in the area and even raising the possibility of moving the facilities to the offshore island of Socotra.[27] After a lull of a few months Sandys raised the issue yet again after taking over from Maudling as Colonial Secretary. Mountbatten responded by declaring on behalf of the Chiefs that 'he did not believe they would wish to change the views they had expressed on previous occasions.' Sandys was unimpressed and told the Cabinet on 1 August 1962 that carving out sovereign enclaves was a better means of retaining access to the base than the negotiation of a defence treaty with an independent federal government. It was Johnston who finally provided a means of circumventing this controversy. He reassured anxious ministers that the federation was not yet on the cusp of independence. In the interval between merger and independence they could rely on the powers which Britain would reserve for herself as the final guarantee of access to the base. The treaty which the British were to sign with the federation fell far short of a grant of independence and it was 'clearly expressed that Britain would be able to remove Aden *in whole or in part* from the Federation, permanently or temporarily at any time.' Thus, although the treaty ended Aden's colonial status and allowed it to join the federation, in the last resort the British retained legal authority to secure their defence facilities even without carving out sovereign enclaves. This did not satisfy Sandys who remained concerned about what would happen when full independence was granted but it was sufficient to clear the final obstacle to merger in Whitehall.[28]

While the enclaves issue appeared to consume an unwarranted amount of time in Whitehall, in southwest Arabia preparations for the shotgun wedding of Colony and federation continued apace. The union did not merely require the blessing of the metropolitan government: at least a token expression of consent from the Colony was also needed. The puzzle for policy-makers was what form this should take. A new election was out of the question, both because the deal that Bayumi struck with the rulers forbade it and because it was unlikely to produce an affirmative verdict on merger. Instead the British relied on the Aden Legislative Council, half of whom had been elected on Luce's narrow 1959 franchise, to endorse membership of the federation. For the purposes of organising a majority, the Aden High Commission decided it should not depend on British *ex officio* members of the Council. It was deemed essential for propaganda purposes to produce a non-official majority.[29] Johnston therefore had the task of constructing a coalition of nominated and elected members of the Council to vote in favour of merger. The latter group could not be insulated from the wider current of nationalist feeling. One of their number, Saidi, insisted that elections should be held prior to any merger and resigned when this option was ruled out. Another, Joshi, proposed that the *ex officio* members should be removed from the Council entirely. Under his plan four replacements would be nominated by the Council prior to their merger vote.[30]

These early signs of independent thinking in the Aden Legislative Council alarmed the federal rulers, who feared that the Aden ministers might seek an early divorce from the federation once they had freed themselves of British colonial control. In July 1962 they met Aden legislators at a conference in London. The rulers were initially adamant 'that Aden belonged to the hinterland states.' They complained to Sandys that the Governor's suggestion that Joshi's proposal 'would give the appearance of a greater measure of popular consent is, in our opinion, baseless since the reconstituted Council could not be said to be any more representative than the present Council.'[31] It was the establishment of strict criteria for secession and British promises to terminate self-government in Aden, should this be required to block a nationalist take-over, which eventually persuaded the rulers to accept the replacement of the official members of the Aden Legislative Council with four nominees selected indirectly by the current members. The federal rulers were reassured by the fact that the British retained reserved powers in the Colony and had a common interest in curbing the nationalists.[32] In this narrow sense they were justified. Three years later the British responded to the escalating demands of Adeni ministers by terminating self-government and imposing direct rule. In the wider sense, however, their concerns about the spread of nationalism in the Colony and about the willingness of the British to cling on in the face of vigorous opposition were to be confirmed.

The issue of Aden's incorporation into the federation dominated the politics of the Colony during 1962. Al-Asnaj led the opposition to the merger proposals and took his nationalist campaign on to the streets of Aden. In response to this challenge the British incarcerated him and made increasing use of regular troops to control the situation in the town. The final vote on merger in the Legislative Council occurred on 24 September and the occasion provided evidence of an imminent bloody confrontation between the British and the Adenis. Seven members of the Council voted for an amendment demanding elections in Aden prior to a final decision on membership of the federation. When this motion was defeated the seven dissenters walked out of the Council, accompanied by another of their colleagues. The remaining members were left free to endorse the merger proposals. This was a Pyrrhic victory for the British and Bayumi: outside of the chamber the debate provoked unprecedented public disturbances.[33] During the three years of negotiations just described the British had sought to manufacture a merger by courting the federal rulers and a tiny circle of Adeni politicians. In the meantime the gap between the aspirations of the bulk of the Arab population and the British had grown still wider.

Nationalism in Aden and Yemen

The rise of Arab nationalism in southwest Arabia took place during a turbulent era in Middle Eastern politics in which local actors competed to free themselves from old ties to the imperial powers and attach themselves to radical programmes of social change. The language of Arab nationalism, with its themes of emancipation from western control and the renaissance of Arab culture, leaked into the politics of southwest Arabia to the point where the terms of political debates were saturated with nationalist concepts. The seepage of these ideas occurred in various ways but two are particularly significant and will be explored here. The most direct route was via the activities of expatriate Yemenis who acquired a sense of the new intellectual current during their travels. It was the Free Yemeni Movement that was particularly influential in this regard. The second route was more reliant on impersonal media and, in particular, the pamphleteering and radio broadcasts emanating from the revolutionary regime in Cairo. This propaganda proved to have general appeal in the Arab world but was especially significant in Aden where a disgruntled working class enthusiastically took up Arab nationalist slogans.

The adoption of nationalist ideas affected the process of British decolonization because their content was explicitly anti-imperialist: the movement was to a large degree defined by its opposition to European rule.[34] By the middle of the 1950s Arab nationalist doctrine had became infused with anti-western sentiment.[35] To the nationalists the Arab world was a cultural unity which had been disassembled by the western powers; it was their task to put it back together again. The existence of a large British base at Aden could only be regarded as an obstacle to this process. From the nationalist perspective it was therefore entirely logical for Nasser to seek to remove the British presence from southwest Arabia. Nasser's foreign policy assumed a basic congruence between Arab nationalist imperatives and Egyptian national interests and the latter also required a confrontation with the British in southwest Arabia. During much of the post-Suez period Egypt was engaged in fearsome competition with Saudi Arabia and Iraq for the leadership of the Arab world. Egyptian influence in Yemen was particularly useful in the conflict with the Saudis as it brought them to the frontiers of the Saudi state. There is a parallel here: just as the British were encouraged to stay in Aden both by strategic interests and their concept of a continuing global role, Nasser was compelled to challenge them by a combination of Egyptian national interests and an ideological commitment to Arab nationalism. This was a conflict of interests but also a clash between differing views of the role which the Arabs and the British had to play in the world.

In one sense, southwest Arabia was not particularly fertile ground for Arab nationalism. In rural areas the primary allegiance of most of the population was to a tribe or a locality. Amongst the educated elites of Sanaa, Ta'izz and Aden there was also a sense that Yemen had a distinctive history and culture which set it apart from much of the Arab world. Thus, Arab nationalism in southwest Arabia generally took on a tinge of Yemeni particularism.[36] It is quite possible to conceive of Yemeni nationalism or nationalisms competing with Arab nationalism. However, with the exception of Imam Ahmad's confrontation with Nasser between 1961 and 1962, this potential conflict remained latent. Yemeni particularists and Arab nationalists found common ground in opposing western imperialism. Daily broadcasts directed to southwest Arabia by Radio Cairo as part of their Voice of the Arabs programming combined with Nasser's political successes cemented the alliance. The British presence in Aden and the Protectorates presented a tempting target for the gratification of local grievances. At no time was this more evident than in the three years prior to the 1962 revolution. During this period the connections between Yemen and the Arab world were becoming ever stronger, partly as a consequence of the increasingly sophisticated operation of Voice of the Arabs but also through the contacts made by local actors with radical groups in Baghdad, Beirut and, particularly, Cairo.

The most conspicuous example of the increasing influence of Arab nationalism in southwest Arabia was the treaty that Ahmad signed with the United Arab Republic. As noted previously, Badr negotiated a form of ancillary membership of the new Egyptian-Syrian state in early 1959. Unlike the agreement reached between Nasser and the Syrian Ba'th, Yemen's treaty with the UAR, which created the United Arab States, did not commit the country to administrative union with Egypt but it did require the Imam to co-ordinate his foreign policy with Cairo.[37] This was largely a defensive measure in response to the punitive actions which the British perpetrated along the frontier. Ahmad was rather more cautious in pursuing his cross-border campaign of subversion after the major British attacks of early 1959 but the frontier with the Protectorates remained the only part of the Middle East where an Arab state was in direct confrontation with the British. The existence of formal ties between Yemen and Egypt did not discourage the Aden authorities from engaging in special operations to undermine Ahmad. In early 1960 they suspected Ahmad of stirring up trouble in the Protectorates and responded by authorising friendly 'Awdhali tribes to undertake their own campaign of subversion inside Yemen in co-operation with the Rassassi tribes on the other side of the frontier.[38]

Although these kinds of incidents illustrated the common interests of Egypt and Yemen in opposing the British, the alliance between Nasser and Ahmad was an exceedingly fragile one. Ahmad remained deeply suspicious of the progressive ideas espoused by Nasser. He was concerned about the increasing appeal of Arab nationalism to the Yemeni population. The break-ing point was the promulgation of the Egyptian National Charter in 1961, which made explicit Nasser's commitment to revolutionary transformation in the Arab world.[39] It was characteristic of the Zaydi tradition which he represented that Ahmad should respond to the new Egyptian constitution with a poem denouncing Cairo's modernism in general and Nasser person-ally. The broadcast of Ahmad's verses set the seal on the enmity between Nasser and the Hamid al-Din. The Egyptians became ever more implicated in the plotting which surrounded Ahmad's court and which culminated in the revolution of 1962.[40] This event brought radical Arab nationalism to Britain's Arabian doorstep and the proxy war between Egypt and Britain was transformed into a direct conflict, albeit one which was conducted in a covert manner.

Prior to the revolution the influence of Arab nationalism upon southwest Arabia was evident from the activities of the Free Yemeni movement.[41] This had its origins in the 1930s when expatriate Yemenis residing in Egypt began to advocate reform of the Imamate. The movement went through various changes of nomenclature and by the 1950s its members were grouped together in the Yemeni Union. From the outset it was a loose, peri-patetic organisation whose leaders travelled frequently and quarrelled fre-quently. Members circulated between Aden, Egypt and Yemen depending on the political climate in each. The organisation's first priority was the reform or dissolution of the Imamate. In later years many of its younger members began to argue for the union of Yemen, Aden and the Protec-torates and the removal of British influence. In these respects it achieved few direct results but it was one of the principal means by which new develop-ments in Islamic, nationalist and socialist thinking were transmitted to southwest Arabia. The very heterogeneity and itinerancy of the movement made it an effective means of propagating various ideas unsympathetic to British imperialism. The first Ba'thist cells in Aden appear to have been established by younger radical members of the Yemeni Union.[42] Even more significantly the Free Yemenis established links during the 1950s with the UNF.[43] After the collapse of the UNF the Aden branch of the Yemeni Union entered into formal alliance with ATUC. One of its leading, and most moderate members, Ahmad Nu'man was expelled from Aden by the British in June 1960.[44]

In order to understand the radicalisation of Adeni politics in the ten years prior to the revolution it is necessary to trace the connections of the town to these broader currents but also the specific local circumstances which led to strikes, demonstration, protests and eventually, armed conflict. Politicians such as Muhammad Luqman and Hasan Bayumi, who the British were willing to acknowledge even if they did not like them, were representatives of Adeni nationalism. Their agenda was far less ambitious than that of the Arab nationalists and concentrated principally on the maintenance of the prosperity of old Aden. These limited goals were not those of the bulk of the population of the town who were encouraged by Voice of the Arabs to think of themselves as part of a broader Arab community. Yemeni immigrants identified a close correspondence between Arab nationalism's portrayal of British perfidy and their own quotidian experiences. Two issues in particular seem to have provoked an authentic sense of outrage among the working population of the town: restrictions on their ability to take strike action and their exclusion from the franchise.

As far as the British authorities were concerned, their opponents were incorrigible in their attachment to Nasser and loathing of western imperialism. Luce argued that it was impossible to compromise with the radicals because they were committed to Arab nationalism and Arab nationalism was unbending in its opposition to British interests. In March 1959 he warned that ATUC 'will become increasingly the principal weapon of Egypt in promoting the latter's political aims in Aden ... The time for persuasion has passed as none of the ATUC leaders will listen to reason nor is there any hope now that they will co-operate with the government.'[45] He proposed a policy of repression codenamed operation SHARK which would begin with the proscription of ATUC. Although this initiative was rejected by the Colonial Office, Luce was clearly determined on a policy of confrontation with the unions and by implication with the industrial work force who manned the oil refinery, the port and the construction industry.[46] There was a temporary lull in industrial unrest in the middle of 1959 and Luce terminated the state of emergency on 1 October.[47]

There was a mere four-day interval between the ending of the state of emergency and the next crisis. The workers in Aden had a range of grievances including low wages, insecurity of employment and poor working conditions. These were seen, in turn, as a consequence of an abundance of available labour; one particularly galling practice was the employers' habit of dismissing longer-serving employees and taking on new arrivals in the town at cheap rates. On 5 October 1959 the dockers' union struck in protest against a series of arbitrary dismissals and the following month the action spread to the refinery, whose workers were unhappy about their terms of employment. Luce reported these events to the Colonial Office but insisted that ATUC's actions were motivated by broader political considerations. When yet another round of strike action began in early 1960 he argued that the disruption was 'part of a deliberate policy of the TUC leaders who were likely to embark on an even more militant policy against government and expatriate employers.' He proposed a typically forthright solution: the imposition of mandatory arbitration and the effective banning of strike action. The Colonial Office noted with some alarm, 'we have no record of legislation of this kind ever being approved in peace time in any Colony.'[48] The proposals which went to the Cabinet contained provisions for an Industrial Court which would impose settlements in the case of labour disputes. It was admitted that the effective proscription of industrial action went 'beyond what has hitherto regarded as acceptable in the UK and other Colonial territories.' Despite this, ministers strongly supported the recommendation and Luce drafted an ordinance outlawing strikes which Hasan Bayumi guided through the Aden Legislative Council.[49]

The subsequent implementation of the ordinance caused a terminal break with the leadership of ATUC, including the moderate al-Asnaj. For much of this period al-Asnaj had been a conciliatory influence, attempting to maintain relations with the Aden authorities while adopting a sufficiently radical stance to maintain his own acknowledged position of leadership against potential challenges from more radical elements. He was not entirely successful and during the strikes of 1960 it was evident that the workers in the Little Aden refinery and at the base were beginning to act independently of the ATUC leadership.[50] Al-Asnaj appealed to Luce to suspend the ban on strike action. Luce was insistent that it should go ahead and informed the Colonial Office the 'Bill must be enacted in accordance with present timetable ... No one here has any faith in ATUC protestations and assertions. They know Government means business this time and are wriggling to play for time.' Al-Asnaj responded with 'veiled threats that no worker would go to the industrial court and that "other union tactics" would be used to achieve labour's purposes.'[51] Over one hundred government employees were sacked in the immediate aftermath of the latest wave of strikes. These punitive measures combined with the ban on strikes hampered ATUC's industrial campaign but prompted the leadership to engage in a still more overtly political role. This role was narrowly defined in Arab nationalist terms.[52]

When further strikes broke out during late 1961 the leaders of the union movement were prosecuted. The defeat over the bill and these arrests forced the unions to alter their tactics and was a contributory factor in the establishment by the ATUC leadership of the People's Socialist Party (PSP).[53] Fewer days were lost to strike action in 1962 but the confrontation between the workers and the Aden authorities shifted on to the streets. The lack of consultation concerning the proposed integration of Aden into the federation and, in particular, the failure to hold a popular election prior to merger, prompted the PSP to initiate an increasingly inflammatory anti-British campaign on the streets of the town. As one commentator with close connections to the Colony observed of the Yemeni population: 'no sense of eloquence could have made headway against their bitterness as second class citizens. And this was the tinder of trouble.'[54] British policy-makers had agreed as early as June 1961 that the Aden Legislative Council elections scheduled for January 1963 would have to be postponed in order to gain time for the completion of the merger arrangements. Their great concern was that a popular election might produce a nationalist victory. In order to avert such a contingency it was agreed that the already narrow franchise 'should be amended to confine the vote essentially to those who can claim by birth or long residence that they belong to Aden Colony.'[55] With the nationalist campaign against merger gathering momentum Johnston cautioned that an early election in Aden would have 'disastrous consequences'.[56] During negotiations with the current Aden Legislative Council there was discussion of postponing elections until 1964.[57] The primary concern of the Aden authorities was that 'al Asnag and his friends might succeed in mustering sufficient outside pressure to secure an alteration of the franchise in such a way that there is a swamping Yemeni majority in the Colony.'[58]

The announcement of the decision to postpone elections until after the merger infuriated al-Asnaj and the nationalists. Their indignation over the continued restrictions on both industrial and political action was encouraged by broadcasts from the Voice of the Arabs. The great British complaint was that the nationalists used industrial relations grievances to further a radical political agenda but it was increasingly difficult for anybody to disentangle resentment about the social conditions of the town from the aspirations of its people for independence and freedom from colonial control. Al-Asnaj created the PSP as the political wing of ATUC and in August 1962 it launched a campaign of action to disrupt the planned merger between Aden and the federation. He made a series of speeches condemning the merger and called for a general strike. His declared determination to march on the Legislative Council building on the day of the merger vote alarmed Johnston who decided to pre-empt him. Citing the increasingly fervid atmosphere in which both the PSP and the Luqmans were conducting their street politics, Johnston ordered al-Asnaj's arrest on 15 September.[59] The British also revoked the licence of a leading nationalist newspaper.[60] By this stage it was difficult to effectively contain the anti-merger protests and regular British army units were deployed when riots broke out on the day of the merger vote. During the course of 24 September one person was killed and five wounded after the police opened fire on crowds in Crater. Over one hundred protesters were arrested.[61] An awareness of these events is a key to understanding the joyous reaction in Aden to the news of the revolution in Yemen that arrived three days later.

In the federation there were no popular protests against merger or any evidence of widespread enthusiasm for the Yemeni revolution. The rulers saw Aden as a valuable asset and regarded its incorporation into the federation as belated justice for the British seizure of the town from the Sultan of Lahj. Unlike the Aden Legislative Council there were no elected members on the Federal Council which consisted of the rulers' nominees. As might be expected the vote on merger in the federation was considerably less controversial and produced an overwhelming majority of 58 to two in favour.[62] Outside these narrow circles opposition to the British was increasing but the genesis of nationalism in these outlying areas was distinct from developments in Aden. Nationalism in the interior developed initially as a consequence of feuds between leading families who were the recipients of British largesse and those who felt a sense of grievance because of their exclusion from the political system which the British were constructing. The latter group followed the precedent set by 'Ali of Lahj and sought support from those opposed to British policy in the wider Arab world.

Pacifying the Protectorates

In many cases it was the advance of British forces into isolated areas accustomed to autarchy that provided the stimulus for the emergence of nationalist feeling in the Protectorates. Significant areas of the Protectorates, such as Mahra and Upper Yafi', had their first sustained contact with European imperialism at a time when outside of the Middle East the European empires appeared to be in full retreat. In those regions where the British had been engaged prior to 1959, such as Upper 'Awlaqi, intensified campaigns of pacification were undertaken. Both the advance into *terra incognita* and the determination to suppress rebellions directed at their long-standing allies in the WAP reflected the belief of local British policy-makers that the conduct of a forward policy was essential to the establishment of a stable political order in which a united federal state could thrive.

The specific tactics employed in pursuing the forward policy contributed to the spread of nationalism. Trevaskis's favoured method of pacification was aerial proscription. This required the quarantining of an area to clear it of insurgents. Leaflets were dropped warning potential rebels and residents to evacuate. Anybody who remained was assumed to be hostile and was subject to bombing and rocket attack. In addition crops and livestock could be destroyed as a means of punishing the general population for assisting insurrection. Aerial proscription was thus both a means of clearing territory of dissident forces and supplying a lesson to those who connived in rebellion. The RAF had employed this approach in both southwest Arabia and Iraq since the 1920s and Trevaskis was not one to abandon traditional methods in order to appease international opinion. It has been defended as much the most humane and effective instrument for controlling the fearsome tribal squabbles which prevailed across southwest Arabia.[63] In fact, although aerial attacks of this kind could be employed in a controlled, graduated manner these tactics were almost uniformly unsuccessful. The evidence suggests that its repeated employment created more problems than it resolved. It had failed to quell the dissident tribes in Oman in 1958. In that case a land campaign was required to dislodge the rebels from their base on the heights of the Jebel Akhdar.[64] The actual deployment of soldiers on the ground was a far more reliable means of clearing an area of dissidents and inflicting punishment on local collaborators. However, in a region with as many trouble spots as the Protectorates there were never sufficient troops to permanently secure the peace. Thus the British fell back on rocketing and bombing from the air as a cheap and practicable alternative, despite its demonstrable ineffectiveness. The problem was that both land and air campaigns inflamed tribal opinion without resolving grievances as the following case studies illustrate.

One of the most intensive pacification programmes took place in Upper Yafi'. Between 1958 and 1962 a concerted effort was made to quell dissidence there through a series of aerial operations. Although a number of temporary lulls did occur after each campaign, the primary result of this activity was to transform a squabble within one of the leading local families into a showpiece confrontation between British imperialism and Arab nationalism. Ostensibly Yafi' was neatly divided into Upper and Lower Sultanates but in actuality it contained numerous competing local potentates and the British were never able to extend their control much beyond the lowland areas. The son of the Sultan of Lower Yafi', Muhammad 'Aydarus, like 'Ali in Lahj, was initially seen as a potential ally in the process of administrative reform. This optimism proved short-lived and following repeated disagreements with British officials and his father, he decamped for the highlands of northern Yafi' in December 1957 taking with him most of the local tribal guard and a large sum of cash from the state treasury. His cause was immediately taken up by Cairo.[65] Over the next five years Muhammad 'Aydarus proved himself an effective spokesman for opponents of the British forward policy and a cunning political strategist. He increasingly adopted nationalist rhetoric to bolster his position as a regional leader both at home and amongst the wider Arab public.[66] Trevaskis became almost obsessed with the threat he posed to British influence. In February 1958 he ordered Shackletons and Venoms to attack Muhammad 'Aydarus's supporters in the highlands. The problems which accompanied the opening day of the operations are evident from Trevaskis's diary: 'The results of the bombing are tragic. We do not seem to have touched a dissident; instead we have killed a woman and two children and destroyed a perfectly innocent camel caravan.' The aircraft had lost their bearings and a Venom pilot had mistaken the caravan for a rebel force. Despite Trevaskis's admission at the outset that 'the margin for error is very great' the British continued to rely on aerial proscription to defeat Muhammad 'Aydarus.[67]

These RAF campaigns appear only to have increased opposition to British influence amongst the tribes of the region and they brought a local conflict to the attention of Britain's opponents in the Arab world. In early 1960 a new round of aerial attacks began and in July Trevaskis boasted that Muhammad 'Aydarus was 'now cutting a pretty sad figure.'[68] However, even during this lull the dissidents continued to circulate anti-British propaganda which portrayed the British campaign as a consequence of Trevaskis's vengeful instincts and the resistance to the bombing as part of the wider global struggle against colonialism. One leaflet claimed that Trevaskis 'has become now like a madman by his actions in Yafa in particular and the South in general . . . owing to his foolishness he did not realise the fact that colonialism has passed away from all parts of the World and that he himself is passing away with colonialism.'[69] Material such as this indicated that attempts to curb tribal independence had the potential in the long term to create revolutionary, anti-colonial feeling in the Protectorates; in the short term it presaged a new round of disturbances.

Muhammad 'Aydarus was not content merely to denounce the atavism of British policy in leaflets and he secured the assistance of the Imam in distributing arms to his tribal supporters. During the summer of 1960 he raised a force of 2,000 tribesmen and in October launched a new campaign of dissidence. The British again responded to the rebel offensive with bombing and rocket attacks. In one incident Muhammad Aydarus's house and a nearby mosque were destroyed.[70] The insurgents were undeterred and in April 1961 Trevaskis warned that 'the threat developing in Yafa is poten-tially much more formidable than anything we have had to deal with in the past.' His solution was to order further aerial attacks against the dissidents. The aim was 'to kick Muhammad Aidrus out of Yafa and into the Yemen' by proscribing those regions in which his supporters were active. In the longer term it was hoped to build up British influence in the strategically vital Hilyan area as a prelude to the construction of a landing strip inside rebel territory. After the first month of bombing it was reported 'the band of dissidents in the proscribed area are still in being ... There are suggestions that opinion in Upper Yafai and among Yafais in Aden is hardening against government for its actions.' Although Muhammad 'Aydarus decamped to Yemen it was evident that the only really effective means of permanently pacifying the region was the construction of the air strip at Hilyan. This required the conduct of a ground campaign but such an arduous operation was beyond the means of the British forces.[71]

In the aftermath of the failure of the 1961 campaign new tactics were adopted in January 1962. These were based on the targeting of economic resources, particularly the qat crops. Punitive action of this kind succeeded in containing dissidence, although the harshness of the methods employed was of some concern to the Colonial Office.[72] The final result of this four-year campaign was a stalemate. Muhammad 'Aydarus was never able to extend his control beyond his mountain strongholds but the British were unable to establish any permanent measure of control over Upper Yafi'. One political officer who spent six months of his career co-ordinating RAF sorties against rebels and parachute drops to friendly tribes in the mountains of Yafi' recorded that despite his efforts the territory, 'remained unconquered and hostile, its valleys alive with vigorous, arrogant Yafais' up to British withdrawal in 1967.[73] The only military historian to have examined these campaigns concluded that 'the dream of the WAP office had become a nightmare' and that the conflict in Upper Yafi' was illustrative of 'the mag-nitude of the task that the Aden Government had undertaken in bringing the tribes into the new Federation.'[74] The inefficiency of proscription in this instance was demonstrated not only by the loss of life and the destruction of crops and property but also by the failure to make any real progress with pacification.

The inability of air action alone to pacify highland regions was further demonstrated by events in Upper 'Awlaqi. The defeat at Robat in the Upper 'Awlaqi Sultanate had demonstrated at an early stage the difficulties of controlling an area without the deployment of adequate land forces. In September 1960 a land-air operation codenamed Operation NIGGARD was finally launched in order to punish the Rabiz for their continued recalcitrance.[75] This succeeded in clearing the Rabiz out of the region, but without the permanent deployment of land forces it was impossible to stop them returning as they did in 1962 and then again in 1963. As in Yafi' the British opted to target the tribes' means of livelihood, in this instance their sheep and goats, and this alleviated the problem of tribal disturbance without of course, securing a permanent settlement.[76] The Rabiz were cowed after ten years of campaigning but they were never reconciled to British control.

To the east of the Sultanate the British confronted an even more serious difficulty as a consequence of a disagreement between two leading families. The Ahl Muhsin had been selected as partners in the process of pacification and became the recipients of British largesse while the Ahl Bubakr, who had once maintained a position of parity, were neglected. On one occasion the Political Officer responsible for affairs in 'Awlaqi recorded the receipt of 24 rifles and 20,000 rounds by the former.[77] The leading Shaykh of the Ahl Bubakr, Muhammad, was dissatisfied with this dispensation and in the late 1950s entered into an alliance with the Jifris and the SAL. In early 1959 he went a step further by visiting Cairo to enlist the support of Nasser for a major rebellion. Trevaskis responded by proscribing those areas of the Shaykhdom suspected of Ahl Bubakr sympathies. Initially, the RAF engaged in desultory bombing but this proved wholly ineffective.[78] As in Yafi' the experience of British aerial attacks encouraged the leaders of the insurrection to place their parochial quarrel in the context of the wider struggle against the British. The start of the campaign was characterised by the newly formed 'Awlaqi Liberation Army as 'a victorious day for the South in general and for you Awlaqis in particular . . . the day when the English and their slaves Ahl Muhsin bin Farid arranged a conspiracy and an attack against the leaders of the Peaceful Resistance.'[79]

The failure of the very limited aerial policing operation to do any more than elicit a flood of anti-British rhetoric from the tribes prompted the Aden authorities to plan the largest scale bombing campaign yet undertaken in the Protectorates. On 11 and 12 April 1960 the RAF, with the assistance of aircraft from an offshore carrier, conducted a two-day blitz against supporters of the Ahl Bubakr, codenamed operation DAMON. In the aftermath of DAMON it was reported that the dissidents 'are said to have suffered some, though not very appreciable damage to their equipment and Ali Bubakr is said to have sustained a slight wound from a rock splinter.' The rebels responded with a renewed offensive which killed six Federal National

Guards.[80] This necessitated the dispatch of the Aden Protectorate Levies and with RAF assistance they succeeded in driving the rebels across the Yemen frontier during May. Bernard Reilly, whose knowledge of WAP politics surpassed that of Trevaskis, concluded that the DAMON attacks proved that air action alone was insufficient to suppress determined dissidents.[81] One can go further and suggest that such campaigns changed the nature of provincial power struggles between the elites of the Protectorates and encouraged those whose positions were undermined by the forward policy to portray their struggles as a front in the wider conflict between British imperialism and Arab nationalism.

Conclusions

It is the continuity of British policy which is the most striking aspect of the three-year period between the founding of the federation and the revolution in Yemen. Despite the scepticism of many Colonial Office officials concerning his background in the diplomatic service, Charles Johnston did not radically change the course of British policy in southwest Arabia. His policies were continuous with those of his predecessors. Like Luce he identified tribal dissidents and Arab nationalists as Britain's foes in the region and he was quickly persuaded of the merits of Trevaskis's plans for merger and independence. Although he lacked quite the singleness of purpose of Hickinbotham, Trevaskis or Luce his detached manner and literary fluency enabled him to articulate the dilemmas of British policy more clearly than any of them. He was responsible for persuading a reluctant Conservative government to accept the incorporation of Aden into the federation. Like his predecessors, he was determined that Britain should continue to play a role in the Middle East including southwest Arabia but was not always confident of success. In May 1962 he wrote to Maudling advising that, while the incorporation of Aden into the federation was necessary and inevitable, it was 'not an easy matter to provide for. It is a bringing together not only of urban and rural but of different centuries as well: modern Glasgow say and the eighteenth century Highlands.'[82] The controversial vote in favour of merger in the Aden Legislative Council hardly did much to resolve this disparity; while in the Protectorates the suppression of one set of tribal disturbances seemed only to presage the outbreak of new insurrections elsewhere. Had the British been able to seal off their corner of Arabia from events in the wider world then there may have been some prospect of success but within hours of the ratification of Aden's incorporation into the federation, events occurred on the other side of the Protectorate frontier which were to make Aden's status a defining issue in Middle East politics and to focus the attention of both the British House of Commons and the United Nations General Assembly upon Britain's last Arabian outpost.

Notes

1 Trevaskis records that after a meeting at the Colonial Office he 'came away leaden-hearted. Only by preserving British sovereignty of Aden, it was argued could the security of the base be assured ... Whitehall's faith in the Victorian formula of Union Jack over Aden's barren rocks and a cordon sanitaire of friendly tribes remained unshaken. I might have been speaking to Captain Haines in modern dress.' K. Trevaskis, *Shades of Amber* (London, Hutchinson, 1968), p. 161.

2 G. Balfour-Paul, *The End of Empire in the Middle East* (Cambridge, Cambridge University Press, 1991), p. 70.

3 PRO: CAB 134/1557, CP(18)16th mtg., minute 2, 22 December 1958.

4 PRO: CO 1015/1911, Aden (Luce) to Secretary of State, 4 December 1958, Amery to Secretary of State, 8 December 1958, DEFE 4/114, COS(58)102nd mtg., minute 1, 16 December 1958.

5 PRO: CO 1015/1910, Secretary of State to Luce, 24 December 1958.

6 PRO: DEFE 4/116, COS(59)16th mtg., minute 2, 3 March 1959, DEFE 6/55, JP(58)174, DEFE 11/400, Lee to Chief of Defence Staff, 6 March 1959, Dickson to Minister of Defence, 10 March 1959.

7 PRO: CO 967/359, Campbell minute, 20 February 1959.

8 PRO: DEFE 4/117, COS(59)23rd mtg., minute 6, 2 April 1959.

9 PRO: CO 1015/1912, Luce to Lennox-Boyd, 14 April 1959 with attachments, Amery to Secretary of State, 27 April 1959, Watt minute, 23 April 1958, Gorell Barnes minute, 24 April 1959.

10 PRO: CAB 128/33, CC(59)51st mtg., minute 4, 8 September 1959, CAB 134/1558, CP(59)12, 14 August 1959, CO 1015/1912, Watt minutes, 23 July 1959, 28 August 1959, Lennox-Boyd to Luce, 18 September 1959, Luce to Melville, 13 October 1959.

11 PRO: CO 1015/2392, Simmonds to Johnston and Melville, 3 January 1961, Melville to Johnston, 25 January 1961.

12 D. Holden, *Farewell to Arabia* (London, Faber and Faber, 1966), ch. 4; T. Little, *South Arabia* (London, Pall Mall, 1968), p. 69.

13 PRO: CAB 131/23, D(60)11th mtg., minute 2, 29 October 1960, CAB 131/24, D(60)53, 27 October 1960, CO 1015/2392, Luce to Melville, 3 September 1960, Watt minute, 13 September 1960, Kirkman minute, 15 September 1960, Melville minute, 30 September 1960, Watt to Martin, 21 October 1960.

14 PRO: CO 1015/2392, Watt to Melville, 27 October 1960, Melville minute 23 November 1960.

15 Charles Johnston Papers, 2/25, Trevaskis to Johnston, 19 October 1961, Johnston to Trevaskis, 23 October 1961, Trevaskis to Johnston, 27 October 1961.

16 PRO: CO 1015/2392, Trevaskis Note on Aden-Federal Relations (ud), Melville to Johnston, 24 January 1961, Johnston to McLeod, 3 March 1961.

17 PRO: CO 1015/2392, Watt minute (ud), Watt minute, 10 March 1961, Note for Secretary of State on Aden Developments, 15 March 1961, Melville minute 16 March 1961.

18 PRO: CAB 134/1560, CPC(61)5th mtg., 5 May 1961, CPC(61)6th mtg., 16 May 1961, CPC(61)10, 3 May 1961, CPC(61)11, 12 May 1961, CAB 128/35 CC(61)29th mtg., minute 8, 30 May 1961, CAB 129/105, CP(61)68, 26 May 1961, CP(61)70, 29 May 1961, CO 1015/2392, Amery to Macleod, 30 March 1961.

19 PRO: CO 1015/2386, Minutes of Meeting of the Supreme Council of the Federation, 12 November 1960.

20 PRO: CAB 134/1560, CPC(61)22, 30 June 1961, CO 1015/2386, Colonial Office Departmental Brief, 14 June 1961, Aden (Johnston) to Secretary of State, 14 June 1961, CO 1015/2387, Record of First Meeting with Federal Delega-

tion, 19 June 1961, Record of second meeting, 20 June 1961, Records of Meeting of Federal Delegation with CO officials, 22 June 1961, 24 June 1961, Secretary of State to Aden (Johnston), 23 June 1961, Record of First meeting of Aden and Federal delegates, 3 July 1961, Record of Delegates' meeting with Melville, 5 July 1961, Secretary of State to Aden (OAG), 6 July 1961.

21 PRO: CO 1015/2387, Johnston to Melville, 11 August 1961, 18 August 1961, CO 1015/2388, Johnston to Watt, 31 August 1961.

22 PRO: CO 1015/2388, Aden (OAG) to Secretary of State, 20 September 1961.

23 PRO: CO 1015/2388, Watt minute 29 September 1961, Aden (OAG) to Secretary of State, 26 September 1961, Aden (Johnston) to Secretary of State, 4 October 1961, Secretary of State to Aden (Johnston), 6 October 1961, Watt minute, 6 October 1961, Martin minute, 7 October 1961, Aden (Johnston) to Secretary of State, 11 October 1961.

24 PRO: CAB 134/1560, CPC(61)13th mtg., minute 3, 20 December 1961, CPC(61)31, 14 December 1961, CO 1015/2388, Bourdillon to Gough, 20 November 1961, CO 1015/2389 Johnston to Secretary of State, 26 January 1962.

25 PRO: DEFE 4/136, CO(61)41st mtg., minute 1, 29 June 1961, DEFE 4/137, COS(61)53rd mtg., 15 August 1961, DEFE 5/116 COS(61)273, 18 August 1961, DEFE 6/71, JP(61)63, 10 August 1961.

26 C. A. Macleod, *The End of British Rule in South Arabia 1959–1967* (Edinburgh, PhD thesis, 2001), pp. 78–81.

27 PRO: CAB 134/1561, CPC(62)4th mtg., minute 1, 16 February 1962, CPC(62)8, 14 February 1962, CO 1015/2388, Wright to Watt, 7 December 1961, CO 1015/2389, Formoy minute, 26 January 1962, CO 1015/2389, Morgan to Johnston, 29 January 1961, de Zulueta to Howard-Drake, 15 February 1962, Minister of Defence to de Zulueta, 15 February 1962, DEFE 4/142, COS(62)9th mtg., minute 6, 6 February 1962, DEFE 5/124, COS(62)65, 7 February 1962, DEFE 6/78, JP(62)11, 29 January 1962.

28 PRO: CAB 128/36, CC(62)52nd mtg., minute 1, 1 August 1962, DEFE 4/145, COS(62)41st mtg., minute 2, 19 June 1962, COS(62)47th mtg., minute 4, 19 July 1962, COS(62)50th mtg., minute 3, 31 July 1962, COS(62)52nd mtg., minute 1, 7 August 1962, DEFE 5/127, COS(62)254, 5 July 1962, DEFE 5/129, COS(62)338, 7 August 1962, DEFE 6/80, JP(62)19, 13 June 1962, JP(62)93, 3 August 1962, CO 1015/2390, Fisher to Secretary of State, 3 August 1962.

29 PRO: CO 1015/2389, Formoy minute, 5 March 1962.

30 PRO: CO 1015/2389, Johnston to Eastwood, 18 April 1962, 4 May 1962, Aden (Johnston) to Secretary of State, 13 May 1962, 18 May 1962.

31 PRO: CO 1015/2390, Record of a Meeting between the Secretary of State and Federal Delegation, 19 July 1962, Mohammed Farid to Sandys, 21 July, 1962.

32 IOR: R/20/B/3332, Record of 13th mtg. at the CO, 9 August 1962. This file contains a full record of the London talks.

33 PRO: CO 1015/2391, Aden (Johnston) to Secretary of State, 14 September 1962, 25 September 1962, 26 September 1962.

34 A. Dawisha, *Arab Nationalism in the Twentieth Century* (Princeton, Princeton University Press, 2003) p. 243.

35 Y. M. Choueiri, *Arab Nationalism: A History* (Oxford, Blackwell, 2000), pp. 117–20.

36 F. Halliday, 'Formation of a Yemeni Nationalism' in J. Jankowski and I. Gershoni (eds), *Rethinking Nationalism in the Arab Middle East* (New York, Columbia University Press, 1997), pp. 25–41.

37 A. A. Rahman, *Egyptian Policy in the Arab World: Intervention in Yemen* (Washington, University Press of America, 1983), pp. 59–61; J. Jankowski, '*Nasser's*

Egypt, Arab Nationalism and the United Arab Republic (London, Lynn Rienner, 2002), p. 140.

38   PRO: CO 1015/2157, Phillips to Watt, 26 April 1960, Luce to Pirie-Gordon, 16 May 1960.

39   A. A. Rahman, op. cit., pp. 241–2.

40   R. W. Stookey, *Yemen: The Politics of the Yemen Arab Republic* (Boulder, West-view, 1979), pp. 231–2; E. O'Ballance, *The War in the Yemen* (London, Faber and Faber, 1971), pp. 67–8.

41   J. Leigh Douglas, *The Free Yemeni Movement* (Beirut, American University Press of Beirut, 1987).

42   Ibid., pp. 218–19.

43   Ibid., pp. 209–15.

44   Ibid., pp. 228–31.

45   PRO: CO 1015/2018, Governor to Secretary of State, March 1959.

46   PRO: CO 1015/2018, Secretary of State to Aden (Luce), 27 March 1959, Foggon minute, 2 April 1959, Aden (Luce) to Secretary of State, 6 April 1959.

47   PRO: CO 1015/2088, Watt to Gorell-Barnes, 28 May 1959, Watt to Luce, 18 August 1959, Luce to Watt, 25 August 1959, Aden (Luce) to Secretary of State, 24 September 1959.

48   PRO: CO 1015/2014, Aden (Luce) to Secretary of State, 6 October 1959, 7 October 1959, 9 October 1959, 11 November 1959, 29 November 1959, CO 1015/2566, Aden (Luce) to Secretary of State, 5 February 1960, 8 March 1960, Watt to Oates, 28 March 1960.

49   PRO: CAB 134/1559, CPC(60)5th mtg., 12 July 1960, CP(60)15, 6 July 1950.

50   C. A. Macleod, *British Rule*, p. 98.

51   IOR: R/20/B/3035, Record of a Meeting with ATUC, 10 August 1960, Gover-nor (Aden) to Secretary of State, 12 August 1960, Notes of a meeting at Government House, 16 August 1960.

52   IOR: R/20/B/3036, Governor (Aden) to Secretary of State, 5 September 1960.

53   C. A. Macleod, *British Rule*, p. 100.

54   T. Little, *South*, p. 85.

55   PRO: CO 1015/2386, Watt to Johnston, 9 June 1961.

56   PRO: CO 1015/2388, Aden (Johnston) to Secretary of State, 4 October 1961.

57   PRO: CO 1015/2389, Johnston to Eastwood, 18 April 1962, Simmonds to Morgan, 3 July 1962.

58   PRO: CO 1015/2390, Simmonds to Morgan, 3 July 1962.

59   PRO: CO 1015/2390, Aden (Johnston) to Secretary of State, 24 August 1962, 7 September 1962, CO 1015/2391, Aden to Secretary of State, 14 September 1962, 18 September 1962, 21 September 1962.

60   T. Little, *South*, pp. 85–6.

61   C. Johnston, *The View from Steamer Point* (London, Collins, 1976), pp. 118–23; K. Trevaskis, *Shades*, pp. 179–80; PRO: CO 1015/2596, Aden to Secretary of State, 26 September 1962.

62   PRO: CO 1015/2391, Aden (Johnston) to Secretary of State, 27 September 1962.

63   H. Ingrams, *Arabia and the Isles* (London, Kegan Paul International, 1998); R. Bidwell, *The Two Yemens* (Harlow, Longman, 1983), pp. 86–7; D. Lee, *Flight from the Middle East* (London, Ministry of Defence, Air Historical Branch, 1980), p. 39.

64   Lee, *Flight*, ch. 7; D. Smiley, *Arabian Assignment* (London, Leo Cooper, 1975), chs 1–7; J. E. Peterson, *Defending Arabia* (London, Croom Helm, 1986), pp. 85–8.

65   IOR: R/20/C/2323, Intelligence Committee Precis of 'Aydarus revolt, 8 Sep-tember 1958; C. A. Macleod, *British Rule*, p. 51.

66 J. Kostiner, *Struggle*, pp. 27–8.
67 Kennedy Trevaskis Papers Pt. 2, s546, Box 2a, Diary entries for 14 and 15 February 1958; IOR R/20/C/3232, Young to BA (WAP), 12 June, 3 July, 19 July 1958.
68 IOR: R/20/C/2324, Young to BA(WAP), 22 March 1960; Richard Holmes Papers, Box 2, Trevaskis to Assistant Advisers, 9 July 1960.
69 IOR: R/20/C2324, Leaflet issued to the 'Sons of Yafa', 6 November 1961.
70 Richard Holmes Papers, Box 2, Trevaskis to Assistant Advisers, 20 November 1960; PRO: CO 1015/2157, Aden (Johnston) to Secretary of State, 4 December 1960.
71 Richard Holmes Papers, Box 2, Trevaskis to Assistant Advisers, 29 May 1961; IOR: R/20/C/2325, Trevaskis paper on 'Policy in Yafa' (ud), R/20/C/2397, Johnston to British Agent, 8 March 1961, Trevaskis minute, 25 March 1961, Trevaskis to Chief Secretary, 13 April 1961, 8 May 1961, 31 July 1961, Aide-Memoire on Operations in Upper Yafa, 23 June 1961; PRO: CO 1015/2157, Aden (Johnston) to Secretary of State, 23 May 1961.
72 PRO: CO 1015/2157, Aden (Johnston) to Secretary of State, 19 February 1962, Formoy minute, 5 March 1962.
73 D. Foster, *Landscape with Arabs* (London, Clifton Books, 1969), pp. 93–4.
74 D. Lee, *Flight*, p. 197.
75 Richard Homes Papers, Box 2, 'Political Background to Operation Niggard', 6 December 1960; PRO: CO 1015/2157, Operations in WAP, 23 February 1961.
76 J. Lunt, *The Barren Rocks of Aden* (London, Herbert Jenkins, 1966), pp. 160–6.
77 Richard Holmes Papers, Box 1, 'Upper Aulaqi Sheikhdom: Handing Over Notes' (ud).
78 For details on the more significant aerial attacks in the Shaykhdom during 1959 see PRO: DEFE 11/429, HQ(BFAP) to MoD, 6 June 1959, 24 June 1959, 20 October 1959, 25 November 1959, 23 December 1959.
79 IOR: R/20/B/3219, Phillips minute, 22 July 1959, Colville-Stewart to Trevaskis, 26 June 1959 with 'Awalqi pamphlets.
80 PRO: CO 1015/2158, HQ(BFAP) to Ministry of Defence, 7 April 1960, 22 April 1960; IOR: R/20/B/3219, Minutes of WAP Security Committee, 6 April 1960, Phillips minute, 11 April 1960, Note by WAP Security Committee, 18 April 1960.
81 PRO: CO 1015/2158, Reilly minute 2 June 1960; IOR: R/20/B/3219, Phillips to Kirkman, 26 April 1960, Phillips to Johnson (Mukalla), 29 April 1960, Luce to Watt, 24 May 1960.
82 PRO: CO 1015/2389, Johnston to Maudling, 20 May 1962.

5 War on Arab nationalism 1962–1964

The Republican revolution in Yemen which began at midnight on 26/27 September 1962 was perhaps the most significant event in the twentieth century history of southwest Arabia. The origins of the modern Yemeni state can be traced back directly to the coup instigated by army officers in Sanaa that night. Although the demise of the Imamate was prolonged it was finally dissolved in 1970, just short of its millennium. More immediately, the revolution gave Nasser direct influence in Arabian affairs: from this point the government of the most populous state in the peninsula was committed to a political programme consciously modelled on the Egyptian pattern. British policy-makers reacted to these events with unrelenting hostility. The mutual animosity of the Republican authorities in Sanaa and the High Commission in Aden led to renewed conflict along the frontier between the federation and the nascent Republic. In order to secure the continued influence of the federal rulers after independence, Johnston and Trevaskis launched larger military campaigns against those tribal rebels inside the federation who were willing to accept Republican assistance. They also revamped federal constitutional arrangements to give them the appearance of greater legitimacy. These measures served to radicalise still further anti-British sentiments in Aden. After 1962 the continuation of formal British control in the long term as Lord Lloyd had envisaged six years earlier, was no longer feasible. However, the underlying assumption amongst many policy-makers that Britain could continue to play a substantial role by maintaining close ties to the federal rulers was sustained. The feeling persisted amongst many in Aden and Whitehall that unless they could defeat Nasser any prospect of a continued world role would be lost. There was a widespread desire to retain a very substantial degree of influence in southwest Arabia, even if this could no longer take the form of imperial rule. The fulfilment of this goal required a further effort to defeat the urban radicals of Aden, tribal insurgents in the federation and the Republican government north of the frontier. The policies that issued from this analysis are the subject of this chapter.

Elections and terror in Aden

The impact of the revolution was felt most immediately in Aden. Johnston admitted in his memoirs that the Aden Legislative Council would not have agreed to merge with the federation had they voted on the issue after the revolution in Yemen.[1] The overthrow of the Imamate was a thrilling event for Yemenis living in Aden. For the first time independence and unity for the whole of southwest Arabia under a Republican government appeared feasible. Johnston reported: 'the Yemeni revolution has killed any prospect of reconciliation at present. Opposition are triumphant and our friends more depressed than ever . . . If we are now faced with a pro-Nasser Republic in Yemen . . . the Nationalist winds will begin to howl here.'[2] The strategy which Johnston adopted to deal with the rise of nationalism was outlined six months later: 'As elsewhere we have the choice between two brands of this: the pan-Arab (whether Nasserite or Baathist) or the local; and as elsewhere, it is the local brands (e.g. the Jordanian patriotism of King Hussein) which suits our interests best. In fact we have every motive for assisting the Adenese nationalism of Bayoomi and his friends in order to undercut the pan-Arab appeal of the PSP/ATUC leaders.'[3] Although this was a coherent and even convincing analysis, in actuality it amounted to no more than a continuation of Trevaskis's plans for encouraging South Arabian particularism as the prelude to the creation of an independent state. Furthermore, the choice of Jordan as an analogue for southwest Arabia was misleading for there was nowhere like the town of Aden in Jordan. The British persisted in the attempt to build the institutions of a post-colonial state on a very narrow basis of support which amounted to no more than the small band of old Adeni nationalists. The fragility of this strategy is evident from the tensions between this group and Britain's other band of friends, the federal rulers and their tribal affiliates. In January 1963 Aden finally entered the federation but the new arrangement was very much a marriage of convenience: the two parties were concerned by the continuous howling of the Arab nationalist gale but they had little else in common.

Those who witnessed the reaction to the Yemeni revolution in Aden were struck by the uniform support given to the new Republican government. The journalist Donald Foster, who knew the town well, recorded: 'there was hardly a shop in the Crater bazaar that was not flying the new Republic's flag – a green star on a ground of black, white and red stripes – as close as could be to the Egyptian pattern.'[4] Much encouraged by the revolution in the north, the PSP continued its programme of disturbances in Aden following the merger vote. A further strike was held on 17 November 1962. Johnston responded in his usual manner by deporting Yemeni workers. Over one hundred Yemenis were removed in the three months after the merger riots and 60 more were imprisoned either for breaching the Industrial Relations Ordinance or for acts of public disorder.[5] This was not regarded by the federal rulers as particularly harsh: they were eager to secure the incorporation of

Aden into the federation so they could suppress nationalist sentiment in the town using their own customary methods. They were dismayed but not surprised by the pro-Republican Arab nationalism current in Aden and complained that their faces were being 'blackened' by the failure to suppress nationalist opposition to the newly expanded federation. In considering the development of policy once Aden was formally incorporated into federal territory, they began to talk of securing independence from Britain as a means of removing the restrictions which the imperial power imposed upon them in dealing with their nationalist rivals. Trevaskis responded to their concerns with emollient words and Johnston urged that the merger be pushed through as rapidly as possible.[6] This necessitated discussion of the new treaties between the federation and Britain in the House of Commons.

The future of Aden had been creeping towards prominence in British domestic politics during the course of the early 1960s. The Labour Party generally expressed support for ATUC and the Conservatives stressed the merits of the federation. An early indication of the rise of partisanship on this matter was provided by the visit of two Labour MPs, George Thomson and Bob Edwards, to southwest Arabia in June 1962. Edwards reported that the Industrial Relations Ordinance was the most significant cause of unrest in the Colony and that there was no support for merger.[7] Thomson emerged later as a key figure in Labour thinking on the Aden issue. He met al-Asnaj during the trip and came to regard him as a valuable moderate union leader who would be willing to resist the advance of communist radicalism in the international labour movement. Trevaskis, Bayumi and the federal rulers regarded the contacts between the Labour Party and ATUC as an act of betrayal. As well as consulting al-Asnaj, Thomson and Edwards also met Trevaskis's nemesis, Muhammad 'Aydarus. The effect of this was to undermine confidence in the long-term future of the federation. All the key actors were well aware that British opposition parties eventually became parties of government. The faith of the rulers in a future partnership was vitiated by suggestions that a new administration might look with greater favour on their nationalist opponents.[8]

From a Labour perspective the contrived nature of the merger vote, the punitive measures undertaken in Aden and the consolidation of Republican control in Yemen confirmed their view that current British policy was counter-productive. The arrest of al-Asnaj for a second time in November 1962 for his role in orchestrating further strike action was regarded as essential by the Governor but infuriated the Labour Party. Thomson intervened to secure a grant from the party's Socialist International Fund to assist al-Asnaj with his legal case. The party's national executive dispatched a lawyer to the Colony to organise a defence for the PSP leaders.[9] This was unsuccessful and in December 1962 al-Asnaj and two of his colleagues were sentenced to terms of imprisonment. At the same time, the last barrier to the implementation of the merger was overcome when the *ex officio* members of the Aden Legislative Council were replaced by the nominees of the non-official members. This arrangement had been agreed during the merger negotiations and it had the effect of strengthening Bayumi's position in the Council. Three of the four replacements were supporters of his and he became the new Chief Minister of Aden when the merger took effect in January 1963.[10] In nominal terms Aden was no longer a Colony but merely one of the states of the federation, albeit one which enjoyed a unique constitutional status.

As well as enduring Labour strictures regarding the forced integration of Aden into the federation, the British government also had to withstand increasingly close scrutiny of its Aden policy from the United Nations. General Assembly resolution 1514 of 14 December 1961 had made clear that UN members were obliged to bring colonial territories to independence and in the following year the Special Committee of 24 was established to monitor this process. During 1963 the Committee began hearing submissions from parties interested in the future of southwest Arabia including the federation, the SAL and the PSP. The Committee initially found that the British government was not fulfilling the obligations described in resolution 1514 and gave itself the task of investigating matters further by appointing a five-man sub-committee. This riled Trevaskis who regarded such international meddling as impertinent. The sub-committee was prohibited from entering Aden and had to base its report on the testimony of petitioners and the evidence it accumulated during visits to Egypt and Yemen. Their report censured the British authorities and formed the basis for UN General Assembly resolution 1949 which was passed on 11 December 1963. This called, *inter alia*, for the organisation of UN supervised elections and early independence for Aden and the federation.[11] Although many in Aden felt that the UN could be ignored as an irrelevance, it was difficult for the metropolitan government, as a signatory to the charter, to take quite such a detached view of the matter. Furthermore, the resolution became a shibboleth for nationalist groups in Aden who made its implementation their first demand.

Elections and independence arrangements were on the minds of British policy-makers as well as the Committee of 24. However, their plans did not at all match up with those of the UN and members of the General Assembly would have been horrified had the back stage manoeuvring in Aden and Whitehall concerning franchise reform become public knowledge. Once the merger agreement was secure Bayumi and the British began to devise a strategy to win the postponed elections in Aden. These had been deferred on the grounds that the existing Legislative Council, which consisted of appointees and members elected on a very narrow franchise, would assuredly be more supportive of merger than any possible future elected body. Nevertheless, with both the United Nations and the Labour opposition monitoring constitutional progress, it was impossible to postpone a vote indefinitely. The nationalists were clearly in the ascendant after the Yemeni revolution and this made it difficult to arrange for the election of Bayumi's allies. Bayumi explained to Johnston in March 1963: 'if elections were held next year they would certainly result in a majority for "the other side", i.e. the PSP and other nationalist elements.' He proposed that the vote be delayed for a full five years. As Chief Minister this was greatly in Bayumi's interest but, given parliamentary and international pressures, it was not something which the British government could contemplate.[12] Instead the Aden authorities engaged in an extensive campaign of keeni-meeni directed against the nationalists in the town to secure the required result when the polls were finally opened in October 1964. They first pressed Bayumi to establish a commission of inquiry in order to design a new franchise which, it was hoped, would continue to exclude the nationalist-oriented majority inside the town. The formation of the commission was delayed repeatedly. Bayumi's ill health proved a particular problem and his death in June 1963 was a serious blow to the British.[13] His successor, Baharun had the advantage of being marginally more acceptable to some opposition groups but his concessions to nationalism, such as the lifting of a ban on Egyptian newspapers, were regarded with suspicion by Trevaskis and the federal rulers.[14]

Baharun finally established a seven-man committee of inquiry to examine the franchise in August 1963.[15] Both the British government and the Aden High Commission were attentive to the franchise commission's work. The odds of stymieing the nationalists at any future election depended on the establishment of demanding criteria for voter eligibility which would exclude the predominantly nationalist immigrant community. The proposals which emerged at the end of October caused absolute horror. Although still excluding the most recent arrivals to the Colony from the franchise, the commission's formula gave the vote to those who had been resident in Aden for 20 years and, for the first time, to women. These recommendations prompted a flurry of back of the envelope psephology in the High Commission. Trevaskis, who was now installed as High Commissioner, estimated that the PSP and SAL would attain 70 per cent of the vote and gain additional seats in Shaykh Uthman and Little Aden. Sandys responded: 'it follows from your assessment of the electoral prospects (a) that the recommendations of the Franchise Commission must by one means or another be nullified and (b) that the elections must be conducted on present franchise or on some other franchise of our own devising.'[16] It was this latter course which was followed. Baharun was informed that the proposed recommendations were discriminatory and a new narrower franchise was imposed which gave the vote only to those born in Aden, excluding women.[17]

The need to prevent immigrant Yemenis from being enfranchised was made urgent by the marginalisation of the so-called moderates who were willing to co-operate with the British. During the course of 1963 an urban insurrection or terror campaign began in the back streets of Aden which was to last, with occasional periods of remission, until the British left in November 1967. The ruthlessness with which collaborators were targetted by the radicals and the indiscriminatory nature of British counter-measures further destabilised the insecure platform on which Trevaskis was attempting to build a pro-British state. In late January 1963 a small bomb exploded inside the Khormaksar base. During the remainder of the year the violence spread to civilian areas. In July two people were killed by a bomb at the South Arabian News Agency office. The stakes were raised further in November when the unions organised industrial action at the base.[18] A turning point occurred at Aden's airport in December 1963 when a bomb was thrown at Trevaskis as he prepared to embark on a flight to London. He was uninjured but an Indian woman was killed outright and a much-admired political officer, George Henderson, was mortally wounded. Some of the rulers and their tribal supporters were at the airport and received minor injuries. In the aftermath of the attack Trevaskis declared a state of emergency and 55 people were detained within a week on the grounds that they were PSP activists.[19] Around 300 Yemenis were deported from Aden during December.[20]

The declaration of a new state of emergency alarmed the Legislative Council in Aden and the Colonial Office back in London, while being insufficient to appease the fury of the federal rulers, many of whom had witnessed the airport attack. The Minister of State at the Colonial Office, Nigel Fisher, expressed particular concern about the detentions of PSP activists prior to the collection of any proof of their guilt. He warned Trevaskis that Parliamentary pressure would become intolerable should the suspects be permanently detained without charge.[21] Contemporaneously, members of the Aden Legislative Council complained about the rough treatment of detainees who were incarcerated in federal detention centres outside of Aden. Their threats of resignation secured the transfer of the prisoners back to Aden.[22] These developments enraged the rulers whose views of what constituted condign action against the nationalists were rather different from that of the House of Commons or the Aden Legislative Council. From this point they began to press more strongly for the establishment of an independent federation. This would end British control of internal security issues in Aden and thus allow them to take their own action against the nationalists.

In London there was concern about the impact which the loss of the base would have on Britain's world role and a persistent belief that Trevaskis and his colleagues were being too hasty in submitting to the demands of their local allies for constitutional progress. In early 1963 Johnston had begun to press for the granting of internal self-government to Aden and formal independence for the whole federation within five years. This struck some in the Colonial Office as evidence of 'a tendency on the part of the High Commissioner to anticipate and perhaps over-estimate local pressures for further transfers of political power.' Fisher believed that the advance towards independence should be conducted 'as slowly as possible.' In June 1963, with encouragement from Trevaskis and Johnston, the federal ministers suggested a timetable which would lead to independence in 1969. Initially,

Sandys condemned the proposals as reckless. When Johnston suggested that constitutional advance might be a *quid pro quo* for retaining British sovereignty over the base he noted: 'I have never accepted this is a *quid pro quo*. We have already given the *quo* in the form of merger and the recent constitutional advance. We are now entitled to the *quid* without further payment.'[23] However, unlike a number of his colleagues, Sandys eventually accepted the notion of a target date for independence in return for guarantees of continued British access to the base. Many other ministers still favoured the policy, first expressed by Lord Lloyd in 1956, of retaining British control into the foreseeable future.

During the winter of 1963–64 there was a clash between Trevaskis and the British government over the issue of constitutional advance. One of the first telegrams Trevaskis wrote after taking over from Johnston as High Commissioner recommended that Aden should be granted independent status within the federation on condition that Britain retain full sovereignty of the base areas. This was a far-reaching proposal: it combined the priorities of the High Commissioner, who wished to create a pro-British state in southwest Arabia, and the Colonial Secretary, who was keen to retain British control over the Aden base as a means of securing long-term influence in the Middle East. Sandys had persistently argued for the establishment of enclaves surrounding the defence facilities. Trevaskis was willing to accept enclaves if this was the price which was required to achieve full independence prior to elections. He believed that if elections preceded independence the Arab nationalists would be victorious and that they would refuse to accommodate British concerns about access to the base. Sandys appreciated the danger that a nationalist government might be elected in Aden prior to independence and shared Trevaskis's wish to delay such an election as long as was feasible. Furthermore, Trevaskis's proposal that British sovereignty over the base be retained satisfied Sandys's preference for direct British control of defence facilities. He therefore changed his mind on the *quid pro quo* and endorsed Trevaskis's proposals, suggesting 31 December 1965 as a possible date for independence.[24]

This sudden reversal of long-standing British policy by Trevaskis and Sandys was much too precipitate for other ministers. They were unconvinced of the need for a rush towards independence. On 5 December 1963 Sandys outlined a plan to make Aden a protected state with the same status as the other constituent members of the federation. This could be portrayed as a constitutional advance because the High Commissioner would have to relinquish his reserved powers and Aden would become at least nominally independent. It also had the distinct advantage of transferring to the federal rulers 'the embarrassing responsibility for internal security in Aden, a responsibility which the authorities of the Federation would discharge with greater severity than we could afford to do.' In other words the Aden nationalists could be quelled by Britain's local allies with fewer embarrassing questions for the government front bench in Parliament or British representatives at the United Nations. At the same time Britain would retain direct control of the base.[25] Six days after Sandys's presentation the Defence Committee rejected the proposals. The Prime Minister, Alec Douglas-Home, made clear his unhappiness at the planned changes to the Aden constitution. He went as far as to assert that he 'does not want us to have any constitutional talks with Aden Ministers.' Like his predecessors, Eden and Macmillan, Douglas-Home took a personal interest in developments in southwest Arabia during his short premiership. His policy was continuous with theirs in that he interpreted events there in the context of Britain's wider conflict with Arab nationalism in the Middle East. Both the nationalist government in Sanaa and Adenese ministers were seen from his perspective as potential Nasserite proxies. The nuances of the High Commissioner's arguments initially had little effect on a Prime Minister determined not to be seen to be making concession to nationalism. Trevaskis was therefore informed that the Cabinet would not accept either the surrender of sovereignty over Aden or federal control of internal security matters.[26]

This was problematic for Trevaskis because the postponement of constitutional advance made it impossible to delay elections until after independence and prevented him unleashing the federal rulers upon the nationalists of Aden. When Sandys presented plans for some minor constitutional changes in Aden as a sop to the town's moderate politicians, Trevaskis stated bluntly that he would not support 'a form of constitutional advance which would weaken our control without releasing the Federation from the restrictions implied by British sovereignty.' At the Colonial Office, Fisher was dismayed by Trevaskis's persistence in pressing for major constitutional change. He commented: 'I do not understand Trevaskis. He knows PM won't agree to independence for Aden.' Sandys informed Trevaskis that independence 'is for the present out of court.' In response, Trevaskis expressed 'regret and dismay.'[27] He was not discouraged from persevering with his attempt to educate British ministers about the benefits of independence. The dispute between Sandys and Trevaskis on one hand and the British Cabinet on the other was as much as anything a debate about how much control Britain would exercise in southwest Arabia after the formal demission of power. Trevaskis therefore set about demonstrating just how extensive this could be if his proposals were accepted. His confidence was founded on the belief that he was constructing a viable state in which Britain would retain an influential role. Following another inconclusive visit to London, on 31 March 1964 he sent Sandys a lengthy letter calling once more for 'the early independence of the Federation subject to safeguards for our base in Aden.' He was explicit that in following this course the government would be handing authority to loyal friends: 'what should be envisaged is not a truly independent state operating without British help but a nominally independent Federation which would in practice remain dependent on us . . . In other words what should be envisaged is something akin to Cromer's Egypt.'[28] Although this was an appealing scenario to British ministers, they were not immediately convinced that independence could be reconciled with continued British control.

The first evidence of changed thinking in Downing Street emerged in May 1964 when Home finally agreed to the Colonial Office's suggestion that a constitutional conference should be staged in London the following month. The political parties, such as the PSP, were excluded but all the constituent elements of the federation, including Aden, were to be represented. Such conferences were, of course, commonplace events on the road to independence.[29] However, it was not until a Defence Committee meeting of 12 June that it was agreed that Sandys should offer the delegates independence in five years time.[30] The long-standing Lloyd policy of maintaining British sovereignty indefinitely was finally reversed. It is perhaps best to see this change as the final consequence of slow, incremental changes in the thinking of ministers. The Cabinet had been split on the independence proposals since the previous December but by this stage the position of the diehards had been undermined by the deterioration of the security situation during the six months in which their status quo policy had prevailed. As we shall see the British were at this time co-operating increasingly closely with the federal rulers in combatting the Republicans in Yemen and this too may have weighed in the balance as evidence that they would continue to act as trustees of British influence.

The London conference itself was notable for the demonstrable antipathy between Adeni ministers and the rulers of the interior. The latter had been itching to gain control of internal security matters in Aden and were furious that the British would not bring Baharun into line. For the Fadli Sultan, who had been present at the bombing of the airport, the apparent favouritism shown to the Adeni delegation was the final straw. He told Trevaskis: 'You British always betray your friends ... We should have listened to Nasser in the first place, when he warned us about what hypocrites you were.'[31] It was anger at the British failure to deal with nationalist agitation in Aden which prompted him to fly to Cairo in the middle of the conference and declare his allegiance to Nasser.[32] He was obliged on arrival to pay the usual obeisance to UN resolutions calling for early independence and to declare the London meeting 'a Conservative Government comedy'.[33] However, the conference had brought to fruition a policy which had been bitterly opposed by numerous ministers. On 22 June 1964 Sandys was authorised to offer independence by 1968 on condition that the federal government sign a defence treaty guaranteeing British access to the base.[34] Agreement to this was secured painlessly as both the Adeni and federal ministers had every interest in maintaining a British presence as the only solid guarantee against an upsurge in Arab nationalism. The delegates from Aden and the Protectorates reserved most of their antipathy for each other rather than the British who were criticised principally for forcing them together. On their return to southwest Arabia furious rows ensued over Baharun's insistence that, as Chief Minister of Aden, he, rather than the British, should retain powers over internal security in the town. This was not reconcilable with the rulers' attitude that, while they were just about willing to allow Trevaskis as High Commissioner to police Aden, they would much prefer to do so themselves. Thinking about the licentiousness which would follow the derogation of powers in this area to Baharun, provoked a storm of protest from the rulers which only dissipated after strenuous efforts to persuade them of the need for compromise.[35]

The granting of further concessions to Baharun, on matters such as internal security and the setting of 1968 as the date for independence, was seen as necessary to assist the moderate politicians in Aden in the forthcoming polls. The scuppering of his plans to bring about independence prior to elections induced Trevaskis to resort to a substantial dose of keeni-meeni to undermine the PSP and stave off a nationalist triumph. Should the PSP achieve a majority in the Aden Legislative Council, his strategy, which rested on keeping both the so-called Aden moderates and the federal rulers in power until the achievement of independence, would be wrecked: Abdullah Al-Asnaj would hardly be willing to act as Khedive to Trevaskis's Cromer. In December 1963 Trevaskis laid out a set of conditions which would be conducive to securing the election of the largest possible number of moderates. The first of these was the sowing of discord among the nationalists: that the Aden High Commission would 'be able to bring about a clash between the PSP and SAL which will encourage them to slit each other's throats.'[36] In pursuit of this objective Trevaskis was authorised by the British government to spend £15,000, 'for penetrating their organisations, suborning their key figures, stimulating rivalries and jealousies between them, encouraging dissension and the emergence of splinter groups and harassing them generally, for example by breaking up public meetings.'[37] As election day approached Trevaskis expanded the programme of black operations: *agents provocateur* were employed by the Aden authorities, anti-PSP splinter groups were funded and nationalist organisations were penetrated by means of phone tapping. These measures had the full support of Sandys who explained the need for a more ambitious programme to Home: 'Since the PSP are the main inspirers of anti-British activity, it is essential to take any action which would weaken their influence.'[38] Funds were also available to prop up the moderates. Fearing that the rather frail Chief Minister Baharun was susceptible to nationalist intimidation, Trevaskis gave him £10,000 in April 1964 to spend on recruiting supporters and to deal with his own 'personal and family difficulties'.[39]

Although the policy of confrontation with the nationalist opposition led to an escalation in tensions inside the Colony which manifested itself in the terror campaign, it was successful to the extent that it maintained moderate influence in circumstances which would otherwise have led to a sweeping victory for the Arab nationalists. There had been a hiatus in the anti-British campaign following the airport attack on Trevaskis, but violence resumed in June 1964 with a bomb explosion outside the Federal Council buildings.

This was a relatively minor incident but as the election approached the level of violence increased. The most notable incidents were a bomb explosion at the British base on 1 September and an attack by armed men on two pro-government newspaper presses on 13 October.[40] There was concern that the resumption of political violence might intimidate pro-government voters and Trevaskis responded with a covert campaign to divide opposition groups and bolster Britain's allies. In addition, during the months of September 1964 over 200 Yemenis were bundled out of Aden by the security forces.[41] However, the most significant factor in the elections was the drastic narrowing of the franchise and the tactical error committed by the PSP in responding to Trevaskis's provocations with a boycott. With a tiny electorate of only 8,000 electing 16 representatives, the High Commission could make fairly accurate forecasts. The insubstantial nature of support for the British in Aden at this stage was evident from the fact that even under these extraordinary conditions they expected the pro-British moderates to win only half of the 16 seats.[42] This turned out to be roughly accurate. Around three-quarters of those with the right to vote did so, electing a mixture of moderate and radical candidates including: for the moderates, the current Chief Minister and recipient of British largesse, Baharun; and, at the radical end of the political spectrum, the man accused of perpetrating the assassination attack on Trevaskis, 'Adbullah Hasan Khalifah. The latter was still in gaol at the time of the poll.[43]

Contemporaneous elections in Britain brought Labour into office and, although they were more sympathetic to the PSP, five years of constant conflict between the British and the workforce in Aden had by this stage produced a poisonous atmosphere which proved impossible to clear. There was initially sufficient support for Baharun to keep him as Chief Minister but during the 12 months after the British and Adenese elections the confrontation between the British and the nationalists intensified to the extent that the High Commission was forced to dissolve the Legislative Council in September 1965. By this stage the urban and up-country insurgencies had fused; the origins of this development can be traced to the crucial years which followed the revolution in Yemen.

Development and pacification in the Protectorates

In September 1962 Arab nationalism was less prevalent in the Protectorates than in Aden. However, over the next two years the politics of the interior were transformed by the emergence of a radical alternative to the SAL. A handful of revolutionary cells had already been established in some of the larger towns of the WAP and the EAP but the absence of large economic enterprises precluded the emergence of urban insurrections of the kind with which the British were dealing in Aden. Tribal dissidence remained the most significant obstacle to the smooth implementation of the forward policy in the Protectorates and it proved relatively straightforward for

Nasser and the new Republican government in Yemen to exploit this endemic disorder to increase British discomfort. Like Imam Ahmad in the late 1950s the Republican President, 'Abdullah al-Sallal, supplied tribal rebels with arms; unlike the conservative Ahmad, he also propagated revolutionary nationalist doctrines. British attempts to counter tribal dissidence had by the time of the revolution begun to inculcate a sense amongst the insurgents that they were part of a broader anti-colonial struggle and, with encouragement from Cairo and Sanaa, this began to take more systematic form after 1962. Although some who fought the British in the Protectorates were unaware of it, the terms of the conflict were changing from a defence of tribal autarchy against British infringements to the execution of a social and political transformation across southwest Arabia. This process culminated five years later with a series of revolutions in each of the protected states in which small numbers of radicals utilised tribal discontent to destroy the traditional systems of rule across what was to become the People's Republic of South Yemen.

One of the reasons why the British had been reluctant to see the destruction of the Imamate, despite their hostility to the Hamid al-Din, was that Ahmad and his family were very convenient enemies. They had few reliable allies inside southwest Arabia and none in the wider Arab world. There was almost as much animosity to Ahmad amongst Yemenis living in Aden as there was to the British. His removal and the institution of a Republic allowed radicals in Aden and tribal rebels in the Protectorates to attach their struggle more securely to the Arab nationalist bandwagon. In the immediate aftermath of the coup al-Sallal pursued a policy of restraint in the Protectorates. It was the refusal of the Macmillan government to recognise the Republic and the support provided to the Royalists by the British and the Saudis via the federal state of Bayhan which soured relations. As early as January 1963 Johnston warned of an emerging alliance between the Republicans in the north and rebels in the south. The following month a meeting of dissidents was held in Sanaa under the sponsorship of al-Sallal and Nasser. Numerous different groups from both sides of the frontier were represented at the conference; not surprisingly given the meeting's provenance, it was dominated by pro-Nasserists linked to the Arab Nationalist Movement. A second conference created an institutional structure for the new organisation and on 14 October 1963 the National Front for the Liberation of the Occupied South declared an armed struggle against the British. By this stage the Republicans were already assisting insurgents in Hawshabi, Yafi' and Radfan; these now came to be regarded by both the British and the insurgents as separate fronts in a broader conflict between radical Arab nationalism and the British sponsored federation.[44]

It is evident from NLF propaganda that the terms of political debate in the region were changing. The early literature of the NLF had a didactic purpose: it explained to the tribes that their rebellions were part of a broader struggle. A typical example exhorted: 'Oh masses of our brave nation. Make your world one. Make your opinion one. Be one Arab nation and not the adverse tribes of the pre-Islamic era when tribes used to live bearing the spirit of vengeance while their enemy is clapping, laughing, mocking at them and at their action, stabbing them in the back with the poisonous daggers of conspiracy and treachery.' One such purported conspirator was the Sharif of Bayhan. An NLF leaflet found in his territory explained that he had 'sold his nationalism and become a toy in the hands of colonialism.'[45] The anthropologist and historian of Yemen, Paul Dresch, has noted that, although most conflicts were the product of particular local circumstances, they were given an ideological sheen by the leaders of the revolt: 'The fighting was depicted at the time as war against colonialism and later as class struggle.'[46]

In the Radfan this war took the form of a conflict between the new revolutionary brand of insurgency and British and federal forces who remained committed to the unending task of tribal pacification. The Radfan was a mountainous region, theoretically subject to the Amirs of Dali'. It was almost as inaccessible as the Yafi' highlands but of greater strategic significance because of its proximity to the main north-south trade routes. The extension of administration to the region enraged the local Qutaybi tribes who regarded interference by the Amir into their affairs as thoroughly unacceptable. They complained that the local Na'ib, who represented the Amir in the Radfan mountains, was infringing on their rights: 'We have got nothing from him except oppression.'[47] This resentment provided the NLF with an opportunity. The Qutaybis travelled to the Republic to collect arms and on their return began attacks on the main road. In October 1963 they were designated the first NLF front in the war against the British.[48] On 22 December Trevaskis reported that up to 200 armed tribesmen were participating in attacks and warned the Radfan insurgency 'is now getting seriously out of hand following the return of the tribesmen from the Yemen with arms.'[49]

Trevaskis's solution to the Radfan problem was to prepare a punitive campaign against the Qutaybis. However, the commander of the Federal Regular Army (FRA), which was slated to conduct the campaign, James Lunt, was not persuaded of the need for yet another round of fighting with the tribes. In his opinion the inhabitants of the Radfan did not constitute a serious threat; they were drug-addled recalcitrants 'stupefied to commit any crime' and engaged in 'some of the most vicious blood feuds in all Arabia.'[50] Whereas Trevaskis wished to bring order to the Radfan by force, Lunt was happy to leave the tribesmen to their pernicious way of life. Lunt later claimed that 'a bag of gold would have produced the dissidents in 20 minutes.' It was only on Trevaskis's insistence that he reluctantly agreed to launch the first Radfan campaign at the start of the new year. He gained a measure of revenge by codenaming the operation, with heavy sarcasm, NUTCRACKER. During the course of the campaign the FRA occupied the key strategic points in Radfan at a cost of 17 casualties. Once a measure of strategic control had been attained, however, there was little notion of what should come next. The FRA withdrew from the Radfan in March 1964 and the insurrection reignited immediately.[51] On 7 April Trevaskis reported that rebel activities had once more made the Dali' road unusable.[52]

It was Egyptian support for the Qutaybis which made the Radfan insurrection a particularly potent threat. After the Republican revolution local rebellions were submerged in the wider confrontation between radical Arab nationalism and continued British influence. On 24 December 1963 Nasser declared his support for the southern rebels. Subsequently, Radio Cairo broadcast vitriolic denunciations of British policies in Aden and the Protectorates and recommended the targeting of High Commission personnel.[53] In a further speech on 22 February 1964 Nasser condemned the British government for failing to learn the lessons of Suez and urged Arabs to be wary of the danger posed by British bases in the Middle East, the most prominent of which were in Libya and Arabia.[54] Two months after this, Nasser flew to Yemen to lend his personal support to the campaign against British imperialism. He told a rally in Sanaa: 'We should vow before God . . . to discharge a debt to almighty God by solemnly vowing to support those who have suffered the tyranny of British colonialism.'[55] This was taken as a final declaration of war by many but, in fact, Trevaskis had long regarded the struggle in the Protectorates as a proxy war with Egypt. On 5 April 1964 he cautioned that 'the "new look" given to rebel activity by the UAR could play havoc unless decisive action is taken now to stop the rot.' Three weeks later he sent ground forces back into the Radfan but what Trevaskis wanted was permission to launch a new round of proscription, including aerial attacks on tribesmen.[56]

Trevaskis's request could not have come at a worse time for the government of Alec Douglas-Home. As well as seeking authority for proscription Trevaskis lobbied, with some success, for permission to conduct retaliatory bombing raids across the frontier and an increase in British support for anti-Republican forces inside Yemen. Butler at the Foreign Office feared that openly bombing tribesmen might attract further international condemnation. His concerns became more pronounced in early May 1964 following the condemnation of the RAF's bombing of Harib fort inside Yemen by the United Nations. Britain's representative at the UN, Patrick Dean, urged Butler to seek an immediate moratorium on RAF action in Yemen and the federation. After a series of fractious discussions between Sandys, who supported the reinitiation of aerial proscription in the Radfan, and Butler, who vigorously opposed it, the Cabinet gave formal approval to Trevaskis's request on 12 May. Reservations were expressed about the indiscriminate nature of aerial attacks or, as one member of the Cabinet put it, that 'there would be no guarantee that women and children as well as men, might not be injured or killed.' Sandys missed the crucial Cabinet meeting because he was in Aden discussing the political implications of proscription but Home's support for the Trevaskis-Sandys line was decisive. Authority was given to proceed on condition that everything possible was done to avoid international attention focusing on the punitive measures.[57] During his flight to Aden Sandys had dictated a political directive for the local Commander-in-Chief which called for the establishment of 'zones of military operations'. The Commander was authorised to evacuate the inhabitants of these zones prior to the initiation by land forces of 'harassing attacks on men and livestock in these areas.' On arrival Sandys urged Trevaskis to avoid, as far as possible, any publicity being given to the punitive aspect of the operations, singling out the possibility of 'goat massacres' as potentially embarrassing.[58]

Sandys arrived in the midst of the second Radfan campaign which had begun with a disastrous SAS reconnaissance into the region on 29 April 1964. Two SAS soldiers were killed and initial press reports that they were decapitated were later confirmed despite Ministry of Defence denials.[59] After this inauspicious start a larger assault on rebel positions was launched by a combined force of commandos and paratroopers on 4 May. British troops suffered further casualties but made adequate progress over the next two weeks.[60] In their wake came the Federal Regular Army who were given the task of punishing the inhabitants of the Radfan, while Trevaskis awaited permission to launch a campaign of proscription from the air. The political directive for the campaign outlined the measures the troops were expected to take in proscribed areas: after warning leaflets had been issued they were to attack any remaining inhabitants, burn fodder, destroy crops and kill livestock. Although they were instructed to avoid civilian casualties as far as possible it was acknowledged that, should a village within a proscribed area refuse to surrender, it would have to be assaulted, in which case 'casualties to women and children will have to be accepted.'[61] After the first few days of the campaign, British officials became concerned that the troops were insufficiently harsh in their execution of these punitive measures. In particular there were complaints that they were failing to destroy grain stocks.[62] Following the belated arrival of Cabinet authority, a more systematic campaign of destruction from the air began on 17 May. The RAF were ordered to attack all signs of movement in proscribed areas, shoot up settlements and cause damage to property.[63] These measures threatened the livelihood of the tribes and during the course of the year the various Qutaybi sub-sections surrendered. The British estimated that there were 150 casualties amongst the tribesmen including 50 deaths but the PSP multiplied these figures by a factor of five in their propaganda. Thirteen British soldiers and 15 Arab soldiers were killed in the Radfan campaign.[64] The suppression of dissidence in one region was, as so often before, merely the prelude to outbreaks of rebellion elsewhere. While the Radfan was declared 'mainly quiet' by August, during the next few weeks the RAF targetted insurgencies in Dali', Dathinah and Hawshabi.[65]

Trevaskis's belief in the efficacy of proscription was questionable given the Sisyphean aspect which the military campaign against tribal insurrection had acquired by 1964. One particular problem was that funds for a hearts and minds campaign based on economic development were not available in sufficient quantities. The British High Commission in Aden regarded economic development as a key requirement if they were to leave behind a stable state in southwest Arabia but they were constantly frustrated by the parsimony of the British exchequer. In November 1962 Johnston incorporated plans for new infrastructure projects as part of an overarching strategy for combatting the threat posed by the Egyptians. He lobbied for the construction of a £12m trunk road system as tangible evidence of Britain's commitment to the federation but the proposal was too expensive to gain Treasury approval.[66] Trevaskis returned to the issue of underfunding in March 1964 and requested £3m to improve services and infrastructure. Noting that 71% of British expenditure was devoted to defence and internal security he proposed a 20% increase in the amount spent on education and health and a major new road building programme.[67] As one might expect the £3m figure was whittled down in the course of discussions by officials and ministers. At a Defence and Overseas Policy Committee meeting on 22 July additional spending of £500,000 on development was authorised. To mitigate disappointment in Aden there was also to be an increase of £500,000 in the political grants given to states, a fund of £120,000 was to be established to cover the labour costs of development and a reserve of £500,000 created for the purpose of staving off tribal disturbances.[68]

Some progress was made despite the limitations imposed by the Treasury. More effort went into development during the last decade of British rule than had occurred in the century after Haines's arrival. The Aden authorities allocated £4.16m from their 1964–65 budget to development schemes, principally for improvements in agriculture, health and education.[69] The problem for British officials on the ground was that they were attempting to compensate for years of neglect. A political officer who worked in Dali' summarised the situation: 'Hospitals in Abyan, Lahj and Lodar were very popular and the system of health posts elsewhere was a step in the right direction ... Primary schools varied from well-equipped ones ... to Quranic ones under thorn trees. Secondary schools were spreading more slowly. I remember the Maflahi children boarding on my ground floor while attending the one in Dali' ... We were starting from a low base line but what was done was appreciated and only a little more funding would have made a huge difference.'[70] Additionally some success was achieved in diversifying the local economy and in producing goods for export. Cotton schemes were particularly successful: in the decade after 1952 production increased from 4,000,000 lb to nearly 14,000,000 lb.[71] Fish processing facilities were developed in Dathinah and Qu'ayti; in other regions cigarette, brick and textile manufacturing were successfully encouraged.[72]

The situation in the Eastern Aden Protectorate differed markedly from that in the WAP. The Hadhramawt valley, which included major population centres, was wealthier and its political institutions sturdier than anywhere else in southwest Arabia. In the rural areas tribal dissidence remained a problem but RAF interventions were sporadic compared to the WAP. The Egyptians did not target the EAP as they did the WAP and the area was therefore not in the frontline of the conflict between Arab national- ism and British imperialism. The authorities in Mukalla achieved a degree of success in utilising Ingrams' Peace as an opportunity to achieve develop- ment. During the 1950s the British introduced diesel driven water pumps into those rural areas of the Hadhramawt which had suffered famine in the past. Similarly, the introduction of motorised boats in coastal regions increased the efficiency of local fishermen. However, the funds available remained paltry: a mere £400,000 in Colonial Development and Welfare grants in 1964–65.[73] Local leaders were frustrated at the failure to realise the economic potential of the region. For example, Sultan Ghalib of Qu'ayti was informed by a Norwegian UN official 'that if we could utilise our fisheries resources in a proper, scientific manner, we could have been as rich as any oil state.' It was also widely felt that the British were missing opportunities to develop the state's potential mineral wealth and its attractiveness to tourists.[74]

Despite the rather more stable and sophisticated nature of politics in the Hadhramawt there was a measure of continuity between British policy in the WAP and the EAP. In particular the pursuit of a forward policy involv- ing both the extension of British influence into regions which were previ- ously unacquainted with western forms of governance and the imposition of administrative reform as a prelude to the creation of a more centralised state were areas of commonality. The former was evident from the determination of the authorities in Mukalla and Aden to subdue the wild Mahra region which lay to the east of the Hadhramawt. In October 1963 the Hadhrami Bedouin Legion was instructed to execute Operation GUNBOAT. This was an oddly inappropriate title for an expedition which took place entirely on land over some of the flintiest and most rugged terrain in Arabia. The osten- sible purpose of the mission was to reimpose the rule of the region's nominal suzerain, the Sultan of Qishn and Socotra, and to facilitate oil exploration. Neither the Sultan nor the oil companies provided the real motivating force which was the tidying instincts of British administrators. The British had first sought to impose an administration on the area in the mid-1950s but their plans to spread government to the mainland were frustrated by the unbending determination of the Sultan not to become involved in the affairs of Mahra.[75] Nevertheless, the territory retained an odd allure for the British, as evident from a disconcerting passage written by the political officer who ran the GUNBOAT campaign: 'The Mahra nation was a shy virgin bride. Treasuring their maidenhood yet longing for the delights in store; they were psychologically unable to bring themselves to embrace their benefactor, to invite his drastic penetration.'[76] Aside from the Sultan it was the notorious Kilshat tribe who proved 'surly' and generally resisted the charms of the uninvited British suitor. In spite of their recalcitrance, GUNBOAT was successfully launched and the British established a short-lived administration in the principal Mahra town of Ghaida between 1963 and 1967.[77] At the end of this period the Mahra territory was abandoned almost unnoticed; its four-year period of British administration constituted one of the briefest episodes in the history of European imperialism in the Middle East. Although events there went unnoticed much beyond Mukalla they nevertheless illustrate the encompassing nature of the forward policy and its continuation in the mid-1960s. Further examples of the same phenomenon can be uncovered by examining the extent of British involvement in the civil war between Royalists and Republicans in Yemen.

Proxy war on Nasser

Events elsewhere masked the initial impact of the Yemeni revolution of September 1962 but over the next two years the Conservative government was to devote an inordinate amount of time to the consideration of how the spread of Republicanism in Arabia could be contained. It is not surprising that the prospect of imminent nuclear war over the deployment of Soviet missiles on Cuba in October 1962 overshadowed the death of Imam Ahmad, the accession of his son Badr and the successful Republican coup organised by al-Sallal, the previous month. Nevertheless, British policy-makers began to calculate the consequences which events in the former Imamate had for the future of British influence in the Middle East at a very early stage. On 6 October 1962 Macmillan minuted: 'I am worried about the Yemen since I believe it is a most serious situation. If things go wrong we may be faced with the loss of Aden and therefore of the Gulf . . . Nasser might be intervening openly.'[78] This supposition regarding Nasser's involvement was accurate: he provided the Republicans with military and political support from the outset. The threat to British interests appeared quite as significant as it had been six years earlier and the language of policy-makers was reminiscent of the Suez era. When in February 1963 Macmillan received a telegram from the British ambassador in Cairo recommending a reconciliation with Nasser he minuted: 'For Nasser put Hitler and it all rings familiar.'[79] By the summer of 1964, ministers were spending more energy on arguing over the best means of frustrating Nasser's objectives in the Yemen Civil War than on any other foreign policy issue. Suez had not cured the British of their appeasement fixation.

The Yemeni revolution introduced Republicanism to Arabia. More particularly, it established on the peninsula a regime eager to copy Nasser's programme. Within days of al-Sallal's coup Egyptian troops returned to Yemen for the first time since the early nineteenth century. These events posed a direct threat to the traditional rulers of Arabia and to their British sponsors. Since the Suez war Cairo had become increasingly less cautious in pursuit of regional hegemony and in the early 1960s this tendency was accentuated by significant domestic upheavals. It frequently happens that political and social revolutions postdate changes of regime and this is certainly true in the case of Egypt in the decade after the Free Officers' coup of 1952. Even following his shouldering aside of the country's figurehead leader, Mohammad Neguib, in 1954, Nasser remained cautious in his approach both to domestic reform and intra-Arab problems. The decision to form a United Arab Republic with Syria in 1958 which, from the perspective of London appeared as definite evidence of Nasser's reckless nationalism, was forced upon Nasser by the desperation of Syrian military officers to avoid a communist takeover. It was the demise of this union in 1961 that marked a genuine watershed for Egypt and the Middle East. As Damascus slipped from his grasp Nasser adopted a revivalist policy of socialisation at home, revolution in the Middle East and non-alignment in the Cold War. These policies had wide ramifications: in Arabia their principal consequence was to bring Nasser into direct confrontation with the Kennedy administration, the Hamid al-Din and the Saudis.[80] Both of these royal houses had been traditional opponents of British influence but, with the success of the Republican coup, they entered an uneasy coalition with the British in the hope of executing a counter-revolution in Yemen.

Given Nasser's past successes, the domestic problems of Saudi Arabia and the fragility of the South Arabian federation it was not difficult to imagine the revolution spreading from its base in Yemen. British policy-makers believed such a development would be fatal to British influence in the Middle East. In early March 1963 Macmillan expressed concern that following a Republican victory in Yemen 'the squeeze will begin' and predicted that Saudi Arabia would be Nasser's next target.[81] Later in the year, when evidence emerged that the Egyptian military effort was faltering, the Foreign Secretary, Douglas-Home suggested the Egyptian army should be 'pinned down and harassed' in Yemen until they decided to withdraw.[82] When fortunes changed again and news of a series of Egyptian military successes was received, the Chief of the Defence Staff, Mountbatten, predicted that after victory in Yemen, Nasser would target British assets in Cyprus, Libya and Malta. He warned: 'if we fail to contain Nasser there Saudi Arabia may break up; we shall certainly be pushed out of Aden sooner rather than later; and Nasser will have little difficulty in eroding our position in the Persian Gulf.'[83] Successive British governments were willing to compromise with opponents of many different stripes in order to frustrate Egyptian ambitions, including the Saudis, Imam Badr, the SAL and eventually the radicals of the NLF.

The immediate issue to confront British policy-makers was whether to recognise the new Republic. Initially, this seemed almost unavoidable. On 23 October 1962 the Cabinet agreed, in principle, to recognise al-Sallal's government. The arguments on either side were thoroughly charted at this meeting: recognition would provide Britain with influence over the Republican regime in the north but would damage relations with the federal rulers in the south.[84] The Kennedy administration moved on the issue more rapidly than the British. Their initial non-committal attitude was soon abandoned and Washington pressed strongly for international recognition of al-Sallal's government as a means to achieve an early settlement of the esca-lating conflict between the Republicans and Badr's Royalists.[85] Washington was convinced that the Royalists would be unable to mount any kind of effective resistance to Nasser and al-Sallal. Given that there was little incen-tive to risk American wrath for the sake of backing the Hamid al-Din, who had themselves long been opposed to the British presence in Aden, the failure of the British to proceed with recognition appears anomalous. The decision not to recognise was testament to the overpowering anti-Nasser feeling within the Conservative Party and to the sympathy of the Aden authorities for the federal rulers who shared a frontier with the new Republic.

The most convincing explanation for the policy of non-recognition is pro-vided by the British chargé in Yemen, Christopher Gandy. Although distant from Whitehall, he had the strong impression that the refusal to recognise the Republic was a consequence of anti-Nasser feeling in the Conservative party. The Suez group had now become the Aden group and was represented in the government by Enoch Powell and Julian Amery.[86] Although Johnston had initially been willing to accept recognition as a *fait accompli*, at the end of December he declared that it would be 'a very serious mistake' to which the federation would strongly object.[87] A number of ministers took up John-ston's argument that recognition of the Republic would irrevocably damage relations with the federation and this led in the early months of 1963 to what Macmillan called 'a violent division of opinion' between the Foreign Office and the Colonial Office.[88] Macmillan pressed the Colonial Office's anti-recognition arguments on Kennedy but Washington believed that the British were allowing their parochial concerns to divert them from the necessity of reaching an accommodation with Arab nationalism.[89] Kennedy grew bored with Macmillan's constant agonising over recognition, while the State Department found the explanations for the continuing delays 'thin and unconvincing'.[90] It thus came as something of a relief to Macmillan when al-Sallal resolved his dilemma in February 1963 by virulently denouncing British imperialism and ejecting Gandy from the country.[91]

Al-Sallal's decision to expel Gandy must be placed in the context of the activities of the federal rulers who viewed the Republican revolutionaries as dangerous Egyptian proxies. Sharif Husayn of Bayhan was the most active in the anti-Republican cause. His independence and courage were greatly admired by those British officials who got to know him but they were also well aware that he was the region's most inveterate and successful plotter.[92] Whenever the High Commission wished to subvert tribes inside Saudi Arabia or deliver assistance to the Royalists they turned to the Sharif. In the immediate aftermath of the Republican coup the British secretly encouraged the Sharif and his colleagues in the federal government to make contact with Prince Hasan. As Ahmad's brother and an opponent of Egyptian influence he had long been their favoured candidate for the Imamate. On the assumption that Badr was dead he seemed the most likely leader of the resistance to the Republicans.[93] Johnston told the American ambassador to Saudi Arabia on 1 October 1962 that he 'expected that the United Kingdom and the Saudi government would lend a hand in resisting the revolution and would probably extend that help via Yemeni Prince Hasan.'[94] Four days later Sandys granted Johnston authority to deliver arms and money to Hasan via the Sharif.[95] This effort was not sustained and it may be surmised that the unexpected reappearance of a healthy Imam Badr in the north of Yemen on 9 October caused a reappraisal of British plans. His death had been widely reported and his dramatic resurrection attracted some journalistic interest. The news of the Imam's survival was confirmed by a delegation of reporters, including Kim Philby on his final foreign assignment, who met Badr in the Yemeni highlands on 10 November.[96] This dramatic development forced the abandonment of British plans to organise a counter-revolution on behalf of Hasan. Badr had been the source of many British problems in the region; his previous association with Nasser and tribal suspicion of his motives made him a much less attractive figure to lead the anti-Republican movement.

The withdrawal of support for the Royalists in October was the first in a series of policy reversals concerning the Yemeni Civil War. Sharif Husayn came to regard British inconstancy as maddening. The British government would turn to the Sharif when they needed assistance in bolstering the Royalists but they did not always want to do this and when they did not his activities could be an embarrassment. On one occasion the Sharif declared in a televised interview that Nasser was 'the son of a dog.'[97] This was disconcerting for the American government which was attempting to negotiate a settlement in Yemen and was well aware of the Sharif's support for the Royalists.[98] The Republicans responded to the Sharif's provocations by making border incursions into Bayhan in February 1963. This, in turn, generated a diplomatic incident between Britain and the Republic and further alarmed the federal rulers. The Sharif insisted that the Republicans must be ejected from Bayhan immediately and at one point federal forces became involved in a firefight with Republican troops. Sandys was, as usual, eager to take retaliatory action but this was delayed while the government in London consulted Washington. Fortunately for relations between Britain and the federation, the Republicans withdrew their troops after the RAF were authorised to drop leaflets warning them of an imminent attack.[99]

As well as swinging back and forth between tolerating and encouraging Sharif Husayn's anti-Republican campaign, the High Commission adopted a permissive attitude to David Stirling's efforts to recruit a mercenary force to assist the Royalists. Stirling's biographer claims that in April 1963 Home met Stirling to discuss Royalist prospects in the Civil War and agreed that 'it would be a good idea if something could be done unofficially.'[100] From mid-1963 Stirling directed the creation of an Anglo-French force which trained, equipped and supervised Royalist tribesmen inside Yemen. The force was initially commanded by Johnny Cooper and later by David Smiley.[101] Such operations are designed to leave no trace in the public record and the precise nature of the British government's involvement remains unclear. Stirling was able to recruit among serving SAS officers and, despite the regiment's policy of opposing mercenary operations, these volunteers returned without charge after campaigning with the Royalists.[102] In addition, the High Commission and the SIS have been implicated in assisting Cooper's operations. The main evidence of High Commission support for the mercenaries comes from Egyptian intelligence reports acquired by the Sunday Times and published in July 1964. These revealed that Charles Johnston's aide-de-camp, Tony Boyle, corresponded with Cooper from the Aden High Commission. When questioned in Parliament about the matter Home vehemently denied that either he or Johnston knew of this correspondence.[103]

It has been suggested that Boyle's contacts with Cooper formed part of a wider policy of collusion between the British government and the mercenary force. Julian Amery and another Conservative MP, Neil 'Billy' McLean, have been identified as influential in obtaining SIS assistance for the unofficial mercenary operations.[104] The latter visited Royalist forces so frequently that he was increasingly regarded as the 'Member for Aden'. Recent research indicates these claims may have been exaggerated and that the mercenaries received little assistance from official British sources. The British government did give aid to the Royalists intermittently but, as we shall see, generally preferred to operate against the Egyptians through its own independent tribal connections rather than utilising Badr or the mercenaries. Boyle was clearly implicated in the mercenaries' cause and in September 1963 he secured the use of an RAF Beverley to deliver supplies to Bayhan for onward transmission to the Royalists.[105] However, this appears to have been an isolated event. The SIS were reluctant to become bogged down in the Yemen quagmire and sought to keep their involvement to a minimum.[106] Consequently, the mercenaries had to resort to a range of non-British contacts in order to sustain themselves and their Royalist allies. Contemporary rumours that these contacts included the Israelis have recently been confirmed. From early 1964 the Israelis began flying in supplies across the Red Sea and dropping them by parachute into Royalist areas.[107] More usually the Saudis were the principal suppliers of the Royalists but their support also varied according to political circumstances. The lack of sustained outside assistance meant that the Royalists never had sufficient equipment to launch a sustained offensive.

It has been argued that the role of the mercenaries in the Yemen Civil War was decisive but it seems evident that the unwillingness of the Home government to become directly involved limited Stirling's effectiveness.[108] The special operations which the British government authorised in an attempt to undermine the Republic are in some ways more interesting.

Although generally described as counter-subversive, they were actually part of a broader strategy to undermine Nasser's influence. In November 1962 Johnston warned that the establishment of a Republican regime in Yemen would endanger the federation: success for Nasser in the north would encourage dissidents in the south. He therefore requested funds for military and economic assistance programmes to bolster the standing of the federation and urged that £200,000 be granted to pursue a policy of counter-subversion and retaliation against the Yemeni Republic.[109] At this stage, with the recognition issue still unresolved, the government were slow to respond, much to Johnston's fury. He rehearsed the argument in favour of arming the Royalists frequently over the next few months but it was not until the success of Egyptian military operations threatened to overwhelm the Royalists that the government began to inch towards a policy of greater involvement in the Civil War. The dispatch of Nasser's key military adviser, Field Marshal 'Amr, to Yemen with reinforcements in February 1963 provided final proof of the Egyptians' determination to secure their position in the Arabian peninsula. 'Amr's Ramadan offensive swept Royalist resistance into the margins of the country.[110] This was alarming for Johnston who believed that a Republican victory would be the prelude to an Egyptian attempt to initiate a revolution inside the federation. Constant pressure from the Aden High Commission led in early March 1963 to his being granted authority to supply arms to the Royalists. The Sharif appears to have been reluctant to co-operate with this latest change in British policy and there were significant logistical problems delivering arms supplies across the frontier. Nevertheless, from this date the British had clearly taken the decision that covert means should be employed to prevent a Republican victory in Yemen.[111] Macmillan was concerned that special operations might not be enough to prevent this and wrote on 7 March: 'I fear that there is little more that we can do to help the so-called "Royalists" more than we have already done by "covert" methods.'[112]

Aside from limited authorisation to deliver arms to the Royalists the principal form of covert operations was retaliatory attacks into Republican Yemen. The British had operated a so-called tit-for-tat policy in the frontier wars with the Imam during the 1950s. Renewed authorisation for incursions into Yemen was given in order to punish the Republicans for supporting dissidence inside the federation. The principle adopted was that for every act of subversion which could be traced back to Yemen, the British would inflict twice as much damage inside Republican territory.[113] This retaliatory action took multiple forms. One of the most conspicuous was mine laying. The British held the Republicans and their Egyptian sponsors culpable for supplying mines to federal dissidents and Macmillan personally endorsed Johnston's request to lay mines in Republican areas.[114] In purely military terms this policy achieved some success. An Egyptian soldier was killed when a British mine exploded under an armoured car in January 1963 and this prompted the local tribes to seek additional assistance from the British.

Trevaskis speculated: 'I think you will agree that the first results of our retaliatory action are useful.'[115] However, as we have seen, the tit-for-tat policy did not discourage the Egyptians from stepping up their own campaign of subversion inside the Protectorates.

In the first six months of the war British interventions were of a limited and intermittent nature but nevertheless clearly breached the publicly professed policy of non-intervention. After the Egyptian offensive of February and March 1963 the conflict inside Yemen reached stalemate and the Royalist and Republican military campaigns became increasingly desultory. The United Nations established a mission to monitor Egyptian and Saudi activity in Yemen, while Washington sought to utilise the lull in the fighting to achieve a permanent cease-fire.[116] Although the head of the UN mission witnessed little evidence of British involvement, American policy-makers believed that the Aden High Commission was stoking up tensions along the frontier as part of their anti-Nasser campaign. British officials issued categorical denials that they were assisting the Royalists and Home reiterated these in a meeting with Kennedy on 4 October 1963.[117] Such reassurances were not given credence by all of Kennedy's advisers. His Secretary of State, Dean Rusk, and his principal adviser on Yemeni affairs, Robert Komer, were both suspicious of Britain's role in the Civil War. Komer believed that the Macmillan government was determined to 'stir up as much trouble as they could without getting overtly involved.'[118] He suggested that these actions would only spur Nasser to redouble his efforts which might in turn 'lead to a much greater Soviet presence in Yemen and the UAR.'[119] When Kennedy raised these concerns, Home maintained the official line that there was no British involvement.[120]

The Anglo-American quarrel over the Civil War remained at a subterranean level until the RAF bombed Harib in March 1964. While American officials were willing to keep their misgivings about British policy quiet for so long as the operations were concealed, the British decision to attack a military base inside Republican territory generated a minor crisis in Anglo-American relations. Following the abandonment of the plan to support Hasan, the British had consistently favoured covert action because it was less likely to generate opprobrium in the White House, the House of Commons, or the United Nations Security Council.[121] This frequently put them at loggerheads with the High Commission in Aden, where public displays of retaliation were regarded as a useful means of reassuring the federal rulers of British support. Usually ministers in London restrained the Aden authorities from overt provocations and this pattern repeated itself when on 13 March 1964 three Egyptian aircraft attacked property and livestock in Bayhan. The Sharif demanded redress but was denied it by the Home government. Nevertheless, it was agreed that retaliatory action would be essential to calm federal ministers should the Egyptians ignore British diplomatic protests and organise further attacks across the frontier. Ministers therefore ordered the preparation of a list of potential targets.[122] Before this appraisal could be completed, a further aerial incursion into Bayhan occurred: a Republican helicopter flew into Bayhan and fired at a Federal Guard post. Trevaskis demanded the right to retaliate and Home authorised an RAF attack on the Republican fort at Harib on 27 March.[123]

The attack on Harib inflicted significant damage on the fort and a number of casualties among the occupying Republican troops.[124] It also brought forth domestic condemnation, international protests and American disapproval. The Cabinet were criticised as 'third division Kitcheners' in the British press.[125] In Washington the most moderate of Lyndon Johnson's advisers regarded the action as ill-advised. Komer spoke for the immoderate faction when he declared with some prescience: 'Gyppos will make maximum propaganda of this "assault on Arabism" . . . They'll publicise UK covert activities in Yemen, focus spotlight on Aden, encourage other Arabs to cause trouble etc. . . . we'll inevitably suffer.'[126] As Komer predicted the Arab League denounced the attack and a condemnatory motion was tabled at the United Nations. The Security Council vote left the British almost completely isolated. The only delegate to abstain alongside the British was the American representative, Adlai Stevenson. This was much against his own inclination: he was only persuaded not to cast a vote in favour of the condemnatory motion by the express insistence of the President. Johnson was not sympathetic to the British case but was influenced by the appeals of his Secretary of State, Dean Rusk, who argued that an abstention was required to bolster moderates like Butler in their ongoing battle against the anti-Nasserites of the British Cabinet.[127] The State Department was swayed by personal pleas from Butler and the British ambassador, Lord Harlech, not to vote in favour of the resolution. In the aftermath of the incident Johnson declared 'that he didn't want to get into the habit of getting caught in an abstention when we really didn't believe in it.'[128] When Home sent him a personal letter of thanks for the American abstention, Johnson informed him that he had only done so reluctantly.[129] The strain on the Anglo-American partnership which the Harib incident generated and the international condemnation which followed were precisely the consequences that the British had sought to avoid by their reliance on special operations. While mounting a public defence of their overt retaliation against the Yemeni Republicans, British subversive activities inside Yemen increased.

The spark which reignited the British campaign of special operations against the Egyptians was the attempted assassination of Trevaskis. There was a conviction within the High Commission that Egyptian intelligence had instigated the terror campaign in Aden, including the airport bombing. On 24 December 1963 Trevaskis requested renewed authority for operations across the frontier. Stressing that the proposed measures 'have all been approved by HMG in the past, and in practise have demonstrated their efficacy beyond doubt' he outlined plans to initiate raids across the frontier by friendly tribes, re-commence mine laying inside Republican areas and sabotage Egyptian military facilities.[130] There was the customary delay in approving such measures but it is evident that in the early months of 1964 Trevaskis was given authority to conduct a campaign against the Egyptian presence which encompassed these measures and the subversion of tribes within Yemen. He wrote to the Commander of British forces in the Middle East on 5 April 1964: 'The only really effective means of countering the threat is . . . to cripple the UAR/YAR's capacity for promoting tribal revolts in the Federation by fomenting similar and yet more extensive and more damaging tribal revolts within the Yemen . . . I already have authority for limited action of this kind and I now await HMG's decision on proposals to take more extensive and effective action within the Yemen.'[131]

These proposals were contained in a dispatch of 15 March 1964 in which Trevaskis expressed his dissatisfaction with the continuing restrictions on his freedom to intervene in the Civil War and requested wider authority to target Egyptian forces inside Yemen. He was emphatic that the defeat of the Egyptian military campaign was essential to the goal of securing continued British influence in southwest Arabia. His rationale provides a revealing account of British calculations at this point: 'our position is endangered by the fact that if a Nasserite Y[emeni] A[rab] R[epublic] becomes firmly established, local political and tribal leaders, civil servants and members of the security forces will tend to jump on Nasserite/YAR band wagon.' This danger would be exacerbated given the 'context of an international campaign against our position at UN and elsewhere and in event of PSP gaining political control in Aden and authority of Federal rulers being undermined by large-scale tribal revolts as a consequence of subversion.' These considerations necessitated more extensive involvement in the Yemen Civil War, including the sponsorship of attacks on Egyptian supply lines by Britain's tribal allies from the federation, the provision of aid to isolated anti-Republican factions in the northeast of Yemen and the renewal of tribal attacks on the Yemeni frontier towns of Bayda and Qa'tabah. Trevaskis was confident that he could rid Yemen of Egyptian influence for a cost of £220,000. British intervention in the Civil War would be part of a wider programme of action, including the subversion of the PSP in Aden, the aim of which was to contain the spread of Nasser's influence.[132] These ideas did not appeal to the Joint Intelligence Committee or the Foreign Office, both of whom accused Trevaskis of exaggerating the Egyptian threat. The JIC concluded that the ejection of Egyptian forces was not feasible unless 'outside help went far beyond the supply of equipment they could operate themselves.' Nevertheless, Trevaskis's plans reignited the interest of Conservative ministers in embarrassing Nasser. Home regarded southwest Arabia as the front line in Britain's continuing confrontation with Nasser and Arab nationalism. He was attracted to the idea of supplying anti-Republican tribes with bazookas and insisted that the matter be pursued.[133]

Trevaskis was asked to clarify the nature of his planned intervention in the Civil War. On 31 March he sent detailed plans to Sandys for the supply of 4,500 rifles, 300 mines, 20 mortars, 30 bazookas and £45,000 to anti-Republican tribes in the interior of Yemen. Reliably pro-British Yemeni tribes just to the north of the federation frontier were to receive 2,500 rifles, 200 mines, 20 mortars, 20 bazookas and £25,000.[134] Two weeks later Home instructed ministers to submit their own proposals for action inside Yemen; a request to which Sandys responded with alacrity and Butler with reluctance. The former agreed that the Royalists probably could not defeat the Republicans but argued that the prevention of an Egyptian victory necessitated greater British involvement including the targetting of Egyptian intelligence operatives. Butler was concerned that increased British intervention in the Civil War would merely encourage Nasser to send more troops to Yemen. At a meeting on 23 April a compromise was reached between the Butler and Sandys positions. Existing authority for mine laying, the supply of arms to Yemeni tribes along the federation's frontier and the organisation of sabotage in Bayda and Qa'tabah was reconfirmed. Other proposals such as organised assassinations of Egyptian intelligence officers and the supply of arms to Royalist forces deep in the interior were rejected. However, a more extensive campaign of sabotage and black propaganda was approved and it was agreed that Royalist forces should be supplied with money by the British government.[135]

Such was the planned scale of British intervention that it was decided to abandon the fruitless attempt to hide these measures from the Johnson administration. In Aden Trevaskis informed the American consul on 27 April that they 'were no longer able [to] maintain non-intervention policy [in] Yemen.' On the same day Butler told Rusk that the Cabinet 'will not see the Royalists go down' and, in an obvious reference to Sandys, hinted that 'extremists in the Cabinet' had favoured a more radical course.[136] Restrictions on military assistance to the Royalists appeared anomalous when the British were engaged in a campaign of special operations and supplying funds to Badr's lieutenants. Consequently, in May Trevaskis was given official authorisation to renew the supply of arms to the Royalists.[137] This was the third occasion on which the British government had sanctioned the arming of anti-Republican forces but the first on which the decision had a significant impact. Unlike the policy decisions of October 1962 and March 1963, which were interrupted on the first occasion by the reappearance of Badr and on the second by a combination of Republican successes and difficulties with Sharif Husayn, in this instance all the evidence suggests that Trevaskis utilised the licence given to him to pursue a vigorous policy of intervention inside Yemen.

Trevaskis interpreted his new authority as permitting him to subvert the Egyptian military campaign with the assistance of the federal rulers and anti-Republican factions in Yemen. The Sharif of Bayhan was perhaps the most active in encouraging and facilitating the British campaign. Ta'izz seems to have been a particular target for covert action and there were frequent reports of explosions in the town. On at least one occasion, Sandys, in consultation with Home, authorised the High Commission to supply the

Sharif with bazookas for transmission to dissidents in Ta'izz.[138] Trevaskis also operated a network of agents inside Yemen, principally in Ta'izz but stretching as far north as Sanaa. They disseminated the High Commission's anti-Nasser literature. British black propaganda was specifically designed to damage the morale of the Egyptian forces and promote discontent with 'Egyptian colonialism'.[139] Although it is impossible to assess the impact of such operations, there is little doubt that by the summer of 1964 there was widespread dissatisfaction amongst Yemenis with what was increasingly seen as a foreign occupation.

Nasser's refusal to be rolled back reopened the argument about counter-measures within the British government. The decision to give financial and military assistance to the Royalists did not finally resolve the debate over Britain's role in the conflict. The Home administration was approaching the end of its mandate in the summer of 1964 and the consensus of opinion seemed to be that a crisis with Nasser would assist the Conservatives in fighting the forthcoming general election. The Colonial Secretary, Duncan Sandys, and the Minister of Aviation, Julian Amery, were convinced that a rematch with Nasser would wipe clean memories of the Suez debacle over which the Conservatives had presided and tarnish Harold Wilson's credibility. Amery wrote to Home with a gloomy analysis of Conservative electoral prospects and queried: 'Can we retrieve the situation in some corner of a foreign field?' His reasoning was that 'Nasser is probably the most hated man in Britain. But at bottom his policy and the Labour Party's also towards the Middle East are very closely aligned. If we could identify Wilson with Nasser ... we might greatly strengthen our hand. To do this would mean pressing Nasser to a point where the opposition could come out in his support.' The options discussed by Amery and Sandys were the organisation of additional attacks on Egyptian forces in Yemen and the dispatch of the Royal Navy to the Suez Canal. Little came of these proposals, but it constitutes an interesting illustration of the continuing commitment to a policy of imperial adventurism within the Conservative Party in the mid-1960s.[140] Wilson himself was 'worried that the Home government may be trying to make the Yemen crisis into a little Suez to win public support.'[141]

In Aden Trevaskis remained concerned about the restrictions on British involvement in the Civil War and in Whitehall the Foreign Office was under criticism for its desire to avoid an open conflict with the Egyptians. Home still considered many of Butler's reservations about backing the Royalists to be overly cautious and Sandys was eager to confront the Egyptians. However, the minister who spilt most red ink in the anti-Nasser cause was the usually temperate Secretary of State for Defence, Peter Thorneycroft. The differences between Home, Sandys and Thorneycroft on the one hand and Butler on the other were magnified by the opening of a major Egyptian offensive against the Royalists in June 1964 which initially seemed likely to accomplish a Republican victory.[142] This disturbed Thorneycroft who warned: 'Unless we can contain the Egyptian position inside the Yemen . . . things will go from bad to worse with increasing speed.' He proposed 'a sharp increase in "deniable" support in terms both of arms and money for the Royalist tribes and other tribes capable of interfering with Egyptian plans in Yemen.'[143] The scale of support required was evident from a 'shopping list' of arms supplies which was transmitted from the Royalist forces in Yemen to the British government by Neil McLean. He remained the most ardent partisan of the Royalist cause within the Conservative ranks and maintained contact with sympathisers inside the government, including Nigel Fisher.[144] Meanwhile, Sandys asked Trevaskis for an appraisal of the likely consequences of a Royalist collapse. Trevaskis responded by rehearsing his usual complaints about the hesitancy of government policy and rendered the consequences of further tardiness in his customary apocalyptic manner. He referred to six different occasions on which he had warned of impending catastrophe; grumbled that his proposals for rolling back Egyptian influence had been whittled down; and concluding that unless there was a change of policy 'by the end of the year we shall be heading for certain disaster . . . this is the last warning I can give.'[145]

It was in the context of this gloomy prognosis that on 22 July ministers considered two alternatives: the organisation by the Aden authorities of covert operations against the Yemeni bases from which dissidents in the Protectorates were supplied or the provision of £600,000 and 11,000 rifles to the Royalists to assist with a major offensive.[146] The first of these options was chosen. The British government had always been reluctant to rely on the mercenaries and the makeshift Royalist coalition to contain Egyptian influence and in the aftermath of this meeting there is little evidence of any significant increase in British assistance to them. In August Fisher informed McLean that following the meeting 'there has been no authorisation for anything on the scale of your "shopping list".'[147] Instead of supplying the Royalists directly Ministers opted to utilise reliable anti-Republican tribes who lived either side of the formal frontier as a proxy army which could be used to attack Egyptian forces around Qa'tabah and Bayda. These campaigns had much in common with the frontier war with the Imam in the late 1950s. Once again it was Jaabil bin Husayn of the 'Awdhali who played the leading role in organising these incursions. At the start of August he received 1,000 rifles from the High Commission.[148] On 23 August tribesmen from the Protectorates attacked Egyptian positions around Bayda. It proved more difficult to organise such special operations in the Qa'tabah area but pro-British factions attacked the town on 1 October. Egyptian military camps were a particular target and on occasions pitched battles broke out between the Egyptians and raiding parties from the Protectorates, most notably in the Juba area in late September.[149] The aim of these operations was primarily to deter the Egyptians from continuing with their own campaign of subversion south of the frontier but in late September and early October 1964 the High Commission in Aden was probably responsible for more attacks on Egyptian forces than Imam Badr's Royalist Headquarters. To advocates of a continuing British role in the Middle East British success in the frontier war with the Republic appeared to demonstrate that, with sufficient ingenuity, Britain could continue to play an influential role in the Middle East.

Conclusions

The two years after the Republican revolution in Yemen were decisive in deciding the future of southwest Arabia. The revolution brought increasing domestic and international attention to the region and inspired the nationalists in the south to follow more extreme tactics in pursuit of more radical goals. There was a debate within the British government over how to respond and the outcome was a victory for the uncompromising Trevaskis approach of brushing aside any opposition to the creation of an independent federation under the control of traditional tribal elements who had a common interest with the British in suppressing Arab nationalism. It is a measure of the extent to which the Conservative government had been driven by increments to adopt the aggressive tactics that Trevaskis had long advocated that in late October 1964 he provided an optimistic analysis of the conflict: 'we owe most to the measures we have taken to combat subversion and rebellion . . . Outside Aden we have relied first, on repressive military measures to combat the rebellious Radfan tribes and Egyptian trained mercenaries of the NLF; second, on retaliatory sabotage and subversion designed to hamper Egyptian agents on the frontier, and, thirdly on purchasing tribal support.' This had, in his view, produced a much-improved climate in which the federation might potentially thrive.[150] Such a sanguine analysis appears, in retrospect, to be misjudged. There was, in the context of an ideological clash between British imperialism and Arab nationalism, no feasible solution to the seething discontent of the industrial workforce in Aden or, given Treasury parsimony, any effective means of resolving incessant tribal insurgency. Furthermore, the atmosphere in Britain and the United Nations was not conducive to the kind of neo-colonialism which Trevaskis had in mind.

Notes

1 C. Johnston, *The View from Steamer Point* (London, Collins, 1964), pp. 124–5.
2 PRO: CO 1015/2391, Aden (Johnston) to Secretary of State, 30 September 1962.
3 PRO: CO 1055/111, Aden (Johnston) to Secretary of State, 18 April 1963.
4 D. Holden, *Farewell to Arabia* (London, Faber and Faber, 1966), p. 57; P. Somerville-Large, *Tribes and Tribulations* (London, Robert Hale, 1967), p. 16.
5 PRO: CO 1015/2596, Aden (Johnston) to Secretary of State, 28 September 1962, 19 November 1962, 4 December 1962.
6 PRO: CO 1015/2391, Chairman of the Supreme Council of the Federation to Governor, 18 October 1962, Secretary of State to Aden, 25 October 1962,

PREM 11/4678, Aden (Johnston) to Secretary of State, 4 November 1962, Secretary of State to Aden (Johnston), 5 November 1962.

7 Labour Party Archive, International Committee Aden Files, 2/3/2, Windrich Memorandum, 3 September 1962 enclosing Edwards memorandum, 'Crisis in Aden'.

8 PRO: CO 1015/2390, British Agent (WAP) to Acting Governor, 29 June 1962, Morgan minute, 10 July 1962, Simmonds to Morgan, 3 July 1962, CO Brief for mtg with Federation Rulers (ud).

9 Labour Party Archive, International Committee Aden Files, 2/3/2, Braunthal to Ennals, 12 October 1962, Ennals to Callaghan, 16 October 1962, Ennals to Muhammad S. Ali, 15 January 1963.

10 PRO: CO 1015/2391, Aden (Johnston) to Secretary of State, 20 December 1962.

11 K. Chang, 'The United Nations and Decolonization: The Case of Southern Yemen', *International Organization* 26 (1972), pp. 44–5.

12 PRO: CO 1055/111, Aden (Johnston) to Secretary of State, 7 March 1963, Eastwood minute, 15 March 1963, Secretary of State to Johnston, 9 April 1963.

13 PRO: CO 1055/111, Aden (Johnston) to Secretary of State, 28 June 1963.

14 C. A. Macleod, *The End of British Rule in South Arabia 1959–1967* (Edinburgh, PhD thesis, 2001), p. 127.

15 PRO: CO 1055/111 Aden (Johnston) to Secretary of State, 23 July 1963; IOR: R/20/D/27, Aden (Johnston) to Secretary of State, 2 August 1963.

16 IOR: R/20/D/27, Secretary of State to High Commissioner, 15 October 1963, Aden (Trevaskis) to Secretary of State, 16 October 1963, 20 October 1963, Colonial Office to High Commissioner, 25 October 1963.

17 IOR: R/20/D/27, Aden (Trevaskis) to Secretary of State, 3 November 1963, 6 November 1963, 24 November 1963, CO 1055/88, Aden (Trevaskis) to Secretary of State, 5 November 1963. For details of the imposed franchise see PRO: CO 1055/32, Legal Supplement (No. 1) to the Aden Gazette (No. 17), 26 March 1964.

18 K. Pieragostini, *Britain, Aden and South Arabia* (London, Macmillan, 1990), pp. 44–5.

19 PRO: CO 1015/196, Aden (Trevaskis) to Secretary of State, 10 December 1963, 11 December 1963 Aden (Trevaskis) to Secretary of State, CO 1015/197, C-in-C (Middle East) to Ministry of Defence, 10 December 1963, Aden (Trevaskis) to Secretary of State, 18 December 1963.

20 IOR: R/20/D/155, Deputy Ministerial Secretary minute, 2 May 1964.

21 PRO: CO 1055/196, Secretary of State to Aden, 10 December 1963, CO 1055/197, Secretary of State to Aden, 20 December 1963.

22 PRO: CO 1055/112, Aden (Trevaskis) to Secretary of State, 26 December 1963, CO 1055/131, Trevaskis to Eastwood, 5 February 1964.

23 PRO: CO 1055/128, Formoy minute, 29 March 1963, 21 May 1963, CO 1055/129 Colonial Office memo 'Aden: Future Policy', 7 June 1963 with handwritten Sandys minutes.

24 PRO: CO 1055/129, Aden (Trevaskis) to Secretary of State. 19 August 1963, 28 August 1963, 15 September 1963, Trevaskis to Eastwood, 17 September 1963, Milton minute, 8 October 1963, Secretary of State to Aden (Trevaskis), 11 October 1963.

25 PRO: CAB 128/38, CM(63)9th mtg., minute 2, 5 December 1963.

26 PRO: CO 1055/196, Secretary of State to Nairobi, 11 December 1963, Secretary of State to Aden, 11 December 1963, CO 1055/131, Secretary of State to Aden, 6 January 1964, PREM 11/4678, Trend Brief on DO(63)9 and DO(63)10, 10 December 1963, Trend memo to PM, 18 December 1963.

27 PRO: CAB 148/1, DO(64)5th mtg., minute 2, 29 January 1964, DO(46)6, 27

January 1964, CO 1055/131, Aden (Trevaskis) to Secretary of State, 29 January 1964 with Fisher minute, Secretary of State to Aden, 31 January 1964, Aden (Trevaskis) to Secretary of State, 2 February 1964.

28 PRO: CO 1055/216, Trevaskis to Sandys, 31 March 1964, Appendix 1.

29 PRO: CAB 128/38, CM(64)27th mtg., minute 3, 12 May 1964, CM(64)28th mtg., minute 1, 14 May 1964.

30 PRO: CAB 148/1, DO(64)26th mtg., minute 4, 12 June 1964.

31 K. Trevaskis, *Shades of Amber* (London, Hutchinson, 1968), p. 218.

32 Private information.

33 PRO: CO 1055/81, Rome to Secretary of State, 3 July 1964, Secretary of State to Aden (AHC), 4 July 1964.

34 PRO: CAB 148/1, DO(64)27th mtg., minute 2, 22 June 1964.

35 PRO: CO 1015/123, Aden (Trevaskis) to Secretary of State, 19 July, Aden (AHC) to Secretary of State, 29 August 1964, Secretary of State to Aden, 1 September 1964, Aden (AHC) to Secretary of State, 10 September 1964.

36 IOR: R/20/D/27, Aden (Trevaskis) to Secretary of State, 18 December 1963.

37 Trevaskis Papers Pt.1, s. 367, Box 6, File 1, Trevaskis to Sandys, 31 March 1964, Appendix 5.

38 PRO: CO 1015/216, Roberts to Sussex, 21 April 1964 with draft of Secretary of State to Prime Minister including Annex, 21 April 1964.

39 PRO: CO 1055/122, Secretary of State to Aden, 12 April 1964, Aden (Trevaskis) to Secretary of State, 13 April 1964, 14 April 1964, Minogue minute, 14 April 1964.

40 PRO: CO 1055/201, Aden (Trevaskis) to Secretary of State, 3 June 1964, 21 June 1964, 2 September 1964, 14 October 1964, 15 October 1964.

41 IOR: R/20/D/155, Deputy Ministerial Secretary to Chief Secretary, deportation returns for 1964.

42 PRO: CO 1015/33, Aden (AHC) to Secretary of State, 20 August 1964, Formoy to Monson, 4 September 1964, Aden (Trevaskis) to Secretary of State, 13 October 1964.

43 T. Little, *South Arabia* (London, Pall Mall, 1968) p. 115; D. Ledger, *Shifting Sands* (London, Peninsular Publishing, 1983), p. 59.

44 IOR: R/20/D/34, High Commissioner (Johnston) to Secretary of State, 23 January 1963, 12 June 1963, 17 July 1963; H. Lackner, 'The Rise and Fall of the National Liberation Front as a Political Organisation' in B. R. Pridham (ed.), *Contemporary Yemen: Politics and Historical Background* (London, Croom Helm, 1984), pp. 46–61; J. Kostiner, *The Struggle for South Yemen* (London, Croom Helm, 1984), pp. 53–9; F. Halliday, *Arabia Without Sultans* (London, Saqi Books, 2002), pp. 189–95.

45 IOR: R/20/C/2097, Pamphlet 8, 'Statement of the Arab Nation in Occupied South Yemen' and 'Arab Nationalist Leaflet found in Bayhan'.

46 P. Dresch, *A History of Modern Yemen* (Cambridge, Cambridge University Press, 2000), p. 97.

47 Ibid., p. 97.

48 J. Kostiner, *Struggle*, p. 71.

49 IOR: R/20/D/63, Aden (Trevaskis) to Secretary of State, 22 December 1963.

50 J. Lunt, *The Barren Rocks of Aden* (London, Herbert Jenkins, 1966), p. 53.

51 T. Mockaitis, *British Counter-Insurgency in the Post-Imperial Era* (Manchester, Manchester University Press, 1995), p. 51; J. Paget, *Last Post: Aden 1964–67* (London, Faber and Faber, 1969, pp. 45–50.

52 IOR: R/20/D/63, Aden (Trevaskis) to Secretary of State, 7 April 1964.

53 PRO: CO 1015/255, Beeley (Cairo) to Crawford (FO), 13 February 1964, Note for Secretary of State on Broadcasts, 23 March 1964.

54 R. McNamara, *Britain, Nasser and the Balance of Power in the Middle East* (London, Frank Cass, 2003, p. 193.

55 PRO: PREM 11/4929, Cairo (Beeley) to FO, 24 April 1964, 25 April 1964, 27 April 1964.

56 IOR: R/20/D/51, Aden (Trevaskis) to Secretary of State, 5 April 1964.

57 PRO: CAB 128/38, CM(64)27th mtg., minute 3, 12 May 1964, CM(64)28th mtg., minute 1, 14 May 1964, CAB 148/1, DO(64)17th mtg., minute 2, 8 April, 1964, DO(64)23rd mtg., minute 2, 14 May 1964, CO 1055/194, Aden (Sandys) to Prime Minister, 11 May 1964, PM to Secretary of State for Colonies, 12 May 1964.

58 IOR: R/20/D/63, Harrington to Sandys, 12 May 1964; PRO: DEFE 11/497, Commander-in-Chief (Middle East) to Ministry of Defence, 11 May 1964.

59 Paget, *Post*, pp. 73–5; PRO: DEFE 11/498, Commander-in-Chief (ME) to Ministry of Defence, 13 May 1964, DEFE 13/570, Commander-in-Chief (ME) to Ministry of Defence, 22 June 1964.

60 There are numerous accounts of the Radfan operation; the most detailed is Paget, *Post*, chs 4–10.

61 PRO: AIR 23/8637, Radfan Report, Appendix 1, Political Directive, 29 April 1964.

62 PRO: DEFE 25/129, Commander-in-Chief (Middle East) to Ministry of Defence, 15 May 1964; IOR: R/20/D/63, Baillie to High Commissioner, 12 May 1964.

63 IOR: R/20/D/63, Assistant High Commissioner to AOC (Commanding) Air Forces (Middle East), 17 May 1964, 21 May 1964, 31 May 1964, 16 June 1964.

64 IOR: R/20/D/59, Colville Stewart to High Commissioner, 12 November 1964.

65 IOR: R/20/D/35, Commander in Chief (Middle East) to Cabinet Office, 17 August 1964, 24 August 1964, 31 August 1964, 7 September 1964, 14 September 1964, 21 September 1964.

66 PRO: CO 1015/2597, Johnston to Morgan, 6 November 1962, Aden (Johnston) to Secretary of State, 30 November 1962.

67 PRO: CO 1015/25, Aden (Trevaskis) to Secretary of State, 15 March 1964, CO 1015/216, Trevaskis to Sandys, Appendix 2, 31 March 1963.

68 PRO: DEFE 11/500, Hockaday minute, 29 July 1964, CAB 148/1, DO(64)25th mtg., minute 2, 3 June 1964, CAB 148/2, D(64)47, 1 June 1964.

69 'A Survey of Aden the Protectorate of South Arabia', prepared for the South Arabian Constitutional Commission by the Colonial Office, July 1965, para. 128. I am very grateful to John Shipman for granting me this informative document on long-term loan.

70 Private Information.

71 *Colonial Office List 1966* (London, HMSO, 1966), p. 48.

72 J. Kostiner, *Struggle*, p. 12.

73 'A Survey of Aden the Protectorate of South Arabia', Prepared for the South Arabian Constitutional Commission by the Colonial Office, July 1965, paras 136–42.

74 Interview with Sultan Ghalib, Transcript of 'Fair Play' by Sultan Ghalib written in 1968–69.

75 S. Mawby, 'Britain's Last Imperial Frontier', *Journal of Imperial and Commonwealth History* 17 (2002), pp. 105–30.

76 P. S. Allfree, *Hawks of the Hadhramaut* (London, Robert Hale, 1967), pp. 156–7.

77 IOR: R/20/C/1822, Watts memorandum, 1 September 1963, Watts to Isa, 23 September 1963, 10 October 1963, Extract from Winsum, 19 October 1963.

78 PRO: DEFE 13/395, Minute from PM to Minister of Defence, 6 October 1962, CAB 128/36, CC(62)59th mtg., minute 1, 9 October 1962; Macmillan Diaries, d. 47, 6 October 1962.

79 R. McNamara, *Balance of Power*, p. 183.

80 F. A. Gerges, 'The Kennedy Administration and the Egyptian-Saudi Conflict in Yemen', *Middle East Journal* 49 (1995), pp. 292–311.

81 Macmillan diaries, d. 48, 8 March 1963, 11 March 1963.

82 PRO: FO 371/168808, Brenchley Memo on Yemen, 23 September 1963, Harrison minute, 24 September 1964, Home minute, 25 September 1964.

83 PRO: DEFE 13/570, Mountbatten to Secretary of State, 16 July 1964.

84 Macmillan diaries, d. 47, 26 October 1962; PRO: CAB 128/36, CC(62)59th mtg., minute 1, 9 October 1962, CC(62)60th mtg., minute 1, 15 October 1962, CC(62)61st mtg., minute 4, 23 October 1962.

85 C. Jones, *Britain and the Yemen Civil War 1962–1965: Ministers, Mandarins and Mercenaries* (Sussex Academic Press, Brighton, 2004), pp. 58–60; S. C. Smith, 'Revolution and Reaction: South Arabia in the Aftermath of the Yemeni Revolution' in K. Fedorowich and M. Thomas (eds), *International Diplomacy and Colonial Retreat* (Frank Cass, London, 2001), pp. 193–208; W. Taylor Fain, 'Unfortunate Arabia: The United States, Great Britain and Yemen, 1955–63' *Diplomacy and Statecraft* 12 (2001), pp. 133–4.

86 C. Gandy, 'A Mission to Yemen', *British Journal of Middle Eastern Studies* 25 (1998), pp. 263–4.

87 PRO: FO 371/168768, BM1015/12, Johnston to Secretary of State, 29 December 1962, Crawford minute, 31 December 1962, Stevens minute, 31 December 1962, Caccia minute, 1 January 1963.

88 Macmillan Diaries, d. 48, 21 January 1963; PRO: PREM 11/4356, Samuels to Bligh, 28 December 1962, Barbados (Stow) to Secretary of State, 29 December 1962, Thorneycroft to Macmillan, 8 January 1963, PREM 11/4357, Trend Memo for Macmillan, 13 February 1963.

89 Fain, 'Unfortunate Arabia', pp. 141–2.

90 Robert Komer claims that Kennedy grew so bored during a long phone conversation with Macmillan about recognition that he passed the receiver to him. He continued to press the American point of view while the President put his feet up and smoked a cigar. See Kennedy Library, Oral History, Robert Komer, 16 July 1964, NSF Box 207, Bruce (London) to Secretary of State, 15 November 1962.

91 Macmillan Diaries, d. 48, 17 February 1963.

92 M. Luce, *From Aden to the Gulf* (Salisbury, Michael Russell, 1987), pp. 33–5; D. Holden, *Landscape*, ch. 11.

93 PRO: CO 1015/2597, Aden (Trevaskis) to Secretary of State, 2 October 1962, Secretary of State to Aden (Johnston) 6 October 1962; Kennedy Library, NSF Box 207, State Department to Jeddah, 29 September 1962, London (Bruce) to Secretary of State, 10 October 1962, 13 October 1962.

94 P. T. Hart, *The United States and Saudi Arabia* (Bloomington, Indiana University Press, 1998), p. 137.

95 S. C. Smith, 'Revolution and Reaction', p. 201; P. Dresch, *Modern Yemen*, p. 91.

96 E. Downton, *Wars Without End* (Toronto, Stoddart, 1987), pp. 331–3.

97 Kennedy Library, NSF Box 208, Jones (London) to Secretary of State, 2 January 1963.

98 National Archives, RG59, Box 4146, Eilts to the State Department, 12 March

1963; PRO: FO 371/168787, BM 1015/33, Formoy to Pridham, 8 January 1963.

99 PRO: CAB 128/37, CC(63)14th mtg., minute 2, 28 February 1963, CO 1055/16, Aden (AHC) to Secretary of State, 30 January 1963, 1 February 1963, 3 February 1963, 5 February 1963, Secretary of State to Aden, 14 February 1963, 17 February 1963, Walmsley to Crawford, 22 February 1963, Aden (Johnston) to Secretary of State, 25 February 1963, 26 February 1963, FO371/168790, BM 1015/100, Walmsley minute, 18 February 1963, New York (UK Mission) (Dean) to FO, 7 April 1964, BM 1022/100.

100 Hoe, *David Stirling* (London, Little Brown, 1982, pp. 356–8; S. Dorril, *MI6: Fifty Years of Special Operation* (London, Fourth Estate, 2000), p. 684.

101 D. Smiley, *Arabian Assignment* (London, Leo Cooper, 1975), chs 8–15.

102 K. Connor, *Ghost Force* (London, Weidenfeld and Nicolson, 1998), pp. 127–8; A. Kemp, *Savage Wars of Peace* (2nd ed. Penguin, London, 2001), ch. 7; T. Geraghty, *Dares*, pp. 88–90.

103 *Parliamentary Debates 1963–64*, 5th series, vol. 699, cols 267–9; P. de la Billiere, *Looking for Trouble: An Autobiography* (London, HarperCollins, 1994), pp. 202–7; T. Geraghty, *Who Dares Wins* (London, Book Club Associates, 1980), p. 92.

104 X. Fielding, *One Man in His Time* (London, Macmillan, 1990), ch. 9, T. Bower, *The Perfect English Spy* (London, Heinemann, 1995), pp. 249–54.

105 C. Jones, *Ministers, Mandarins*, p. 132.

106 Ibid., pp. 118–19.

107 Ibid, pp. 136, 147–8.

108 X. Fielding, *Man*, p. 155.

109 PRO: CO 1015/2597, Johnston to Morgan, 6 November 1962, Johnston to Secretary of State, 30 November 1962.

110 E. O'Ballance, *The War in the Yemen* (London, Faber and Faber, 1971), pp. 97–9; D. A. Schmidt, *Yemen: The Unknown War* (London, Bodley Head, 1968), p. 161.

111 PRO: PREM 11/4928, Nairobi (Sandys) to Colonial Office (Fisher), 5 March 1963, Aden (Johnston) to Secretary of State, 6 March 1963.

112 Macmillan, d. 48, 7 March 1963.

113 Private Information.

114 PRO: DEFE 13/398, Macmillan to Commonwealth Secretary, 22 October 1962.

115 IOR: R/20/D/34, Johnston (Aden) to Secretary of State, 23 January 1963; PRO: PREM 11/4357, Aden to Secretary of State, 28 January 1963.

116 Carl Von Horn, the head of the United Nations Yemen Observer Mission blamed the Egyptians for the continuation of the conflict and believed Washington deliberately undermined British influence in the region. See C. Van Horn, *Soldiering for Peace* (London, Cassels, 1966), pp. 354–6.

117 National Archives, RG59, Box 4147, London (Bruce) to Secretary of State, 15 October 1963; PRO: PREM 11/4928, Extract of a Record of a Conversation at the White House, 4 October 1963.

118 Kennedy Library, Oral Histories, Robert Komer, 16 July 1964, Dean Rusk, 21 July 1970.

119 Kennedy Library NSF Box447, Komer to Bundy, 20 September 1963, NSF Box 209, Cairo (Boswell) to Secretary of State, 18 September 1963; National Archives, RG 59, Central Foreign Policy Files, Box 4147, Bruce (London) to Secretary of State, 15 October 1963.

120 PRO: PREM 11/4928, Record of a Conversation at the White House.

121 S. Mawby, 'The Clandestine Defence of Empire', *Intelligence and National Security* 17 (2002), pp. 105–30.

122 PRO: FO 371/174627, BM1022/11, Aden (Trevaskis) to Secretary of State, 15 March 1964, Brenchley Memo, 17 March 1964, Sandys to Butler, 17 March 1964, BM 1022/16, Aden (Trevaskis) to Secretary of State, 16 March 1964, BM 1022/22, Foreign Office to Washington, 21 March 1964, BM1022/23, Brenchley Memo, 18 March 1964, DEFE 25/129, Draft Memo from Secretary of State for Defence to PM, 1 April 1964, PREM 11/4678, Aden (Trevaskis) to Secretary of State, 18 March 1964, 19 March 1964, Secretary of State to Aden, 19 March 1964, CO 1055/29, Secretary of State to Aden, 26 March 1964, CAB 148/1, DO(64)15th mtg., minute 4, 18 March 1964.

123 PRO: FO 371/174627, BM 1022/34, Aden (Trevaskis) to Secretary of State, 27 March 1964; IOR: R/20/D/8, Secretary of State to Aden, 26 March, 27 March 1964.

124 IOR: R/20/D/8, Aden (Trevaskis) to Secretary of State, 28 March 1964, Commander in Chief (ME) to Ministry of Defence, 29 March 1964.

125 R. Bidwell, *Yemens*, p. 152.

126 Johnson Library, NSF Box 161, Komer to Bundy, 2 April 1964.

127 Foreign Relations of the United States [FRUS] 1964–68, Vol. 21, Memo from Bundy to Johnson, 9 April, pp. 623–4, Telephone Conversation between Johnson and Rusk, 9 April 1964.

128 Johnson Library, Ball Papers, Box 6, Stevenson-Ball Telecon 9 April 1964, Bundy-Ball Telecon, 9 April 1964, NSF Files, Box 161, Belk for Bundy, 29 May 1964; PRO: CAB 148/1, DO(64)17th mtg., minute 2, 8 April 1964, FO 371/174628, BM 1022/84, New York (UK Mission) (Dean) to FO, 7 April 1964, BM 1022/100, New York (UK Mission) (Dean) to FO, 7 April 1964, BM 1022/115, New York (UK Mission) (Dean) to FO, 9 April 1964.

129 FRUS 1964–68, Vol. 21, State Department to Secretary of State, Manila, 11 April, 1964, Johnson to Home, 12 April 1964.

130 IOR: R/20/D/8, Trevaskis (Aden) to Secretary of State, 24 December 1963.

131 PRO: DEFE 28/147, Trevaskis to Harrington, 5 April 1964, DEFE 4/167, COS(64)25th mtg., minute 3, 24 March 1964; IOR: R/20/D/8, Shegog to Oates, 9 March 1964.

132 Due to the inconsistent manner in which government records are weeded it is currently necessary to consult the same document in different files to obtain the full details of Trevaskis's plan. See PRO: CO 1055/25, Aden (Trevaskis) to Secretary of State, 15 March 1964, PREM 11/4678, Aden (Trevaskis) to Secretary of State, 15 March 1964.

133 PRO: PREM 11/4678, Butler to PM, 20 March 1964 with handwritten Home minute (ud), DEFE 13/417, Hull to Minister of Defence, 24 March 1964.

134 Kennedy Trevaskis Papers, Pt. 1, s. 367, Box 6, File 1, Trevaskis to Sandys, 31 March 1964 including Appendix 3.

135 PRO: PREM 13/569, Home to Butler, 16 April 1964, DEFE 25/129, Butler to Prime Minister, 21 April 1964, Sandys to Prime Minister, 22 April 1964 The best evidence concerning the decision made at this meeting are the ticks and crosses interpolated by Luce on his copy of a DOPC paper entitled 'Yemen: Range of Possible Courses of Action Open to us' in DEFE 25/129. On the decision to fund the Royalists see also DEFE 11/497, Trotman Brief for Chiefs of Staff, 4 May 1964.

136 Lyndon Johnson Library, NSF Country Files, Box 161, Aden (Wheelock) to Secretary of State, 27 April 1964, Box 213, Memorandum of conversation between Rusk and Butler, 27 April 1964; PRO: CO 1015/200, Washington (Harlech) to Foreign Office, 28 April 1964.

137 PRO: DEFE 13/570, Hockaday for Secretary of State, 20 July 1964.

138 PRO: DEFE 13/570, Butler to Home, 11 September 1964, Moran to McIndoe, 11 September 1964, Peduzie to Wright, 14 September 1964.

139 PRO: DEFE 11/498, Aden (Trevaskis) to Secretary of State, 25 May 1964.
140 Duncan Sandys Papers, DSND 8/16, Amery to Home with Note on Aden/Yemen Problem, 7 May 1964, Amery to Sandys, 7 May 1964.
141 Tony Benn, *Out of the Wilderness: Diaries 1963–1967* (London, Hutchinson, 1987), p. 108.
142 E. O'Ballance, *War*, p. 128.
143 PRO: DEFE 11/499, Thorneycroft memo on 'Maintaining our Position in South Arabia', 13 July 1964.
144 C. Jones, *Ministers, Mandarins*, p. 158.
145 IOR: R/20/D/90, Aden (Trevaskis) to Secretary of State, 18 July 1964; PRO: CO 1055/216, Secretary of State to Aden, 18 July 1964, Aden (Trevaskis) to Secretary of State, 18 July 1964.
146 PRO: DEFE 13/570, Memorandum for Consideration by Ministers at DOPC on 22 July 1964.
147 C. Jones, *Ministers, Mandarins*, p. 159.
148 IOR: R/20/D/9, Aden (Trevaskis) to Secretary of State, 6 August 1964.
149 IOR: R/20/D/35, Commander-in-Chief (Middle East) to Cabinet Office, 31 August 1964, 7 September 1964, 14 September 1964, 21 September 1964, 28 September 1964, 5 October 1964, 12 October 1964.
150 PRO: CO 1055/195, Trevaskis to Secretary of State, 28 October 1964.

6 The Labour reappraisal 1964–1966

Advocates of the metropolitan explanation of decolonization who believe that the pressure of economic and domestic change at home was a seminal influence on the end of empire might find sustenance for their views from the activities of Robin Young on the night of the British general election of 15 October 1964. Young was an experienced Political Officer and hugely admired by his colleagues but they were not convinced by his suggestion that the results of the poll would be crucial to the future of the Middle East. He stayed awake to listen to the returns on the radio and by the end of the following day was convinced that Harold Wilson's victory was the beginning of the end for British influence in the region.[1] The assumptions underlying this analysis have since acquired a degree of orthodoxy. The general view is that, given a more robust attitude than Wilson and his colleagues managed to summon up, something like Trevaskis's plan to model southwest Arabia on Cromer's Egypt might have been feasible. In one sense there is evidence to commend this view, for the new Labour government was unable to devise an effective strategy and, by announcing in February 1966 that previous offers of defence assistance after independence were to be retracted, it made the task of clinging to the remains of British influence more difficult. However, this analysis takes insufficient account of the fact that the watershed had already been traversed by October 1964: nationalist fortunes had been in the ascendant since the late 1950s, international pressures for withdrawal were mounting and the internal security problems in the interior were being magnified by an alliance between the tribes and the Egyptians. Furthermore, there was an element of continuity between Labour and Conservative approaches: although the former were less sympathetic than the latter to the federation and keener to appease the nationalists in Aden, the goals of British policy and even some of the tactics remained unchanged. The Wilson government wanted to play a continuing role in southwest Arabia and the Middle East; in order to do so it employed a variety of means, many of them familiar, to combat Egyptian influence and construct a stable state in which their interests would be guaranteed. Initially, the new tactics in Aden will be explored before the elements of continuity in policy towards tribal insurrections and the Civil War in Yemen are examined.

Context: the base in British and Egyptian thinking

By the middle of the 1960s the bases at Aden and Singapore were established as the cornerstones of British east of Suez policy and therefore of the country's continuing global influence. The initial instinct of the new Labour administration was that this effort should be sustained. Although it is sometimes difficult to disentangle personal views from bureaucratic roles or to penetrate the rationalisations which crop up in ministerial memoirs, it seems evident that on entering office key Labour figures favoured the continuation of a substantial British presence east of Suez. There was certainly no consensus within the new administration that Britain should end its military commitments in the Middle East. There are echoes of the romantic attachment to Britain's world role in the attitude both of Wilson and his *eminence grise*, George Wigg, to the east of Suez strategy. Among the more hard-headed advocates of a continued role for Britain on the world stage were Wilson's second Foreign Secretary, Michael Stewart, and the Defence Secretary, Denis Healey. Three distinct factions challenged the Bevinite advocates of Britain's global mission but in October 1964 they were not in positions of great authority. A group which could be described as defence rationalists made a strong case for finally addressing the yawning and long-standing gulf between British foreign policy commitments and defence resources by cutting the east of Suez role. Though their arguments differed somewhat the most eloquent spokesmen for this group were the Navy Minister, Christopher Mayhew, and the Minister for Aviation, Roy Jenkins. A second grouping had reached the same conclusion by a different route. Many of the more liberal Labour politicians were eager to terminate Britain's remaining colonial relationships on the grounds that imperialism was outdated and discredited. Wilson's Colonial Secretaries, Anthony Greenwood, Frank Longford and Frederick Lee were all broadly of this view but they were excluded from Wilson's inner circle. Finally, there were a number of Labour ministers who had limited knowledge of foreign policy but who regarded the empire as an expensive encumbrance which hindered progress towards the construction of a modern, equitable society at home. The government's two leading diarists, Richard Crossman and Barbara Castle, fell into this camp.

During the first year of Wilson's premiership a review of all British defence spending, including the Aden commitment, was undertaken in order to reduce annual costs to the arbitrary figure of £2,000m. This required the government to prioritise and it initially appeared that the Aden base was likely to survive the defence review on the grounds that it was the key to retaining British influence in the Middle East. At the outset of his six-year term of office as Defence Secretary, Denis Healey 'believed that our contribution to stability in the Middle and Far East was more useful to world peace than our contribution to NATO in Europe.'[2] If Britain was to retain a presence in the Middle East there was a strong case for keeping the

Aden base. The Chiefs of Staff had long been insistent that it was an irreplaceable asset. Although they gradually moderated their view that there was no feasible substitute for the defence facilities in Aden, they continued to warn that the development of a new base in the Persian Gulf would be costly.[3] Wilson's instincts were to avoid cuts that would prejudice the country's ability to participate in interventions overseas. At the Chequers meetings in November 1964 which began the process of reviewing defence costs, the Prime Minister sought to reduce expenditure by cutting weapons programmes rather than east of Suez commitments.[4] While adhering to the goal of defence retrenchment, Wilson declared that Britain needed 'most, if not all, of the bases we now hold.' The importance of Aden to British strategy was reaffirmed in the February 1965 Defence White Paper, which authorised further construction work on the expansion of the base.[5]

Given the balance of power in the new Cabinet, the endorsement of the east of Suez role at Chequers and the centrality of Aden to British strategic planning in the Middle East, the decision to abandon the base may appear paradoxical. It can best be explained as the culmination of two related trends: an increasing recognition of the intractability of the problem which Labour had inherited and a new strategic analysis suggesting that alternatives to the facilities at Aden could be constructed elsewhere. These modes of thought were implicit in the papers produced by the Long Term Study Group which had been established by the Conservative government in May 1964. Their final reports, which were produced in October, stressed that Aden was in many ways a more significant base than Singapore but that the case for keeping it was made less compelling by the political problems on the ground and the fact that, in contrast to southeast Asia, alternative facilities could be established in more stable regions of the Middle East such as the Persian Gulf.[6]

It was the political issues that were the key to the change in policy. A consensus developed around the erroneous assumption that the announcement of a decision to withdraw from the base would help appease moderate opinion in Aden. Whereas the Conservatives regarded the rulers as congenial proxies for the continuation of British influence, the Labour government believed that the promise of military withdrawal would have a transforming effect on the nationalist opposition in Aden. Once the suspicion that Britain was only interested in military facilities was expunged by a policy of judicious concessions, the nationalists, rather than the federal rulers, would act as the responsible anti-Nasserite guardians of continued British influence. Tellingly, Healey claims to have changed his mind about Britain's east of Suez role when he realised that the policy of clinging on to defence facilities was exacerbating rather than resolving Middle East tensions.[7] Although he suggests this realisation first struck him with regard to Kuwait, the case of Aden clearly fits a similar pattern. The initial reaction of Patrick Gordon Walker, Wilson's first Foreign Secretary, was that a defence agreement should only be negotiated after Aden had achieved independence, if at all, and this judgement was endorsed by his successor Michael Stewart.[8] Greenwood told the Cabinet in March 1965 that 'he hoped we did not visualise any permanent retention of the Aden base as this was linked up with his political negotiations.'[9] The decision to withdraw from the base was a consequence not of the fixing of a ceiling on British defence expenditure, but of a new analysis of regional politics. Greenwood's priority was to win over the nationalist opposition in Aden and he mistakenly believed this would be facilitated by the withdrawal of British forces.

The consensus of opinion at the Ministry of Defence, the Foreign Office and the Colonial Office that withdrawal would promote a political settlement inevitably left the base vulnerable to Treasury demands for retrenchment. During the course of the first Labour defence review military planners were forced to reconcile themselves to the likely loss of the facilities in Aden and began to seek out alternatives in the Gulf. They were reluctant to abandon the base because they believed that this would be chalked up as a victory for Nasser. This attitude and the increasing realisation that the loss of the facilities was inevitable in the long term were recorded in a Chiefs of Staff discussion on 11 May 1965: 'A withdrawal from Aden would particularly be regarded as a British defeat so long as Nasser remained in Yemen ... If Nasser were forced to leave the Yemen it would not end subversion in the Federation of South Arabia but our withdrawal from Aden would be made very much easier.'[10] It was only after the decision not to retain the Aden base was agreed in mid-1965 that the Chiefs began to study seriously the possibility of establishing new defence facilities in the Persian Gulf.

Far from mitigating British problems the announcement that Britain would abandon its defence commitments exacerbated them. George Brown would eventually ruefully acknowledge that the decision to cut defence ties to southwest Arabia hindered the attempt to secure an orderly decolonization.[11] By the time of Labour's election factors were at work in both local and regional politics which rendered almost any attempt to secure the continuation of extensive British influence unworkable. The moderates with whom Greenwood wished to work were being eclipsed by more radical figures. Although the nationalist opposition in Aden was rhetorically committed to the eradication of western imperialism, the presence of British defence facilities was not their primary concern. They had been alienated by the industrial situation, the reliance of the Aden authorities on indiscriminate deportations and the restrictions on the franchise. The launch of the terror campaign in Aden further entrenched opposition to the British as a consequence of the often harsh reprisals authorised by the Aden High Commission. Despite this, the prospect of Britain abandoning the base had practically no appeal to the local population who were well aware of the economy's dependence upon a continuing British presence. As Tom Little has noted: 'For shop-keepers, taxi-drivers and officials in government and private business, the British decision was viewed as a calamity.'[12]

In terms of broader trends in Middle East politics Greenwood chose precisely the wrong moment to seek a reconciliation with Arab nationalism. In the mid-1960s Nasser's discontent both with continued western support for Israel and the overt and covert activities of the western powers in the Middle East led him to pursue a more confrontational approach. The founding of the NLF in 1963 and Nasser's trip to Yemen in 1964 provided evidence of his determination to eject the British from their last Arabian outpost. However, the fulfilment of this ambition was made more difficult by divisions amongst Britain's opponents. As was characteristic of Middle East politics, ideological fractures had appeared in nationalist ranks: between advocates of Yemeni or Adeni particularism and pan-Arabists; between Arab socialists and international communists; and between supporters of armed force and proponents of industrial action. In May 1965 Nasser brought together various parties to the conflict, including the leaders of the tribal revolt in the south such as Muhammad 'Aydarus, disenchanted federal rulers including the ex-Fadli Sultan, former Free Yemenis such as Nu'man and the PSP represented by al-Asnaj, to form an umbrella organisation: the Organisation for the Liberation of the Occupied South (OLOS).[13] Elements within both the SAL and the NLF initially remained independent of OLOS. Subsequently, the NLF were at least nominally brought into a new group called the Front for the Liberation of Occupied South Yemen (FLOSY). However, many NLF cadres were moving away from an unquestioning commitment to Nasser and these groups were never fully integrated into any of these Nasserite contrivances.[14] Their refusal to submit to Cairo's lead would eventually lead to open warfare between FLOSY and the NLF and this, in turn, had significant consequences for both Nasser and the British.

At just the time that Nasser was attempting to unite Britain's opponents in southwest Arabia, the Arab Nationalist Movement and the Ba'th party, both of whom had established a presence in Aden during the 1950s, were taking a sharp ideological turn away from Nasser's brand of Arab socialism and towards a more orthodox Marxist position. The NLF in Aden shadowed these developments. A new younger group of leaders, who were known as the Secondary Leadership, were formulating a potent strategy for effecting a revolution in Arabian politics and society. Under the influence of Marxist revolutionary ideology they developed a new reading of Arabian politics which emphasised the need to target local imperialist collaborators. FLOSY and other nationalist organisations were hindered by the difficulties of maintaining a united front among differing interests and the fact that the demands made by Nasser very frequently conflicted with local imperatives. The Secondary Leadership of the NLF were unencumbered by any desire to maintain a united front in opposition to the British or by any loyalty to Egypt; they criticised the past leadership for its servility to nationalism and had no hesitation in identifying those who backed Cairo's line as naïve apologists.[15] Most significantly of all however, they identified and targeted the federal rulers as agents of imperialism and sought to destroy them through exploiting tribal discontent. In the longer term ideological shifts within the

NLF proved useful to the British as it gave them a non-Nasserist alternative to FLOSY. However, in the shorter term it doomed Greenwood's attempt to conciliate the nationalists. Instead of negotiating with the colonial authorities, FLOSY and the NLF entered into a competition with one another to prove their radical anti-imperialist credentials.

Greenwood's new start in Aden

Greenwood doggedly persisted in his attempts to win over the nationalists of Aden until his hopes sank with the reimposition of direct rule in the town and the declaration of a state of emergency in September 1965. By the time that the Labour government announced its decision not to retain a military presence in southwest Arabia in February 1966 the strategy of appeasing opposition groups was already in tatters. As we shall see the Wilson administration was quite willing to employ force in the Protectorates and Yemen in order to uphold British interests, but in Aden they believed a compromise was possible with a nationalist movement which had strong links to the party. British tribulations were the product of a mistaken belief that they could win over the nationalists; this analysis failed to recognise how far the situation in Aden had deteriorated.

The Wilson government rejected the Conservatives' formula for an independent state in Aden and the Protectorates dominated by the traditional rulers. Their disavowal of this element of their predecessors' Aden policy was symbolised by Greenwood's decisions to release Khalifah, who was the chief suspect in the December 1963 airport bombing, from gaol and to dismiss Trevaskis. The attempted assassination of Trevaskis remained a painful memory for all involved and Khalifah's achievement in securing the largest vote for a single candidate in the October 1964 elections caused further anguish.[16] Khalifah appears to have been a gauche, almost doltish, young man, thoroughly unprepared either for his fingering by the British as the mastermind of the airport plot or his subsequent elevation to the role of avatar of Arab resistance to British imperialism. He was undoubtedly at the scene of the attack and the Aden authorities were convinced that he had thrown the grenade at Trevaskis.[17] The death of George Henderson and the continuing trauma suffered by Trevaskis's wife in the aftermath of the incident made the issue of Khalifah's treatment a personal as well as a political matter. For the federal rulers, some of whom were injured at the airport, the assassination plot symbolised British inability to maintain order in Aden.[18] However, the fact that Khalifah was elected despite British manipulation of the electoral system 'gave the lie to the opinion of some British officials that only a gang of Yemenis and others brain-washed by Egypt were responsible for resistance in Aden.'[19] The election results reinforced Greenwood's inclination to release Khalifah. His public justification was that Khalifah had been legally elected and that the other Aden ministers would not take up their responsibilities until this was done. Some new members of the Legislative Council even suggested that Khalifah should be appointed Chief Minister in Aden. Khalifah wrote to Greenwood and Wilson expressing his willingness to assume this role in order to avoid the setting of an 'undemocratic precedent'. Greenwood told his colleagues that Khalifah would have to be freed at some point and that an early release would be a useful means of symbolising the new administration's desire for a rapprochement with the nationalists. He therefore ordered the release while endorsing Trevaskis's efforts to secure the reappointment of Baharun as Chief Minister.[20] Trevaskis made no attempt to camouflage his disgust at the 'unpalatable decision' to free Khalifah. Following much intrigue and counter-intrigue Trevaskis rallied sufficient support in the Aden Legislative Council to secure Baharun's appointment as Chief Minister.[21]

The Khalifah affair soured relations between the Aden authorities and the new Labour administration. On 27 October Trevaskis wrote to Greenwood that 'Khalifa's release, against which I clearly advised you, has had the most embarrassing consequences.'[22] Trevaskis regarded the decision as a significant victory for the radical opponents of British influence. By contrast, Greenwood believed that at least some members of the PSP could be persuaded of the benefits of the British connection and that they would prove more durable allies than the federal rulers, who were unlikely to ever be recognised as anything other than British proxies. The tension between Greenwood and Trevaskis culminated when Trevaskis returned to London in order to assist his wife's recovery from the continuing trauma induced by the airport incident. He was absent from Aden for the whole of November and Greenwood decided to appoint a replacement. His rationale was that Trevaskis 'may well be too committed to the earlier policy to be able to steer the new one through successfully and with the necessary appearance of personal conviction.'[23] Richard Turnbull was quickly selected as Trevaskis's successor but the choice was not an entirely fortunate one. Turnbull was an African specialist and soon came to regard the complex machinations that characterised Arab politics as both bewildering and distasteful. He inherited an almost impossibly difficult situation and over the following two years oversaw the further deterioration of Britain's position. After his dismissal in May 1967 he, like Trevaskis, felt embittered at his treatment by the British government; unlike Trevaskis he did not publish an extended indictment of Labour policy.

There was justifiable annoyance among Labour ministers about the extent of the problems which were inherited from the Conservatives and a much less justified belief that the Aden nationalists provided an alternative basis for continued British influence. Gordon Walker's first thought on taking over from Butler as Foreign Secretary was that the federation did 'not appear ... to have the makings of a viable state.'[24] Subsequently, at a crucial point in the debate over Aden's future, Wilson suggested that the federation itself was 'a sacred cow'.[25] The problem for Wilson and his colleagues was to establish an effective alternative political structure and this was never achieved. Greenwood's instinct was to seek a reconciliation with the Aden nationalists. He travelled to Aden at the end of November and, on his return, pressed for a number of concessions, including the lifting of restrictions on newspaper publishing and right of assembly, the release of detainees, the return of exiles, and some reform of industrial relations legislation.[26] The natural partner in this enterprise was the cautious, flexible leader of the union movement and the PSP, al-Asnaj. Just a few months before the elections he had impressed the Labour Party's Commonwealth and Colonies Group as a potential ally.[27] One of Greenwood's first acts as Colonial Secretary was to offer him a nominated seat on the Aden Legislative Council. His refusal indicated the absence of trust between the Aden authorities and even the more moderate members of the opposition.[28] Still more significantly, the escalation of the terrorist campaign in the last months of 1964 further polarised attitudes. The Aden High Commission was reluctant to implement Greenwood's policy of reform at a time when they were under direct attack, while al-Asnaj and his supporters risked alienating their natural constituency if they showed any signs of appeasing the British. Al-Asnaj was eventually marginalised by the radicals of the NLF precisely because of his willingness to consider some form of compromise over Aden's future.

The prospect of an urban insurrection in Aden on the bloody model of Algiers was made apparent when NLF activists threw grenades into a coffee house on 30 November 1964. Two British servicemen were killed and 14 other people injured as a consequence of the attack. The following month the daughter of a British Air Commodore died when grenades were lobbed through a window into the midst of a children's Christmas party at the British base in Khormaksar.[29] During 1965 grenade and bazooka attacks became a regular feature of daily life in the town.[30] It was convenient for the Aden authorities to explain the new campaign as a reaction to the Labour government's change of policy. However, political violence had been a part of the life of the Colony since 1958 and its origins were in continuing disputes over the status of the immigrant Yemeni community and the frustration of the more educated elements within Aden society at continued British manipulation of their affairs. Greenwood might have wished to plot a reverse course but he was unable to secure any significant relaxation in industrial relations or internal security legislation. His great difficulty was that the continuation of the violence produced an atmosphere that was not conducive to reform. As the Aden authorities accurately indicated, any offer of compromise was likely to be seen as a sign of weakness by the increasingly militant nationalist movement whose overriding ambition was to force the British to implement UN resolutions calling for elections and independence. The first half of 1965 was therefore dominated by a four-way struggle between Greenwood, who prioritised reform; the Aden authorities, whose primary goal was the restoration of order in the town; the federal rulers, who were disturbed by Labour's desire to appease the PSP; and the nationalist movement, which increasingly regarded acts of violence as evidence of commitment to the anti-British struggle. Perhaps the most significant schism was between the new government in Whitehall and Colonial Office officials in Aden. The Observer commented: 'probably never in Britain's history has a secretary of state been represented in a crisis spot by men on the ground whose philosophy is so directly opposed to his own.'[31]

Greenwood initially invested his hopes in a constitutional conference at which the various parties to the conflict would be represented and believed that he had achieved provisional agreement to this idea during his initial visit to Aden in late 1964. This was standard procedure in the process of decolonization but he diverged from the norm by attempting to gather support for the idea of a unitary state to replace the federation.[32] Such a proposal would give more weight to Aden, which had by far the greatest concentration of population, and threatened to marginalise the rulers of the protected states. As such it was designed to appeal to Adenese sentiment. The insuperable obstacle was the attitude of the rulers who were sharp enough to realise that constitutional niceties mattered. Their objections to the proposed end of federalism in turn provoked the Aden Legislative Council who threatened to resign *en masse* in protest at federal obstructionism.[33] The conference had to be postponed and Baharun, whose negotiations with the rulers had embittered both parties, resigned his post as Chief Minister in February 1965.[34] In this polarised atmosphere, the British found it almost impossible to find reliable collaborators. Turnbull chose 'Abd al-Qawi Makawi as Aden's new Chief Minister in the belief that he might co-operate with British plans, while retaining some influence with the nationalists. However, almost from the outset it was evident that Makawi valued his credibility in nationalist circles more than the opinions of British policy-makers.[35] He never established himself as an independent force and his career in Aden politics was to end in tragedy.

Greenwood's solution to the collapse of the putative constitutional conference initiative in February 1965 was twofold: he pressed ever more strongly for concessions to the nationalists in Aden and began work on the establishment of a British commission to devise a constitution which could be presented to the Adenese and the rulers as a basis for negotiation. Both issues were controversial. Turnbull's first few weeks in Aden coincided with the height of the terror campaign and he was blunt in his assessment of the new Labour government's plans for reconciling the urban nationalist movement to continued British influence in the post-independence period: 'Greenwood is wrong as Arabs in Aden will not support us against Arab world. Rulers in the federation would pack up but for our military support.'[36] The American consul in Aden reported widespread astonishment amongst British officials at the ambitious nature of the new government's plans to create a unitary state.[37] For his part, Greenwood was not convinced that the Aden authorities were making sufficient effort to appease nationalist sentiment. In March 1965 he urged Turnbull to try once more to persuade al-Asnaj to join the Aden government.[38] The High Commissioner was recalled to London for consultations and Greenwood reiterated the importance he attached to measures such as freedom of association and franchise reform in Aden as well as the establishment of a broader party system across the federation.[39] Turnbull remained hostile to al-Asnaj who he regarded as a 'puppet of the Egyptians.'[40] His principal concern was the security situation inside Aden and in June Greenwood again expressed dissatisfaction at his failure to proceed with any substantial measure of liberalisation.[41]

The creation of a constitutional commission proved an even thornier problem than the proposed liberalisation measures. British ministers endorsed the idea on 31 March, in the belief that it was a necessary expedient to convince the nationalists that the government was determined to make some progress towards reform.[42] The dissenting voice was that of Denis Healey, who was in the midst of reviewing British overseas commitments. He argued, with a measure of prescience, that any suggestion that Britain was about to abandon its military presence in Aden would aggravate still further the security situation. It was suggested that even the establishment of a commission could be interpreted as a weakening of British determination to resist Egyptian pressure. This raised the danger that local collaborators would decide to 'immediately reinsure with Nasser.'[43] To circumvent such possibilities it was essential to carefully select the members of the commission. Initially Greenwood proposed that, to appease international and Adenese opinion, there should be a Muslim member from Pakistan, Malaysia, Sudan or Tunisia and a nominee of the UN Secretary General, U Thant.[44] There was some scepticism among ministers about the idea of Muslim and UN nominees and months of speculation ensued concerning the likelihood of the Commonwealth or the UN producing acceptable candidates. Negotiations with U Thant proved fruitless because, on the one hand, the British were determined that 'we in fact if not in form should have the final say in their selection', while on the other, U Thant was under pressure from the Committee of 24 not to compromise with British colonialism.[45] Greenwood later recalled: 'I tried very hard and expected more from the Committee of 24, perhaps I was naïve.'[46]

U Thant's rejection of British requests that he produce a list of candidates in mid-May made the appointment of a Muslim member to the Commission both more urgent and more difficult. This issue was complicated by the activities of the Aden Legislative Council and the politics of the Commonwealth, from where the British hoped to find a reliable candidate. Makawi was a captious alternative to Baharun and was anxious not to be seen to be collaborating with the British. He gave a 'very cold reception' to Turnbull when he first raised the idea of constitutional commission at the start of April 1965. It was at his instigation that the Aden Legislative Council voted the following month for the immediate implementation of UN resolutions. In a further act of provocation Makawi accused British troops in Aden of behaving 'like madmen'.[47] Turnbull recorded on 24 May that the Aden government had 'ostentatiously nailed its colours to the UN resolution.'[48]

Makawi's efforts to hinder the establishment of an effective constitutional commission culminated in July. After much haggling Greenwood had eventually settled upon a Sudanese candidate who, he hoped, would have more credibility in the Arab world than a Nigerian or Pakistani. Makawi responded to the announcement that the Sudanese government had appointed a delegate to the commission by writing to Khartoum urging them to withdraw their candidate. To the consternation of the British, the Sudanese government acquiesced.[49] Makawi then surpassed even this provocation by banning the two newly appointed British commissioners, Noel Coulson and Evelyn Hone, from entering the Colony on the grounds that they were 'illegal immigrants'.[50]

Following the collapse of the planned London conference in February and the damage inflicted to the commission by Makawi in July, the constitutional resources available to Greenwood were threadbare. Nevertheless, he made a second trip to Aden and with considerable ingenuity a third and final constitutional contrivance was fashioned: the summoning in London of a working group to establish the agenda for future negotiations.[51] Greenwood was eager that opposition figures should attend.[52] He continued his pursuit of al-Asnaj and wrote him a personal letter requesting that he represent the PSP on the working party. Shaykhan al-Habshi of the SAL was also invited to attend.[53] Greenwood was delighted that both accepted but when the working group met in London at the start of August al-Asnaj was insistent that the agenda for any future conference must be predicated on the full implementation of UN resolutions. He gained strong support for this line from the delegation representing the Aden Legislative Council. Greenwood explained that the government could not accept UN resolutions because they were incompatible with the emergency measures which were essential to the maintenance of order in Aden. By 7 August it was clear that the meetings of the working group were generating further animosity and Greenwood terminated proceedings.[54]

The inability of the government to realise any political solution emboldened the urban guerrillas recruited by the NLF and OLOS leadership. Without any prospect of a negotiated settlement the British counterinsurgency campaign in Aden proved ineffective. This was only partially a consequence of the absence of any concessions with which to win over moderates. The ruthless targeting of British personnel and Arab collaborators by the radical nationalists was brutal but effective. From the outset of the campaign British intelligence operations were unsatisfactory and this failing was compounded by the astute decision of the guerrilla groups, probably guided by Egyptian intelligence, to assassinate Arab members of Aden's special branch. After the NLF and OLOS killed a number of his colleagues the most senior Arab working for Special Branch defected to Yemen in February 1965.[55] By the end of July all of the Arabs employed by the Aden Intelligence Committee either informally or with Special Branch had resigned or been assassinated.[56] The foundering of diplomacy and the flourishing of political violence finally convinced Greenwood's colleagues that his strategy had failed. During the first few days of September 1965 the British Speaker of the Aden Legislative Assembly, Arthur Charles, was fatally wounded by a sniper outside his local tennis courts; a British police-man, Harry Barrie, was shot dead in his car; and the British head of the dwindling Special Branch, Bob Waggitt, narrowly escaped a similar fate.[57] To the fury of Turnbull, Makawi refused to condemn the killing of Charles. Federal ministers were even more incensed by the apparent collapse of order in Aden and by the continuing insistence of the Aden Legislative Council that UN resolutions should be implemented. Muhammad Farid, who was gradually assuming the dominant role previously played by Sharif Husayn in federal circles, told Turnbull that the rulers 'had come to the end of their tether and would not be fobbed off with words any more.' Turnbull recom-mended the imposition of direct rule on the grounds that 'we must devise some immediate means of getting ourselves off the hook upon which we now seem to be dangling.'[58]

On 23 September 1965 ministers agreed to suspend the constitution and impose direct rule. Greenwood felt humiliated by this repudiation of his policy. His first reaction to events in Aden was to minute that he hoped 'there will be no threat to suspend the constitution'.[59] After his advice was ignored he warned Wilson that the suspension of the Aden government was 'a grave mistake' and that 'repression is unattractive under any circum-stances but it is quite insufferable if it is not accompanied by a political initiative.'[60] However, the abandonment of the carefully negotiated Aden constitution was a product of longstanding British inability to reconcile the Aden moderates with the federal rulers. The former group had always resented their forced integration into the federation. In the increasingly violent atmosphere that prevailed during 1965 they had no incentive for compromise with the British. After 12 months of attempting to fashion a deal between the Adenis and the Sultans through concessions to the former, from September 1965 the Labour government found themselves committed to the federal rulers by default. They were the only group that could potentially act as agents of continued British influence after independ-ence. The source of their reliability was the common interest which they shared with the British in resisting Egyptian ambitions. Events in the Pro-tectorates and Yemen during the first year of the Labour government demonstrated that, despite the chance of tactics adopted by Greenwood in Aden, the containment of Nasser remained the first priority of British strate-gists.

Sowing rancour

The Wilson administration continued the Conservatives' policy of non-recognition of the Republican regime and pursued a counter-insurgency strategy in Yemen and the Protectorates, which was quite as vigorous as that of the Home government. Wilson, Greenwood and George Brown have been criticised for their allegedly supine attitude towards Arab nationalism, not least by the outgoing High Commissioner, Kennedy Trevaskis.[61] Greenwood's failure to placate Adenese opposition groups and Brown's subsequent correspondence with Nasser are said to have demonstrated the bankruptcy of appeasing Arab radicals. However, as the imposition of direct rule demonstrated, the policy of conciliation was pursued by fits and starts and needs to be set alongside British actions in Yemen and the Protectorates. The campaigns conducted there suggest that the Labour government was willing to embrace military as well as diplomatic methods in fending off the nationalist threat to British prestige. From the fragmentary records available for the post-1964 period it is evident that the conflict between the Egyptians and the British escalated in these years. The details of the policy debate amongst Wilson's ministers over the Yemen Civil War are absent but it is possible to construct a rationale for the increased use of special operations across the frontier and also to provide evidence of the covert activities conducted by the British. An analysis of this kind indicates that British policy-makers remained determined to prevent the Egyptians gaining a toehold on the Arabian peninsula.

The first and most obvious explanation for an increase in keeni-meeni over the border was to counter the terror campaign in Aden. There is little reason to doubt the repeated asseverations of the authorities in Aden that the Egyptian Intelligence Service in Yemen co-ordinated and armed opposition groups in Aden and the Protectorates. An official report into internal security issues which was completed in January 1965 stated: 'Nasser's activities and his announced intention of driving the British out of the Aden base leave no doubt that the real enemy of the Federation is Egypt.' It recommended an expansion of federal forces to deal with the threat.[62] With casualties in the urban warfare in the south mounting, it was natural that the British should strike back against Nasser in the north. The usual policy of the British was to follow the two-for-one principle: for every mine planted in the Protectorates or grenade thrown in Aden, the British distributed double the number along the Yemen frontier or in Ta'izz; for every raid south of the border, two raids were conducted into the north.[63]

Perhaps more significant than the imperative to punish the Republicans for sponsoring insurrection in Aden and the Protectorates was the need to get the Egyptians out of Yemen altogether in order to secure the future independence of the whole region. The Labour government did not have the same ideological affinity with the Royalists or the federal rulers as the Conservatives but they were equally determined to encourage some form of Yemeni particularism as an alternative to Nasserite pan-Arabism. In Aden this tendency manifested itself in an unsuccessful attempt to cultivate 'moderate' nationalists; in Yemen the emergence of a 'third force' attached to neither Republicans nor Royalists attracted British support. The 'third force' had its origins in the Free Yemeni movement, which had campaigned for the reform of the Imamate since the 1930s. It consisted of Republicans disillusioned with the overbearing manner of the Egyptians and tribal leaders who had no sympathy for Republicanism but who had their own grudges against the Hamid al-Din. They established their independence from Egyptian control when a number of politicians associated with third force ideas, including Muhammad al-Zubayri, Ahmad Muhammad Nu'man and the future North Yemeni President, Abd al-Rahman al-Iryani, resigned from al-Sallal's Cabinet in December 1964.[64] In that month the Aden authorities advised Greenwood that 'to give some encouragement to anti-Egyptian Republicans may be at least as effective as our recognition ... of the Royalists.' Gordon Walker and Greenwood sanctioned an approach to the Saudi monarch, Faysal, suggesting co-operation in support of the third force.[65] Although Faysal was unenthusiastic at this stage, this did not discourage the British from giving various forms of support to anti-Egyptian elements within Yemen.

Covert operations were perhaps the most significant element in British opposition to the Republicans and Egyptians. On 29 January 1965 Stewart set out the range of options available for the conduct of special operations inside Yemen. There appears to have been broad support for continuation of the kind of tactics adopted by the previous government, which had been code-named RANCOUR. A new round of covert operations entitled RANCOUR II was authorised.[66] This encompassed British support for the Royalists and tribal dissidents opposed to the Egyptian presence in Yemen. The reliance on unaffiliated tribal elements that were hostile to the Egyptians did not entirely preclude some continuing assistance to the Royalists. The Conservative government had begun to provide the Imam's forces with substantial assistance in the spring of 1964 and the continuation of this policy under Labour is evident from the complaints of the key Royalist general 'Abdullah bin Hasan during a visit to Aden in November 1965. He was provided with accommodation by the High Commission but protested that the British would only supply his forces with grenades rather than guns.[67] Partly because of these tensions between the British and Badr's marshals the majority of British covert support appears to have been directed to tribes which were not officially a part of the Royalist coalition.

The Americans were well aware of RANCOUR and their consul in Aden, Curtis Jones, provided his government with details concerning the substance of these operations. In October 1965 he was contacted by a Shaykh from the Sabir tribe in Yemen who arranged to meet him in one of Aden's many back alleys. The Shaykh had been employed by the Republican government but told Jones that 'he became convinced several months ago that the Sallal-Amri clique is exploiting the Yemeni people.' He was a typical representative of the third force and, as an influential local leader, an attractive figure to the British. Jones provided a detailed and revealing account of the British role in the affair. He recorded that the Shaykh 'had formed a clandestine organization of 200 people from the Subir area which during the next three months had carried out token bombings near the homes of officials like Sallal and Egyptian intelligence chief Safwat ... the explosives had been obtained secretly from the British in Aden and smuggled into Yemen through Subayhi country. However, things had gone wrong. Some of his relatives in Aden who had been acting as intermediaries in the acquisition of arms had openly appropriated some money and some rifles for their own purposes.' Worse followed as the Shaykh was detained by the Republican authorities and found his connections to the British severed. He appealed to Jones for American arms and money. Despite the Shaykh's useful intelligence Jones rejected this plea.[68] Although the Sabir Shaykh's testimony indicates some of the problems attending RANCOUR II operations, Labour ministers seemed satisfied that they were effective in undermining Nasser's designs. While preparations were being made for British withdrawal in 1967 Lord Shackleton gave an appreciation of their impact: 'RANCOUR operations in the Yemen have been extremely successful. They have been effective both in driving the Egyptians back from parts of the South Arabian frontier and in causing the Egyptians considerable inconvenience by tying down a disproportionate number of Egyptian forces. Information we have received demonstrates that as a result the Egyptians have even been near to losing control in some areas.'[69]

Special operations against the Egyptians in Yemen were complemented by a counter-insurgency campaign in the Protectorates designed to defeat Cairo's surrogates amongst the tribes inside the federation. British policy-makers calculated that Egyptian influence in southwest Arabia could be contained through the employment of counter-measures on both sides of the frontier. Despite the tactical victory in Radfan earlier in the year, by the end of 1964 insurrections were breaking out all across the federation. Egyptian intelligence agents in Ta'izz shipped arms and money to the rebels. On 11 January 1965 the British Commander-in-Chief reported that they were preparing a 'major offensive against British presence here.'[70] Labour ministers and the Chiefs of Staff were informed of the deteriorating situation and in March 1965 authorisation was given for a further round of proscription against dissident tribes inside the federation. Once again the Dali' area was selected: the new campaign took place north of the Radfan in the border district occupied by the Sha'iri tribes.[71]

Operation PARK began in March 1965. The political directive issued by the Ministry of Defence replicated the orders given during the Radfan campaign and required the strict enforcement of proscription. In contrast to the earlier operation, instructions were given to avoid publicity as far as possible.[72] During his tour of Aden and the Protectorates in June 1965 Denis Healey visited the Sha'iri area and expressed strong support for the campaign. Robin Young recorded: 'Mr. Healey himself has said that top priority must be given to defeating this offensive and if in the course of doing so we have to continue our somewhat unpleasant measures as far as the locals are concerned, then I doubt there will be any strong reactions from London.'[73]

As indicated by Young, the Sha'iri tribes suffered considerable hardship following forcible ejection from their homes, British estimates of the number of casualties inflicted are similar to those for the Radfan campaign. Calculations made in December 1965 indicate that approximately 69 dissidents were killed and 101 wounded in the western area of the federation during the previous nine months, the majority of whom would have been Sha'iri tribesmen.[74] The intention of the campaign was to ensure that they suffered considerable privation and, as in the Radfan, this involved the destruction of crops and livestock. On one occasion Sha'iri tribesmen attempted to save their flocks by sending them back to the proscribed grazing grounds accompanied by women and children. The Federal Army was ordered by its British commanders to fire at the returning parties but this caused considerable discontent among the troops after a woman and a baby were wounded during one of these encounters.[75] The federal forces and the RAF also destroyed local property. A Political Officer who toured the region in the aftermath of the campaign recorded that one village 'was destroyed completely by the military, and from what I can gather mistakenly'. In two other villages he found that houses which appeared still to be standing were 'ruined internally'.[76] Although this campaign was ostensibly designed to bolster the authority of the Amir its real purpose was to demonstrate to the tribes that collaboration with the Egyptians would have disastrous repercussions. The Amir of Dali' thought this counter-productive: he feared that, 'by increasing military action against the people of Dhala and by disrupting their lives we would not defeat the dissidents but instead drive people to support them.'[77] The NLF appeared to concur in this analysis and key elements within the Secondary Leadership including Muhammad 'Ali Haytham exploited the issue of RAF bombing during their efforts to proselytise amongst the tribes.[78] These activities demonstrated their worth in 1967 when the majority of the central states, including Dali', fell under NLF control.

The WAP rulers were insistent that the main threat to their authority came not from tribal dissidents but from over the frontier. Egyptian land and air forces continued to make occasional forays into federal territory and the question of how to tackle these transgressions remained a source of tension between the British and the federal authorities. The response of the Wilson government to the demands of the rulers for overt punitive action was continuous with those of their Conservative predecessors: limited authorisation for immediate retaliation and the avoidance, as far as possible, of major incidents likely to attract international attention. On 11 November 1964 Greenwood renewed automatic authorisation for retaliatory fire and counter-battery action by land forces along the frontier. In the aftermath of Harib, however, the British government was wary about authorising RAF raids into Yemen. Although Greenwood did not forbid such measures he insisted on prior authorisation from Whitehall before the Aden authorities initiated any such action.[79] Bayhan remained the focus of the frontier war;

the Egyptians continued to target the Sharif because of the assistance he proffered to Royalist forces and the Sharif continued to complain about British failure to retaliate in sufficient strength. In the aftermath of an attack into Bayhan by Egyptian MiGs on 29 June 1965 the argument between the federal leaders and the British reached a new pitch. The former demanded punitive action. Greenwood responded that he would not be 'rushed by the Federal Supreme Council'. Turnbull was infuriated by Greenwood's attitude and refused to relay his reservations about retaliatory action to the rulers. At this point the Sharif wrote to Greenwood to complain that the British government had 'broken the agreements and failed to honour her pledges.'[80] This marked the final break between the Sharif and the British. The former withdrew from federal affairs and sought to insure his personal position by strengthening his links with the Saudis.

Marking time in Aden

The deterioration of the internal security situation in Aden had forced the Wilson government to reconsider its policies during its first year in office. By the middle of 1965 a consensus was reached that the base ought to be abandoned after independence on the grounds that this would simplify the tasks of rapprochement with the nationalists and the creation of a viable state after independence. This decision was not made public until February 1966 and, when it was announced, it had precisely the opposite effect. In the interim, further attempts to find partners in the process of decolonization foundered on the incompatibility between British desires to establish a non-Nasserite government in waiting and the commitment of all major nationalist figures in Aden to Nasser's agenda. Subterranean forces were at work in Yemen and the federation which would eventually sunder the nationalist movement and allow the British to hand over to a transformed non-Nasserist NLF in November 1967 but, in the aftermath of the decision to impose direct rule, such an eventuality appeared most unlikely. Between September 1965 and February 1966 there was a marked deterioration in Britain's relations with both the nationalists and the federal rulers.

On hearing news of the suspension of the Aden constitution Nasser cancelled plans for a meeting with the visiting Foreign Office Minister of State, George Thomson, to discuss the continuing sour state of Anglo-Egyptian relations. Instead Makawi visited Cairo, in his new role as a nationalist hero, to consult with other opposition leaders. Over the next few months he was influential in bringing about a short-lived compromise between al-Asnaj of OLOS and Qahtan al-Sha'bi of the NLF. Having lost his position as Aden's Chief Minister, Makawi became the publicly declared leader of the new umbrella organisation, the Front for the Liberation of Occupied South Yemen (FLOSY); however, real influence continued to lie with al-Asnaj, Qahtan and Nasser.[81] Makawi's departure prompted yet another British effort to locate moderates within the Adeni nationalist movement with whom they could reach a deal. This task was given urgency by the continuing atmosphere of insecurity generated by nationalist attacks and British reprisals. The declaration of direct rule sparked off a new round of strikes in Aden and Turnbull was forced to make provisional plans to detain the leaders of the opposition. When Wilson received this news he complained that the situation was 'getting out of hand'.[82] He and Greenwood were still eager to find local collaborators in the process of decolonization. Wilson ordered a review of British commitments to the federal rulers. Unsurprisingly, it was found that there was no alternative group willing to deal with the British but they nevertheless persisted in their attempts to develop links with independent opposition figures.[83] The Under-Secretary at the Colonial Office, Lord Beswick, was the most persistent advocate of this approach. He visited the region to assess the situation and later recalled his disbelief that 'the Colonial Office at the time apparently still thought it would be feasible to administer the territory as a Colony.' He favoured 'a fresh start' in contrast to the efforts of the local authorities to 'leave some of these sheikhs in power.'[84] Beswick's criticisms of the reactionary attitude of the Aden High Commission prompted Greenwood to write once again to Turnbull to urge restraint in dealing with the civilian population and to show leniency towards trade unionists with nationalist sympathies.[85]

The corollary to the search for new partners in Aden was a continuing scepticism amongst Labour ministers about the federal future for southwest Arabia that the Conservative government had plotted out. There were differences between the men on the spot and policy-makers in Whitehall concerning the viability of the federal rulers as agents of British influence. While in private ministers hoped that some independent force might emerge between the federal rulers on the one hand and the Nasserites on the other, their public hopes rested on the constitutional commission which, following Makawi's removal, was now free to visit Aden. By this stage the members of the commission had been reduced to two: the former Governor of northern Nigeria, Gawain Bell, and the specialist on east African constitutions, Ralph Hone. The composition of the Hone-Bell commission was strikingly different from Greenwood's initial conception, which had required the inclusion of international delegates whose credentials might carry some weight with Britain's critics. Although the two men were professional in their approach, their status as officials of the British government mitigated against the possibility that their report would gain international acceptance. Nevertheless, after the suspension of the Aden constitution responsibility for producing a formula for constitutional progress devolved to them. Turnbull recorded: 'All our hopes for a rational and traditional solution to South Arabian problem are now centred in Hone and Bell.' The federal rulers were impatient with what they regarded as British temporisation but Wilson instructed them to await the commission's recommendations.[86]

Despite the importance attached to the commission by British officials its deliberations proved ultimately of less significance than the debate taking place in Whitehall over when and how to announce the plan for British withdrawal from the base. On 24 November 1965 ministers made the definitive decision to abandon the base and revoke all defence commitments at independence.[87] They were uncertain about the precise impact that such an announcement would have but the general view was that it would assist them in reaching a compromise with the elusive, moderate, independent Adeni nationalists. Greenwood was convinced that an early announcement was necessary in order to facilitate negotiations with the opposition. He told Wilson there was 'no prospect of any useful political initiative until we can announce our decision about the base.'[88] Turnbull's main concern was that the termination of British military commitments would be interpreted by the federation as an admission of surrender to their enemies. He reminded his superiors that the British were wholly responsible for the federation which 'was an artificial creation brought into being essentially in order to buttress the Aden base; it was economically unviable, socially underdeveloped, politically unstable. By inducing the Federal Rulers to join it we had inevitably brought upon them the hostility of the United Arab Republic (UAR) and much of the rest of the Arab world. At best the announcement of our withdrawal would create great consternation among them.'[89]

Turnbull's warnings about the reactions of the federal rulers were prescient and a number of policy-makers in Whitehall who were aware of the likely impact of the announcement sought to have it postponed. However, the new Colonial Secretary, Frank Longford, and his predecessor, Greenwood, reiterated the argument that public clarification would assist with the process of decolonization. On their account, it would concentrate the minds of local actors on the constitutional talks. Longford suggested: 'if we continued to equivocate we should be open to a charge of bad faith from the Federal Rulers.' As we shall see, it was the alarming content of the announcement rather than any equivocation concerning its timing that was to infuriate the federal rulers. The Cabinet Secretary, Burke Trend, warned of the likely strength of reaction against the proposed military withdrawal but this was not seen as a reason to delay: this difficulty would have to encountered at some point and the Foreign Office case for a postponement was based on the need to continue the policy of containing Nasser. They argued that by declaring an intention to withdraw they risked undermining anti-Nasser leaders in the Gulf, most particularly the Shah of Iran. It might also encourage the Egyptians to halt the putative withdrawal from Yemen to which they were committed following the negotiation of a deal with Faysal. However, the practical objections to postponement proved decisive. Healey successfully argued that delay would complicate the presentation of the Defence White Paper and that the news was almost certain to leak in any event. In light of these considerations, ministers agreed to include plans to withdraw from Aden when the Defence White Paper was published on 23 February 1966.[90] Unlike Greenwood, who visited Aden twice, Longford opted to send Beswick to Aden with the difficult task of explaining the decision to the federal government. As his biographer notes, 'Longford, fundamentally much more interested in domestic than overseas policy and a lifelong reluctant traveller, passed the buck to Beswick.'[91] This was unfortunate in the sense that the rulers always preferred to speak to senior figures but it is doubtful whether Longford's presence would have made any difference to their reaction. The revelation that the base was to be abandoned and that Britain would not defend the federation after independence would, as we shall see, have a detrimental effect on British efforts to conduct an orderly withdrawal but, by this stage, the prospects of a successful decolonization had been diminishing by the year for at least a decade.

Conclusions

The shifts in policy after Labour's election were rather subtler and exhibited a greater degree of ambiguity than has been suggested by those critics who have accused Wilson of scuttle in Aden. Although there was a faction in the Labour Party which regarded the remains of the empire as an embarrassment and a liability, others were committed to the continued world role. Some within the government, including Wilson himself, shared the romantic attachment to notions of imperial responsibility that had marked Conservative policy. They were not persuaded to abandon the Aden commitment as a result of a deliberate calculation of material costs and benefits but because they believed the maintenance of the base was hindering attempts to reach a rapprochement with local nationalists. Wilson and Healey initially argued that retrenchment in defence was compatible with the continuation of a substantial British presence in the Middle East. It was only when the scale of the local problem in southwest Arabia became evident that a dual track strategy emerged: concessions to local opinion in Aden alongside confrontation with Egypt's surrogates inside the federation and across the frontier in republican Yemen. The great obstacle to the success of this strategy was that by the time of his appointment there was actually little Greenwood could do to ameliorate local tensions. The legacy of bitterness generated in Aden by deportations, union legislation, manipulation of the franchise and the shotgun wedding with the federation could not be overcome. Greenwood's mistake was to believe that an offer of complete withdrawal from the base would facilitate a smooth hand over of power to local nationalists. Labour ministers hoped that this could be achieved as gracefully as possible but the overriding aim after February 1966 was to escape from the commitment, while preventing a Nasserist take-over.

Notes

1 Private information.
2 D. Healey, *The Time of My Life* (London, Michael Joseph, 1989), p. 279.
3 PRO: DEFE 4/175, COS60th mtg., minute 3b, 13 October 1964.

4 S. Dockrill, 'Britain's Power and Influence: Dealing with Three Roles and the Wilson Government's Defence Debate at Chequers in November 1964', *Diplomacy and Statecraft* 11 (2000), pp. 211–40.

5 G. Balfour-Paul, *The End of Empire in the Middle East* (Cambridge, Cambridge University Press, 1991), p. 84; K. Pieragostini, *Britain, Aden and South Arabia* (London, Macmillan, 1990), pp. 105–8.

6 S. Dockrill, *Britain's Retreat from East of Suez* (Palgrave/Macmillan, Basingstoke 2002), pp. 51–3.

7 D. Healey, *Time*, p. 280.

8 PRO: FO 371/179751, B1052/5, Brenchley minute, 14 January 1965, Gordon Walker minute, 14 January 1965, Stewart minute, 1 February 1965.

9 B. Castle, *The Castle Diaries 1964–1970* (Weidenfeld and Nicolson, London, 1984), p. 27.

10 PRO: DEFE 4/184, COS 24/65, minute 5, 11 May 1965.

11 According to Castle, Brown later admitted there was 'some truth' in the view that the federation was unsustainable without British military support. See B. Castle, *Diaries*, p. 235. Crossman also recorded that Brown felt 'desperate' about the outcome in Aden. See R. Crossman, *Diaries of a Cabinet Minister, Vol. II* (London, Hamish Hamilton and Cape, 1976), p. 538.

12 T. Little, *South Arabia* (London, Pall Mall, 1968), p. 149.

13 J. Kostiner, *The Struggle for South Yemen* (London, Croom Helm, 1984), pp. 112–13.

14 F. Halliday, *Arabia Without Sultans* (Saqi Books, London, pp. 210–11.

15 J. Kostiner, 'Arab Radical Politics: Al-Qawmiyyun al-Arab and the Marxists in the Turmoil of South Yemen 1963–1967', *Middle Eastern Studies*, 17 (1981), pp. 454–76.

16 PRO: CO 1055/33, Trevaskis (Aden) to Secretary of State, 17 October 1964.

17 D. Ledger, *Shifting Sands* (London, Peninsular Publishing, 1983), pp. 50–2. Ledger provides an extraordinarily detailed account of the planning and execution of the attack which broadly represents the official British version. It is impossible to judge its veracity without corroborating evidence.

18 PRO: CO 1055/89, Trevaskis (Aden) to Secretary of State, 19 October 1964.

19 T. Little, *South*, p. 117.

20 PRO: CAB 148/17, OPD(64)1st mtg., minute 3, 21 October 1964, CO 1055/89, Trevaskis (Aden) to Secretary of State, 20 October 1964, Khalifa letter to Wilson, 21 October 1964.

21 PRO: CO 1055/89, Trevaskis (Aden) to Secretary of State, 22 October 1964, 24 October 1964, 26 October 1964, Secretary of State to Aden, 24 October 1964.

22 PRO: CO 1055/89, Trevaskis (Aden) to Secretary of State, 27 October 1964.

23 PRO: CO 967/433, Poynton to Caccia, 16 December 1964.

24 Lyndon Baines Johnson Library, NSF Country Files, Box 213, Memorandum of a conversation between Rusk and Gordon-Walker, 26 October 1964.

25 PRO: PREM 13/113, Wright to McIndoe, 21 September 1965.

26 PRO: CAB 148/17, OPD(64)16, 30 December 1964.

27 Benn, *Out of the Wilderness: Diaries 1963–1967* (London, Hutchinson, 1987), pp. 117–18.

28 PRO: CO 1055/89, Secretary of State to Aden, 28 October 1964, 9 November 1964, 11 November 1964, Trevaskis (Aden) to Secretary of State, 28 October 1964, Aden (AHC) to Secretary of State, 10 November 1964, 11 November 1964.

29 PRO: CO 1055/202, FO to Cairo, 30 November 1964, Aden (AHC) to Secretary of State, 24 December 1964.

30 K. Pieragostini, *Britain*, pp. 103–4.

31 Ibid., pp. 145–6.
32 PRO: CO 1055, 124, Greenwood to Oates (Aden), 30 December 1964, Secretary of State to Aden, 31 December 1964.
33 PRO: CAB 128/39, CC(65)12th mtg., minute 2, 25 February 1965, CAB 148/18, OPD(65)11th mtg., minute 1, 24 February 1965, CAB 148/20, OPD(65)36, 22 February 1965.
34 PRO: CO 1055/89, Aden (Turnbull) to Secretary of State, 23 February 1965, 24 February 1965, Record of Greenwood-Turnbull conversation, 24 February 1965.
35 T. Little, *South*, pp. 139–41.
36 Mountbatten Papers, MB1/J658, Mountbatten's Handwritten note of Meeting in Aden, 9 February 1965.
37 National Archives, RG 59, Bureau of NEA, Box 2, Wheelock to Aden (Davis), 15 January 1965.
38 C. A. Macleod, *The End of British Rule in South Arabia 1959–1967* (Edinburgh, PhD thesis, 2001), p. 155.
39 PRO: CO 1055/124, Marnham to Turnbull, 9 February 1965, Secretary of State to Aden, 17 March 1965, Aden department note, 19 March 1965, Note of a Meeting with Turnbull, 23 March 1965, Greenwood to PM, 29 March 1965.
40 K. Pieragostini, *Britain*, p. 141.
41 PRO: CO1055/124, Greenwood minute on Aden department note, 15 June 1965.
42 PRO: CAB 148/18, OPD(65)19th mtg., minute 4, 31 March 1965, CAB 148/20, OPD(65)64, 29 March 1965.
43 PRO: PREM 13/112, Greenwood to PM, 30 March 1965, Trend to PM, 30 March 1965, Wright minutes, 31 May 1965, 1 April 1965, Healey to Colonial Secretary, 31 March 1965, 1 April 1965, CO 1055/124, Marnham minute, 31 March 1965.
44 PRO: CO 1055/142, Greenwood to PM, 25 March 1965.
45 PRO: PREM 13/112, Greenwood to PM, 15 April 1965 with Wilson minute, Greenwood to PM, 4 May 1965, Stacpoole (CO) to Wright, 7 May 1965, CO 1055/142, Secretary of State to Aden (Turnbull), 7 May 1965, Aden (Turnbull) to Secretary of State, 8 May 1965, CO 1055/143, Secretary of State to Aden (Turnbull), 22 May 1965.
46 K. Pieragostini, *Britain*, p. 112.
47 Ibid., p. 98.
48 PRO: CO 1055/142, Aden (Turnbull) to Secretary of State, 7 April 1965, 22 April 1965, 29 April 1965, 4 May 1965, 16 May 1965, Turnbull to Marnham 24 May 1965.
49 PRO: CO 1055/143, Aden (Turnbull) to Secretary of State, 17 July 1965, Secretary of State to Aden, 18 July 1965, CO 1055/145, Secretary of State to Aden, 27 May 1965, Khartoum to FO, 1 June 1965, Secretary of State to Aden, 1 June 1965, 5 June 1965, 19 July 1965 with Greenwood minute, 19 July 1965.
50 PRO: CO 1055/90, Aden (Turnbull) to Secretary of State, 20 July 1965.
51 K. Pieragostini, *Britain*, pp. 122–3.
52 PRO: CAB 148/18, OPD(65)33rd mtg., 28 July 1965; CAB 148/22, OPD(65)119, 27 July 1965.
53 IOR: R/20/D/147, Aden (Turnbull) to Secretary of State, 25 July 1965, 28 July 1965.
54 IOR: R/20/D/147, Secretary of State to Aden, 3 August 1965, 4 August 1965, 5 August 1965, 6 August 1965, 7 August 1965.
55 C. A. Macleod, *The End of British Rule in South Arabia 1959–1967* (Edinburgh, PhD thesis, 2001), p. 150.

56 IOR: R/20/D/212, LIC(Aden) Weekly Intelligence Summary, 26 July 1965.
57 Ledger, *Sands*, pp. 65–6; K. Pieragostini, *Britain*, p. 128.
58 PRO: CO 1055/126, Aden (Turnbull) to Secretary of State, 14 September 1965, 16 September 1965, Marnham to Poynton, 17 September 1965, PREM 13/113, Aden (Turnbull) to Secretary of State, 16 September 1965, 21 September 1965.
59 PRO: CO 1055/126, Greenwood minute, 6 September 1965.
60 PRO: PREM 13/113, Greenwood to Wilson, 24 September 1965, CAB 148/18, OPD(65)37th mtg., minute 1, 23 September 1965, CAB 148/22, OPD(65)133, 22 September 1965.
61 J. B. Kelly, *Arabia, the Gulf and the West* (Weidenfeld and Nicolson, London, 1980), ch. 1; K. Trevaskis, *Shades of Amber* (London, Hutchinson, 1968), p. 238; M. Crouch, *An Element of Luck* (London, Radcliffe, 1983), p. 207; S. Harper, *Last Sunset* (London, Collins, 1978), pp. 70–2; J. Paget, *Last Post* (London, Faber and Faber, 1969), pp. 113–15; D. Ledger, *Sands*, p. 100.
62 PRO: DEFE 4/181, COS10th mtg/65, minute 4, 23 February 1965 including WAP Security Committee report, 1 January 1965.
63 Private information.
64 Nu'man was appointed Prime Minister by Sallal in April 1965 but resigned for a second time in June in protest against Nasser's continued interference in Yemeni politics. On the emergence of the third force see: R. Bidwell, *The Two Yemens* (Harlow, Longman, 1983), pp. 209–10; P. Dresch, *A History of Modern Yemen* (Cambridge, Cambridge University Press, 2000), pp. 102–4; E. O'Ballance, *The War in the Yemen* (London, Faber and Faber, 1971), p. 134; D. A. Schmidt, *Yemen: The Unknown War* (London, Bodley Head, 1968), pp. 224–5; T. Little, *South*, pp. 136–7.
65 PRO: CO 1015/6, Aden (AHC) to Secretary of State, 21 December 1964, Jedda to FO, 26 September 1964, Secretary of State to Aden, 1 January 1965.
66 PRO: DEFE 13/710, Healey to PM, 9 February 1965, Wright to McIndoe, 26 March 1965, Peduzie to Reid, 12 October 1965, Poynton to Trend, 15 October 1965. All material pertaining to the details of RANCOUR operations has been removed from this file.
67 National Archives, RG59, Central Foreign Policy Files 1964–66, Box 1864, Jones (Aden) to State Department, 12 November 1965, Box 3024, Tai'zz (Clark) to State Department, 9 December 1965.
68 National Archives, RG 59, Central Foreign Policy Files 1964–1966, Box 1865, Aden (Jones) to State Department, 25 October 1965.
69 PRO: DEFE 13/572, Paper by Lord Shackleton (ud).
70 IOR: R/20/D/36, Commander-in-Chief (Middle East) to Cabinet Office, 11 January 1965.
71 PRO: CAB 148/18, OPD(65)17th mtg., minute 3, 24 March 1965, DEFE 4/183 COS 65/15th mtg., minute 2, 23 March 1965.
72 IOR: R/20/D/158, Chaplin to Commander, Federal Regular Army and Commandant, Federal Guard, 15 March 1965, including Annex A, Political Directive, Baillie to Young, 17 March 1965.
73 IOR: R/20/C/2437, Young to Somerfield, 24 June 1965. For Healey's brief account of his trip see D. Healey, *Time*, pp. 283–4.
74 IOR: R/20/C/2442, Minute of Special Security Meeting in Dali', 14 December 1965.
75 IOR: R/20/C/2437, Somerfield to British Agent, 20 September 1965.
76 IOR: R/20/C/2437, Somerfield to Young, 15 December 1965.
77 IOR: R/20/C/2442, Minute of Special Security Meeting in Dali', 5 May 1966. For the Amir's complaints during the course of the campaign see IOR: R/20/D/2437, Young note for file, 30 June 1965, Somerfield to British Agent, 6 July 1965.

78 J. Kostiner, *Struggle*, p. 100.
79 PRO: DEFE 11/501, Secretary of State to Aden, 16 November 1964.
80 PRO: CO 1055/24, Aden (Turnbull) to Secretary of State, 29 June 1965, 30 June 1965, 2 July 1965, Greenwood minute (ud), Secretary of State to Aden, 4 July 1965, 5 July 1965, Aden (Turnbull) to Secretary of State, 8 July 1965, Amir of Bayhan to Greenwood, 3 July 1965.
81 T. Little, *South*, p. 14; R. Bidwell, *Yemens*, pp. 170–1; J. Kostiner, *Struggle*, p. 114.
82 PRO: PREM 13/113, Eirene White memorandum, 6 October 1965 with Wilson minute (ud).
83 PRO: CAB 148/22, OPD(65)133, 22 September 1965, CO 1055/91, Poynton minute for Secretary of State, 22 September 1965.
84 K. Pieragostini, *Britain*, pp. 149–50.
85 PRO: CO 1055/127, Aden (Turnbull) to Secretary of State, 10 December 1965.
86 PRO: CO 1055/127, Aden (Turnbull) to Secretary of State, 23 October 1965, record of meeting with Federal leaders at Government House, 20 October 1965, Wilson to Chairman of the Federal Council, 13 November 1965.
87 PRO: CAB 148/18, OPD(65)52nd mtg., minute 1, 24 November 1965, CAB 148/24, OPD(65)183, 22 November 1965.
88 PRO: PREM 13/704, Greenwood to PM, 9 December 1965.
89 PRO: CAB 148/78, OPD(O)(AS)(66)1st mtg., 4 January 1966.
90 PRO: CAB 148/25. OPD(66)8th mtg., minute 1iv, 23 January 1966, CAB 148/27, OPD(66)22, 19 January 1966, FO 371/185178, B1052/16, Speares Minute, 6 December 1965, B1052/29, Brenchley minute, 20 January 1966.
91 P. Stanford, *Lord Longford: A Life* (London, Heinemann, 1994), p. 349.

7 Decline and fall of the forward policy 1966–1967

It is sometimes suggested that colonial issues were rarely the subject of con-troversy or even interest in British domestic politics after 1945. Neverthe-less, British policies in Africa and the Middle East did occasionally spark heated debates in Parliament and the press: Palestine, Suez, Biafra and Rhodesia still have resonance even if the details of the events which made them headline news have been forgotten. The case of Aden is somewhat dif-ferent for, although it generated a significant degree of public interest during the 1960s, the episode appears to have faded almost entirely from the popular memory. By contrast, those British officials who were personally involved in the end of British rule in Aden and the Protectorates retained an interest in the affairs of the region and, for them, the decisions made by the Wilson government generated an almost unprecedented degree of bitterness. The Labour government was charged by its critics with causing unnecessary loss of life and of carelessly throwing away British prestige by the decision embodied in the February 1966 Defence White Paper to abandon its defence commitment to Aden and the Protectorates at independence. J. B. Kelly later described it as 'a betrayal of all past undertakings, a betrayal of the trust placed in British steadfastness, a renunciation of an imperial power's recognised responsibilities to its subjects.'[1] Responding to Kelly's criticisms, Thomas Mockaitis pointed to the legacy which the Wilson government had inherited from their Conservative predecessors: an unpopular federation dominated by tribal leaders and an unsuccessful counterinsurgency cam-paign.[2] There is substance to both the Kelly and Mockaitis positions: the Conservatives did build a gimcrack political system with a narrow base of support and the Labour government's decision to suddenly retract the offer of defence assistance did impair efforts to achieve a political resolution. Policy-makers in Britain eventually acknowledged this latter problem and an examination of the post-February 1966 period suggests that they retreated on the policy of decisively cutting commitments. The further dete-rioration of the security situation in Aden after this date, which was aggra-vated by the decision to abandon the base, eventually precipitated an even hastier withdrawal than that envisaged in February 1966. Consideration of these controversies forms a necessary prelude to a discussion of the impact of the Defence White Paper on the ground in southwest Arabia in the first half of this chapter; the second half examines the escalating urban insurrection in Aden, the overthrow of the rulers in the interior and the last minute negotiations which preceded Britain's exit in November 1967.

Labour in retreat

The repeated failure of the various short-term expedients designed to secure wider acceptance of the federation, the continuing lack of any viable alternatives and the deterioration of the internal security situation inside. Aden, led the Labour government to alter long-term planning for southwest Arabia during 1966–67. Under pressure both from the opposition in Parliament and from their own officials on the ground in Aden, they compromised on the goal set in the Defence White Paper of terminating British commitments immediately at independence. The concessions offered were limited by an unwavering determination not to offer a formal defence treaty but nevertheless they did involve the assumption of additional costs at a time of economic retrenchment. The various proposals made to the federal government during this period illustrated the government's desire to fortify local opinion against Nasser's intimidating propaganda. While continuing to tackle Egyptian influence on the ground there was, for the first time since Suez, a commitment at the highest levels of government to some form of rapprochement with Cairo. However, this diplomatic initiative was not universally popular and during the course of the June War of 1967 the anti-Nasser instincts of key officials were once more on display.

After Healey outlined the contents of the Defence White Paper to the House of Commons on 22 February 1966 the Conservative opposition and some key former officials accused the Wilson government of appeasing Nasser. Conservative MPs responded to Healey's statement with noisy denunciations.[3] They argued that in July 1964 Sandys had, on behalf of the British government, promised to defend the federation after independence and that the retraction of this offer would leave Britain's allies defenceless against Egyptian subversion or even armed attack. Hickinbotham and Trevaskis, who was still furious at his dismissal by Greenwood, both criticised the decision in separate letters to the Times.[4] Consideration of the Defence White Paper in general and Aden in particular resumed on 7 March during a Parliamentary debate on a critical opposition motion. Although the Conservatives lost the vote of the following day, Enoch Powell provided an effective critique of Healey's policy and Sandys drew attention to Labour's failure to abide by the commitments to defend Aden and the Protectorates that he had offered federal ministers.[5] This was not an issue of great interest among a wider constituency and it did not feature in the general election campaign which led to the return of Labour to power on 31 March. However, the Conservatives' electoral reverse fortified their determination to discover new ways of embarrassing Wilson and in Aden they believed they had a foreign policy issue which could be exploited to their benefit.

At Prime Minister's questions on 10 May 1966 Lambton asked Wilson whether he accepted that the decision not to offer a defence treaty meant that the federation would now 'have very little chance of survival.' In a poorly conceived rejoinder Wilson suggested that Conservative politicians in London seemed more concerned about this matter than federal ministers in Aden.[6] Two days later Trevaskis wrote to Sandys, with whom he had once had rather frosty relations, enclosing a copy of the reply which federal internal security minister, Sultan Saleh, had made to the message Beswick had delivered in February. This had been supplied to him by another federal minister, Muhammad Farid, and provided damning evidence of the federal government's anger at the decisions contained in the White Paper.[7] The document clearly contradicted the Prime Minister's reply to Lambton and Sandys was delighted by the provision of an unmissable opportunity to embarrass Wilson. On 16 May, with the Saleh statement in his pocket, he asked the Foreign Secretary, Michael Stewart, why Wilson had understated the degree of discontent within the federation in his reply to Lambton. Stewart struggled to find an answer and the press, who were supplied with a copy of the Saleh statement by Sandys, accused Wilson of misleading the House. Sandys obtained 140 signatures for a censure motion but the Conservative front bench were divided over the utility of such action. The Conservative leader, Ted Heath, opted instead to ask Wilson to clarify his position. By this stage Wilson 'was in a towering rage at the carefully planned Conservative plot to discredit him.' He made an unapologetic statement to the House on the matter. His reply to Lambton was justified, he claimed, on the grounds that federal ministers had modified their position since the Beswick visit. Despite the jesuitical character of this response, the unyielding character of his speech broke the nerve of the opposition front bench. Conservative backbenchers continued to snipe at the government over Aden but a full-scale crisis was averted.[8]

The narrowness of Wilson's escape drew ministerial attention once again to the matter of the federation's future. Although they had never had much confidence in this creation, those ministers traditionally committed to the east of Suez role felt that a sudden collapse would damage British prestige in the Middle East. Others saw the demise of the federation as a natural consequence of the manipulation of previous Conservative governments and were eager to wash their hands of an unwanted commitment. The former group had the advantage because the parliamentary situation and constant pressure from the authorities in Aden militated against the complete abandonment of the federation at independence. Over the course of the next year the rulers attempted to embarrass the British government into offering additional protection. When federal ministers visited London during the summer of 1966 they were offered further concessions in order to establish the basis of a viable state for the post-independence period. Initial discussions centred on federal demands for a defence agreement, the re-equipment of federal forces and a guaranteed ten-year aid programme. The Cabinet were not prepared to negotiate on the first point but the last two were carefully considered. Some ministers were concerned at the damage which would be inflicted on British prestige should the federation collapse in the face of Arab nationalism. Prestige had always been a valuable commodity in the thinking of British policy-makers and remained so despite their reluctance to add further to Britain's financial commitments overseas at a time when domestic economic revival was a priority. The best hope of maintaining some British influence was through the nascent armed forces of the federation. These had been gradually expanded and reformed during the previous decade as part of Trevaskis's plans to create a stable pro-British state. In 1961 the Aden Protectorate Levies were redesignated the Federal Regular Army (FRA) and came under the nominal authority of federal ministers. By 1966 this force had expanded to five battalions; it was intended to form the basis of the planned South Arabian Army (SAA) which would have responsibility for internal security and defence following British withdrawal.[9] The rulers regarded the expansion and re-equipment of the FRA as an urgent matter and the fear of an immediate nationalist take-over made the British receptive to these pleas. In May 1966 Stewart proposed that the FRA be expanded to ten infantry battalions and that small coastal and air forces should be created. He insisted that the British Treasury was the only possible source of funding. The Chancellor, Callaghan, doubted the utility of additional expenditure but, despite his protests, Wilson authorised an increase in the British capital grant to the federal forces of £5.5m and additional recurrent military expenditure of £2.5m per annum.[10]

The degree of satisfaction provided by the government's decision to fund the expansion of the federal forces was offset by discontent amongst British officials in Aden and federal ministers with Labour's efforts to reach an accommodation with Nasser. This expressed itself in attacks upon Stewart's replacement as Foreign Secretary, George Brown, as 'Nasser's pen pal'.[11] From Brown's point of view, Nasser was the source of British problems in southwest Arabia and his Egyptian diplomacy constituted an attempt to deal with the source of the problem, rather than contain its effects, which was an approach which had led to Greenwood's downfall. For the first time since 1955 the post of Foreign Secretary was occupied by a politician who was broadly sympathetic to Nasser and to Arab nationalism.[12] His efforts to improve relations with Cairo were hindered by a legacy of mistrust dating back to the creation of the Baghdad Pact in 1955, the most recent manifestation of which was Nasser's decision to break diplomatic relations with Britain on 17 December 1965. Nasser demanded that British diplomatic staff leave Egypt in order to show solidarity with other African states who were campaigning against Wilson's policy of passivity towards the Smith regime following Rhodesia's unilateral declaration of independence. This made the simple tasks of negotiation difficult and required an unconventional approach to diplomacy that Brown was well equipped to supply.[13] During a visit to the Soviet Union in November 1966 Brown discovered that Egyptian Field-Marshal al-'Amr was in Leningrad. He quickly arranged a meeting at which the two men discussed the problems in Anglo-Egyptian relations. The seizing of this opportunity led to a formal correspondence between Nasser and Brown which exhibited agreement on the necessity for improving relations but no consensus regarding Aden's future.[14]

The false optimism regarding the salutary effects of an early British military withdrawal from Aden which Greenwood had generated continued to linger within government after February 1966 and found expression in a desire to expedite evacuation and independence. The likely economic and diplomatic benefits such a policy would yield were made more attractive by the continued stagnation of the British economy and the opportunity for an Anglo-Egyptian rapprochement. The Foreign Office had set 1 January 1968 as a provisional date for independence and withdrawal but in late November 1966 George Thomson suggested moving the date forward to 1 July 1967.[15] This was regarded as impracticable but, with the situation on the ground deteriorating and the prospect of improved Anglo-Egyptian relations available, on 16 March 1967 Brown presented a package of new measures to the Cabinet designed to expedite British withdrawal and federal independence. His plan was to move the date of independence forward two months to 1 November 1967, while offering compensation to the federation in the form of defence guarantees for the first six months of the post-independence period. Thomson was dispatched to Aden with instructions to persuade the federal ministers to accept the earlier date. However, they responded angrily to these new proposals and refused to consider the November deadline. According to their analysis, the federation would not be ready for independence until late 1968 and, in order to have any long-term future, it would require additional military assistance from Britain in the post-independence period. Thomson was shaken by this reaction and recommended the plan be put into 'cold storage'.[16] Back in London, the Cabinet diarist Richard Crossman was dismayed by the refusal of the federal ministers to co-operate in securing an early British exit. He recorded: 'Unfortunately the locals spotted what we were up to. If it paid us to advance the date of independence and get out first and off the land, they were bound to spot this and cause trouble.' The federal reaction was so vitriolic that Brown, who of all the Labour ministers seemed most concerned about breaking previous obligations to the federal rulers, withdrew the proposal.[17]

Following the failures of the Greenwood, Beswick and Thomson missions the next Labour minister sent to Aden in search of a solution was Lord Shackleton who became the informal minister for Aden during the last months of British rule. He arrived in Aden in early May 1967 and soon concluded that the most significant factor contributing to the political turmoil was a lack of confidence in the federation's future. Without any foreknowledge of the impending catastrophic defeat for Nasser in the Sinai but with an acute awareness of the fragility of the federal system which the British had built, he recommended that the government retreat further from its stated policy of terminating any kind of defence relationship at independence. He argued that concessions to the rulers were essential in order to strengthen the federation sufficiently to resist Egyptian pressure and warned that a decision to fix the date of independence at 1 November 1967 'would be too shattering a blow to the confidence of the Federal Government'. As an alternative, he proposed offering either 1 February 1968 or 1 January 1968 as the target date for independence. In an effort to give the federal government a greater appearance of long-term robustness, he advocated the retention of an RAF force of six aircraft at the Khormaksar base for two years after the withdrawal of British ground forces. The Labour Cabinet were not prepared to go this far but they did concede that the federal government required a further offer of assistance in the immediate post-independence period if it was to regain the confidence of the local population.[18] Their ingenious, and economical, solution was to offer air cover from offshore carriers for the first six months after independence. This was too flimsy a concession to appeal to federal ministers who by this stage had lost all confidence in the Labour government. They told Shackleton that his government's latest proposals 'would open the door to massacres and endless trouble.'[19]

As well as increased defence assistance, Shackleton also recommended a change of personnel in Aden. He and George Wigg believed that Turnbull had lost his grip on the situation and that an experienced diplomat was required. Turnbull was ordered to return to London in May 1967 where Brown summarily sacked him. Humphrey Trevelyan, was chosen as Turnbull's successor because of his experience as ambassador in both Cairo and Baghdad.[20] His support for a reconciliation with Arab nationalism can be traced back to his forthright denunciations of Eden's plans to destabilise Nasser during the mid-1950s.[21] Trevelyan's bluntness could be disturbing to friends and foes: Brown complained that the manner in which he presented the conditions of his acceptance of the Aden appointment was 'bloody rude'.[22] Having had his terms met it was evident immediately on his arrival that Trevelyan intended to inject a dose of Foreign Office realpolitik into Adeni politics. The pragmatic manner in which he approached the Arab nationalist threat did not appeal to strident opponents of Egyptian influence inside the federal government. Up to this point, British policy in Aden and the Protectorates had been dominated by the notion that Britain ought to play a continuing role in the region after independence; an idea propagated by the men on the spot and ingested by policy makers in Whitehall. The Conservatives regarded the federal ministers as potential agents of British influence in the post-independence period, while Labour attempted to construct a coalition of moderate nationalists and traditional rulers who would adopt a pro-western, anti-Nasser policy. Trevelyan appears to have calculated that Britain had few material interests at stake in southwest Arabia and his thinking was shaped by the requirement for a successful military evacuation. Although this necessitated continuing vigilance against Nasser and a final effort to bolster the federation these were now means to an end rather than ends qua values. From the outset Trevelyan was eager to expedite the process of withdrawal and informed Brown: 'When a colonial power turns its back it presents its bottom to be kicked. I conclude that we should go as early as possible.'[23]

The first evidence of the greater priority that Trevelyan gave to a successful withdrawal rather than to the defence of the federation was his repudiation of Shackleton's suggestion that Britain ought to retain aircraft at the base. He believed that this would require the continued deployment of two battalions on the ground and that these units would be hostages to fortune. Instead he suggested that it was 'better to concentrate on such offshore support as we can give combined with strengthening the Federal forces.'[24] This did require some concessions to appease federal ministers: on 17 June Trevelyan presented them with a package of proposals which had been approved by the British government two days earlier. They were based closely on his own recommendations and presented with the gloss that this was the best deal yet offered for the post-independence period.[25] On 19 June Brown outlined these latest proposals to Parliament. The offer consisted of new equipment for the federal forces, including armoured cars, field artillery and eight Hunters for a nascent South Arabian air force; a military aid mission; a promise to fund the Hadhrami Bedouin Legion for two years after independence which was conditional upon the EAP rulers agreeing to join the federation; the commitment of a carrier-based fleet to south Arabian waters for six months after independence; and a somewhat vague promise of protection from a V-bomber force stationed at Masirah for an unspecified period.[26]

The reinstatement of January 1968 as the target date for independence and the offer of sea-based air power did not strike the federal government as very convincing evidence of a long-term British commitment to their welfare but they were quite sufficient to alarm the Parliamentary Labour Party who feared that Brown intended to put domestic recovery at risk in order to maintain burdensome east of Suez commitments. Christopher Mayhew accused Brown of 'unconditional surrender to the Conservative Opposition' and Michael Foot expressed 'a great sense of shock' at Brown's apparent desire to extend British commitments. From the opposition benches, Sandys added to Brown's misery by declaring 'once or twice I thought I was listening to myself'.[27] At a meeting of the Parliamentary Labour Party on 28 June further brickbats were hurled at Brown. His thoroughly ingenuous comment that 'we wanted to leave Aden at the earliest possible moment; we wanted to leave in good order; and we did not want to leave "a Congo" behind us' was greeted with overwhelming scepticism. He was urged to limit the V-bomber commitment to six months and chastised for pursuing Conservative policies.[28] These criticisms took little account of events in southwest Arabia which, as so often before, were developing with a speed which left politicians in Whitehall trailing lamely behind.

The federal rulers had been unimpressed with Labour's latest offer of defence assistance and continued to press for further concessions. Trevelyan explained that 'they still seem to want something more.'[29] The 'something more' was a defence treaty. However, their interest in Brown's Commons speech was eclipsed when, on the day after its delivery, the Aden police force and the newly established South Arabian Army mutinied. This was the final watershed moment for British rule in southwest Arabia. It demonstrated decisively that the federation was now dominated by elements hostile to the British and the rulers. After the long succession of disappointing announcements regarding the date of independence and the continuing refusal of the British government to agree to a post-independence defence treaty, the mutiny convinced the federal rulers that they could not hope to maintain the federal system after 1968. They were so demoralised that they offered little resistance to the nationalist take-over of the various federal states during the second half of 1967. In order to account for this sudden collapse it is necessary both to trace the failure of attempts by the federation to acquire greater local and international legitimacy and to consider the inability of the British administration to effectively counter the continuing terror campaign in Aden. It was these developments which provided the context for the mutiny and the subsequent semi-abdication of the federal rulers.

South Arabia after the White Paper

Mistrust of the British government's intentions amongst the population of Aden and the Protectorates had been increasing for some years. Many of the tribal leaders whom the British had transformed into federal ministers had nursed suspicions about the dependability of the British as allies at least since the dismissal of Trevaskis. However, this did nothing to mitigate their anger when in February 1966 Beswick explained that they would receive no military assistance after independence. Shaykh Muhammad Farid, who emerged as a key actor in the remaining months of British rule, described the announcement as 'disgraceful' and 'unbelievable'. Shaykh Husayn Mansur of Dathinah indicated his intention to decamp to Cairo and urged his colleagues to follow him. The general view was that an early compromise with Nasser was a better option than lingering while the British withdrew and the nationalist tide engulfed them. The black mood amongst the federal rulers was matched by that of British officials who were acutely aware that local politics had been manipulated in order to suit Britain's continuing ambitions in the region. They recalled that those who supported the British forward policy 'went right out on a limb. We are now telling the world and them that they will have to fend for themselves.'[30] The danger was that they would suffer the same fate as the Hashemite kings of Iraq, the last of whom was gunned down in his own palace courtyard in Baghdad. One British Political Officer who had advised different ruling families in the WAP and the EAP articulated the widely felt sense of betrayal which the Defence White Paper generated: 'it was seen as the weak climax to a series of disastrous political posturings on the part of our British masters. It gave quite the wrong signal to those who were all too ready to believe the worst of a faded imperial power. It was at the least embarrassing to Britain's supporters and, at worst, death to those friends of ours who were caught in South Arabia.'[31] From the distance of Whitehall there was little sympathy for this case. Aside from his unfortunate Parliamentary performance concerning the Beswick offer, Wilson's only recorded reaction to the gathering dissent on the ground in Aden and the Protectorates was to express disappointment that a lunch offered to the federal rulers at 10 Downing Street two months previously had failed to propitiate them.[32]

Despite Wilson's complacency, British policy-makers hoped to fashion a government which would have a degree of international respectability. This task was complicated by the disillusionment of the federal rulers: after the announcement of the Defence White Paper they had no interest in discussing the proposed constitutional reforms of Hone and Bell. Instead they began searching for some constitutional formula which would have broader support in the Middle East and at the United Nations. The implementation of resolution 1949, which called for British withdrawal and early elections, remained the key nationalist demand. Paradoxically, the Wilson government's decision to terminate defence commitments increased hopes that the federation would be recognised as an independent, rather than neo-colonial, state. Labour ministers had always wanted some form of UN co-operation and in March 1966 the government indicated that it was willing to accept the resolution with a number of provisos.[33] Federal ministers were increasingly concerned about the international climate in the post-independence period once British guarantees of protection had been withdrawn and they therefore welcomed British flexibility on this point. Following consultations with King Faysal of Saudi Arabia, who was regarded as their most valuable potential ally, on 13 May 1966 the Fadli Sultan declared that the federation would accept UN resolutions. On behalf of his colleagues he proposed that their implementation should be discussed at a conference of all political parties. It was hoped this gesture would encourage the more moderate opposition groups to join the government and facilitate international recognition of any new dispensation.[34]

The delusion that the UN would be willing to compromise with the federation was quickly exposed as such. The Wilson government insisted that their acceptance of UN stipulations must be qualified by references to Britain's continuing responsibility for the internal security situation in southwest Arabia.[35] This was insufficient for the Committee of 24 which continued to denounce the British designed federation and stood by its demands for strict and immediate implementation of resolution 1949. On

15 June 1966 they condemned the federal government as unrepresentative, denounced the proposed conference plan and called on the Secretary-General to appoint a special mission to Aden to enforce a solution. This caused dismay in Whitehall. Fred Lee, Wilson's latest and last Colonial Secretary, strongly opposed any compromise with the UN. However, the Foreign Office successfully argued that it was necessary to co-operate with U Thant's mediatory efforts if the new state was to obtain international legitimacy. The Wilson government accepted the proposed special mission on the understanding that its activities should not prejudice either internal security or Britain's treaty obligations.[36] These concessions were sufficient to produce temporary deadlock between the militants and the moderates on the Committee of 24.[37] Continued squabbling inside the UN gave the British and the federation an opportunity to pursue their efforts to broaden their support inside southwest Arabia.

Plans to widen local support for the federation by inviting new elements into the government were a continuation of longstanding British efforts to find non-Nasserite politicians committed to South Arabian particularism rather than Arab nationalism. In May 1966 Turnbull reiterated his commitment to this objective in a message to the Colonial Office which outlined his priorities: aside from creating a constitution which was 'respectable enough not to disgrace us' and the successful conduct of a military withdrawal, he listed his third key aim as the creation of 'a successor Government that will be sufficiently stable and sufficiently well disposed towards HMG ... to prevent the Egyptians from making our position in the Gulf too hot to hold.'[38] The fractious nature of opposition politics had always made the accomplishment of these goals a matter of superior skill and a great deal of luck. Nationalist groups tended to compete with one another in demonstrating the trenchancy of their anti-British convictions and this made them wary of negotiations with the imperial power. Nevertheless, in the last two years of British rule this divisiveness did have some compensating advantages. While maintaining a public front of obduracy, some key figures began to consider compromise with the British. Although nothing of substance came of these efforts, the increasing drift away from Nasserism tended to soothe British worries about a nationalist domino effect in Arabia. There was always a strong element of Adeni, rather than Arab, nationalism in the town, while in the Protectorates the tribes remained resolutely more concerned about their own kith and kin than the wider struggle. The incorrigible parochialism of politics in southwest Arabia was evident from the course of the Civil War in Yemen, where Egyptian attempts to consolidate their influence were constantly undermined by the priority which local actors gave to local disagreements. Between February 1966 and November 1967 a series of realignments occurred amongst the Egyptian sponsored opposition movements which eventually resulted in the triumph of a radicalised NLF committed to a socialist programme and shorn of its pro-Nasser cadres. The decisive split occurred at the Khamir conference in November 1966 when the Secondary Leadership of the NLF repudiated the merger with FLOSY which had been negotiated three months previously.[39]

Ideological disagreements and personal rivalry generated differences between and within opposition parties. The detailed manoeuvres of the various groups remain opaque but the British were aware of the extent of the disagreements in the opposition camp and were eager to exploit this factionalism as part of their campaign to contain Egyptian influence. The SAL was dominated by Protectorate notables and continued to favour a moderate programme that balanced anti-imperial politics with a desire to prevent a social revolution or Egyptian domination. The key figures in the SAL were Muhammad al-Jifri and the expelled Sultan of Lahj, 'Ali abd al-Karim. In light of recent history they were cautious about any rapprochement with either the British or the current set of federal ministers. Nevertheless, their activities were of interest to the British and contemporary intelligence assessments indicated that the SAL had increased their influence as an alternative to Egyptian dominance. At the other extreme, the so-called Secondary Leadership of the NLF were committed to a programme of radical social change which appealed to those in Aden and the Protectorates who were disillusioned with the British, Nasser, the federal rulers and the Adeni politicians. Their spokesman Qahtan al-Sha'bi had previously been responsible for agricultural policy in Lahj and was a bitter rival of al-Asnaj.[40] Although the precise reasons for the NLF split from FLOSY were ill-defined, the British had a broadly accurate picture. They were aware that: 'A proportion of the NLF in Aden seem to have resisted Egyptian attempts to include it in FLOSY, and may pursue its own campaign possibly by violent means.' However, British intelligence estimated that it was a third group, consisting of those FLOSY cadres loyal to Nasser, which was most likely to win the struggle for power in Aden and the Protectorates. It was expected that, as a first step in this direction, the Egyptians would attempt to establish FLOSY as a provisional government in exile.[41]

On the basis of this assessment of the opposition groups, the British and the federal leaders first courted the previously ostracised SAL leadership and later the NLF in order to forestall a FLOSY victory which would effectively mean a triumph for Nasser. Federal ministers held a first round of secret talks with SAL leaders and dissident FLOSY elements in Beirut in April 1966. The willingness of such groups to attend raised hopes that a provisional government could be formed consisting of the current federal government, the SAL leaders and FLOSY dissidents.[42] Turnbull suggested that such an administration might contain ten federal ministers, four representatives from Aden and 'Half a dozen "Progressives".'[43] In pursuit of this goal, the British were assiduous in cultivating their old SAL adversary, Muhammad al-Jifri, who was issued with a British passport which enabled him to return to Aden, eight years after the British had expelled him.[44] The most prominent of the potential FLOSY dissidents, al-Asnaj, did not attend the Beirut meeting but was contacted by Muhammad Farid on behalf of the

federation in June. Labour politicians in Britain had always regarded negotiations with al-Asnaj as a significant prize. During his trip to Aden Healey
enquired personally about the prospects of a deal with al-Asnaj. Cornering
him proved no easy matter in the context of an increasingly bitter and
violent struggle within the nationalist movement: his elusiveness was attri-
buted to fear that he would be killed if he visited Aden.[45] Despite the difficulties in achieving a rapprochement with al-Asnaj, the British achieved
some tangible successes in their efforts to exploit divisions within FLOSY:
following a second secret meeting of federal ministers and nationalist leaders
in July, two FLOSY notables were lured back from Cairo. The ex-Fadli
Sultan, who had fled to Cairo in the midst of the London constitutional talks
two years previously, and the prominent 'Awdhali leader, Jaabil bin Husayn,
renounced their alliance with Nasser. Nevertheless, the British were disappointed that the latest round of talks failed to secure a formal alliance
between SAL and the federation.[46] Prior to a third round of discussions in
Beirut in October, Turnbull noted that the 'important thing' for the federal
rulers was to encourage 'Ali and the Jifris to join a reconstituted government
'because whatever their other views they oppose the Front and oppose the
Egyptians.'[47] At this final meeting the SAL leaders insisted they would not
accept posts inside the federal government. Sultan Saleh, who had taken the
lead in this long series of negotiations, reported that they were 'not prepared
to join the Federal Government at this juncture or to partake in discussions
on constitutional reform.'[48]

The continuing coyness of both the Committee of 24 and the SAL despite
the long courtship of the federal government left the British authorities
with no alternative but to proceed with the requisite constitutional reforms
with the federal government on a bilateral basis. On 22 October 1966 Turnbull suggested to Sultan Saleh that the federation's political system should
be centralised. The new federation should have a Head of State or President
and a Prime Minister; the former would be from the Protectorates and the
latter from Aden.[49] Unfortunately, the natural choice for Head of State,
Sharif Husayn had retreated to Bayhan nursing the conviction that the
British could not be trusted. This left two rival candidates: Sultan Saleh of
'Awdhali and Shaykh Muhammad Farid of 'Awlaqi.[50] A further complica-
tion was the desire of the authorities in Whitehall for some form of elections
in southwest Arabia prior to independence. This inclination was associated
with the persistent hope that UN involvement would be useful either in
securing a more broadly based government prior to independence or, at
least, in implicating the international community in whatever solution
emerged from the morass of local politics.[51] Following disagreements in the
Committee of 24 over the prospects for the Secretary-General's putative
special mission to southwest Arabia, representatives of local parties were
called to New York in November 1966 to parade their credentials before the
relevant General Assembly Committee. As the suavest of the current ministers Muhammad Farid defended the federation's record but his case for

building a new administration on the base of the current dispensation was rejected. On 12 December the General Assembly passed resolution 2183 calling again for the implementation of previous UN resolutions and for the appointment by the Secretary-General of a special mission to advise on the holding of elections.[52]

The notion of any form of ballot prior to independence was anathema to British officials in Aden. Their hopes continued to rest on the calling of a constitutional conference. Following consultations between Turnbull and Brown in December 1966 a timetable was drawn up which suggested that a UN mission could be accommodated in February or March 1967, prior to the holding of a constitutional conference on southwest Arabia.[53] By this stage there was a pervasive atmosphere of pessimism surrounding the likely future of the region. Robin Young reported: 'South Arabia is a like a Shakespearean stew, full of strange ingredients and giving off at times a not very savoury aroma . . . There is an increasing danger of the potage boiling over and leaving little more than a very nasty mess'.[54] At the other end of the chain of decision-making Harold Wilson noted that the latest reports of the Joint Intelligence Committee made 'pretty gloomy reading' and sought a way out with 'the minimum of damage and discredit.'[55] This pessimistic outlook accounts for the decision to co-operate with the UN mission despite the fact that the commissioners were unwilling to accept the legitimacy of the federal government.[56] By this stage, the Wilson government was prepared to consider almost any alternative which promised some form of resolution. The three commissioners appointed by U Thant on 23 February 1967, Manuel Perez-Guerrero of Venezuela, Abdul Sattar Shaliza of Afghanistan and Mousa Leo Keita of Mali, were not regarded as sympathetic to British goals but it was hoped that they could be persuaded of some of the impracticalities involved in the immediate application of the UN formula.

The commissioners visited London on 21 March prior to flying to Cairo and Aden. Brown urged them to 'encourage opposition elements to join in a constitutional conference on the basis that the task was to broaden the basis of power and not merely to destroy authority.' The cautious optimism that the commissioners might prove useful in securing international recognition of a new government was dissipated by the farcical events that ensued following their first appearance in Aden on 2 April.[57] Their arrival was presaged by an almost unprecedented downpour the previous day. The subsequent floods temporarily subdued the expected popular protests but by 3 April strikes and riots were in full swing across the Colony. Turnbull's intention was to offer the commissioners a welcome lunch and then introduce them to federal ministers but they refused to have any contact at all with representatives of the current government. Instead they retreated to the Seaview hotel which was a reasonably safe distance from the gathering disturbances. After a couple of days in purdah on 5 April they asked to speak to the nationalist detainees. Turnbull transported the commissioners to the detention camp but riots broke out as soon as the prisoners became aware of their presence. They escaped the violence by making an undignified exit in a British helicopter. The commissioners blamed the British for the fiasco and vented their frustration by taping a statement which condemned the federation as a vehicle for British imperialism. At this point, the patience of federal ministers snapped. When they discovered that the mission intended to broadcast their diatribe in support of the opposition nationalist movement they ordered the confiscation of the pre-recorded tape. Consequently, when the commissioners sat down in their hotel room, eager to listen to their broadcast, they heard instead the jaunty theme tune to the popular television western series, Bonanza. This provocation persuaded the commissioners to pack their bags in order to avoid any further humiliation. In this they were again disappointed for a major argument broke out at the airport when the RAF police insisted on searching their luggage. Invective and cursing flew back and forth between the commissioners, the policemen and delighted journalists before Perez-Guerrero finally agreed to have his baggage inspected. The mission retired to Geneva never to return.[58] During the following months they conducted interviews with relevant parties but, like the British, they found themselves drifting in the wake of the decisive developments of June 1967 which were the culmination of the ongoing struggle which they had witnessed on Aden's streets.

The battle of Aden

The political atmosphere during the last two years of British rule in Aden was contaminated by violence and intrigue. There were numerous sources of this mephitis: from the base at Khormaksar and the centre of British administration at Steamer Point issued forth a stream of *agents provocateur*, mercenaries destined for Yemen and intelligence officers working on the dirty tricks to be employed along the frontier; on the streets of Aden, British servicemen rapidly grew disillusioned with the British civilian leadership and contemptuous of the Arab population and their counter-measures became correspondingly brutal; in the frontier town of Sheikh Uthman and inside the volcano of Crater, terror organisations planted bombs, threw grenades and plotted against one another and the British. Although the majority of the residents wished to keep out of the way of both sides this was increasingly difficult when neither the British army nor the terrorists were willing to take much time in distinguishing between neutral bystanders and potential enemies. The blurring of lines of authority and, in particular, the difficulty of distinguishing those actions which were endorsed by the British government from those undertaken on individual initiative makes it difficult to assign responsibility for specific incidents but it is evident that the Aden government and the British armed forces were unable to maintain security in the town and were responsible for casualties amongst the civilian population.

From late 1965 violent attacks on British facilities and clashes between rival factions became persistent features of life in Aden. Individuals from many different backgrounds became caught up in the fighting, including the mass of unskilled manual workers and the army of clerks and bureaucrats who staffed the offices of private companies and governmental institutions. Contemporary interviews with detainees who admitted their involvement in the opposition groups provide some insight into their membership. Among those who confessed to NLF or FLOSY membership were a 24 year old Yemeni who had been employed by Cable and Wireless but subsequently became 'committed to the terrorist campaign against the British' and a 36 year old illiterate road sweeper who joined the NLF after being sacked from a job at the BP refinery because of his involvement in trade union activities. Other detainees belonged to the aristocracy of old Aden and included the scion of 'a well-to-do and respected Aden family' who had spent a year at St John's College, Oxford, before becoming a civil servant and a 25 year old Adeni footballer of Indian extraction who had worked for the Post Office. Their accounts illustrate the connections between the politics of Aden and the wider Arab world: a number told the British that their organisations had close connections to George Habash's Arab Nationalist Movement, while most had received training in either Cairo or Yemen.[59]

There is little evidence to suggest any significant differences in the social composition of the opposition groups. It was on ideological and personal grounds that the Secondary Leadership of the NLF, who were committed to a Marxist programme, refused to integrate into FLOSY, which remained broadly pan-Arab in its official ideology. Following the failure of Nasser's attempt to impose unity on the opposition, fighting between the factions intensified in early 1967. The Egyptians responded to the NLF's intractability by forming a para-military branch of FLOSY, known as the Popular Organisation of Revolutionary Forces (PORF) which targetted rival organisations. Egyptian intelligence agents in Ta'izz were responsible for supplying and co-ordinating PORF attacks. They continued to plant mines and hurl grenades at British defence facilities but, in addition, PORF cadres attempted to assassinate NLF leaders. The latter responded in kind and the situation was further complicated by the activities of the SAL. Both the SAL and the NLF had close contacts with the federal administration. The history of the terror campaign in Aden is too complex to recount in detail but the fate of the prominent FLOSY leader and former Aden Chief Minister, Makawi, is illustrative of the anarchy into which Aden began to descend in early 1967. From January Makawi and the other FLOSY leaders were in open competition with the NLF for the support of the Aden population. All were well aware that the victorious party would have the opportunity to replace the British at independence. Strikes, demonstrations and the assassination of collaborators and rivals were the currency of the struggle.[60] The eighth anniversary of the federation on 11 February 1967 was portentously named the Day of the Volcano and singled out for a test of strength between the opposition groups. In response, the Aden authorities deployed British regular troops on the streets of Crater to break up assemblies and impose a curfew after dark.[61] The thwarting of mass action on the Day of the Volcano placed a greater premium on assassination and Makawi was singled out by the NLF as a prominent FLOSY target whose death would demonstrate the inability of Britain to contain the increasing mayhem in Aden. On the night of 27 February a bomb was found outside Makawi's house. It exploded before it could be defused and three of his children were killed in the blast. Large crowds turned out for the funerals and this provided the pretext for armed combat between rival activists which culminated with a siege of SAL headquarters by FLOSY supporters. The former group were widely suspected of involvement in the Makawi assassination. British regular forces were again called upon to break up the demonstration, which they did only after the SAL fighters suffered significant casualties. The British could take no comfort from the determination of the opposition groups to attack one another because they remained targets themselves. On the night of the funerals a landmine exploded in the midst of a cocktail party in Ma'ala attended by British officials. Two women were killed outright by the explosion. Egyptian propaganda was more concerned to assign responsibility for the deaths of Makawi's children, which they blamed on a conspiracy between the British, the federal rulers and the NLF.[62]

The disillusionment of Aden's residents with British rule was not merely a consequence of Egyptian propaganda and intimidation. Indeed, what made the exaggerated reports of atrocities which filled Radio Cairo convincing was that they mirrored the experience of the population living in Aden. The anti-British feeling of the town's large Yemeni community had been the foundation upon which the successes of the Trades Union movement had been built. After the declaration of the state of emergency the final fringe elements of support for the British amongst the older families disintegrated under the combined pressure of the nationalist terror campaign and British counter-measures. The activities of Egyptian intelligence agents operating from Yemen were a source of concern for the small number of Adenis who were inclined to support the imperial power. British statistics indicate that it was the local civilian population which suffered the most during the fighting. It was estimated that during the course of 1966 five British servicemen were killed in Aden and 216 wounded, while 33 civilians were killed and 315 wounded.[63]

As far as a clear British counter-insurgency strategy existed it consisted of making use of deportations, internment and tough action on the streets in order to capture or kill those responsible for the terror campaign. Deportations had always been a controversial weapon in the British arsenal of counter-measures but they remained a measure of first resort for the authorities. The murder of an Adeni delegate to the Federal Council in August 1966 raised British fears that the campaign of intimidation against those seen to be collaborating with them might further damage already battered confidence in the Aden authorities. Turnbull told the Foreign Office that he was responding by 'doing what we can to step up our periodical action to deport Yemeni undesirables (human riff-raff, unemployed etc.).' The authorities rounded up 105 unemployed Yemenis and transported them over the border into Yemen, despite the absence of any evidence of their involvement in terror attacks.[64] Approximately 200 people were deported from Aden during the month of August and a further 90 during September.[65]

The second element of the British counter-insurgency strategy was internment. As in the case of deportations, a latitudinarian approach was adopted to the evidence required to detain a suspect. The experience of detainees was designed to be as unpleasant as possible. The lack of trained intelligence officers meant that crude interrogation techniques were employed. A British Political Officer recalled: 'We had torture in Aden. There was no doubt about it. A Maltese from the territorial army came out and they were just trying to get their hands on any one who would come and work in intelligence because we were so short of intelligence officers.'[66] Although the Amnesty International investigation into torture allegations appears to have been markedly incompetent, even the official British inquiry conducted by Roderick Bowen noted significant irregularities in the treatment of prisoners. The methods employed by interrogators from Aden appalled SAS troops deployed in the region. One soldier who served with the SAS in Aden later gave an account of an incident that caused him particular alarm. Having captured a suspected insurgent, his squadron requested an interrogator from the detention centre at Fort Morbut: 'After a few hours an overweight, half-caste Arabic speaker turned up by helicopter. He said he was Maltese . . . He was carrying an officer's swagger stick, and when he was taken to the prisoner, the interrogator proceeded to beat him with his swagger stick all over the body including the soles of his feet . . . Some members of B Squadron were only restrained with the greatest difficulty from shooting the interrogator. He beat up the prisoner for ten or 15 minutes, then said "He knows nothing," got in the helicopter and went back to Steamer Point.'[67]

There is no doubt that the greatest hostility was generated not by either deportations or internment but by the harsh measures employed by British servicemen on the streets of Aden for which there was no redress. The fear caused by FLOSY and NLF inspired bombings and shootings should not be underestimated and it is probably true that the Aden authorities did not instigate a general policy of reprisals. However, the shortage of intelligence, a lack of trained manpower, the belief that the restrictive rules of engagement were unworkable and a certain contempt for the Arabs of the town ensured that the urban counter-insurgency campaign in Aden became increasingly brutal and indiscriminate. A journalist who was sympathetic to the efforts of the British army recorded the violence which accompanied the visit of the UN commissioners in April 1967. He noted that the Northumberland fusiliers 'are in ugly mood . . . There's a lot of boot, gun butt and fist thumping. It isn't a display of brutality – it's a show of righteous human anger.'[68] Frequently, the victims were entirely non-political or even sympathetic to the British cause. On one occasion the loyal bodyguard of a British political officer was beaten and stamped upon in a random attack by British soldiers during a visit to Aden.[69] Alongside this open violence, the British continued to pursue a covert campaign designed to undermine what was seen as an Egyptian offensive in the town. The Chiefs of Staff were keen to maintain and intensify the 'counter-offensive against the UAR' in Aden which included political action, counter-propaganda, psychological operations and covert action.[70]

The internal security situation declined further following the Arab-Israeli war in June 1967. Despite Brown's efforts to inject a degree of cordiality into the frosty British relationship with Nasser, the authorities in Whitehall and Aden were delighted by the prospect of his likely humiliation by the Israelis. Conversely, an Egyptian victory could potentially overturn the efforts of the previous ten years to block the spread of Nasserism in Arabia. The Foreign Office informed Trevelyan on 5 June: 'we are very aware that if President Nasser came out of the Middle East crisis on top our chances of promoting satisfactory terminal arrangements in South Arabia will be even slimmer than they are now. Can you at any point give any indication of federal thinking on this?' Trevelyan responded on 7 June that the federal ministers were 'wholly cynical in their support for Nasser, whom they would like to see battered, but if he came out on top against Israel . . . they would probably compete to see who could get to Cairo first.'[71] Despite the continuing hostility to Nasser in Britain and the fact that Brown sketched out plans to exploit Nasser's weakness in order to bolster Britain's position in the Middle East, there was no substance to the assertions of Egyptian propagandists that Britain and the United States were actively involved in assisting the Israelis during the conflict.[72] Nevertheless, Cairo's accusations were widely believed in the Middle East and contributed to the discontent in southwest Arabia that led to a dramatic mutiny two weeks after the end of the Arab-Israeli conflict.

The mutiny of 20 June 1967 constituted the final dramatic dip in the downward movement of British fortunes and was recalled with a sense of shock by those who witnessed it.[73] Its causes were complex and compounded of Arab anger at British support for Israel during the June war, friction generated between British and local forces as a consequence of the difficulties associated with the counter-insurgency campaign and rivalry between different tribal factions following the creation of the South Arabian Army earlier in the month. It began with protests by local troops at 'Awlaqi domination of senior positions in the SAA and, in particular, the designation of Nasir Burayk as future commander of the force. Complaints by non-'Awlaqi officers about the new appointment had led to their suspension and this was taken as further evidence of British partiality towards the 'Awlaqis. The initial demonstrations on the morning of 20 June became increasingly disorderly and spread from the army in Lake Lines to the police force in Champion Lines and then to the armed Aden police in Crater. Regular British forces were dispatched to restore order and became involved in a series of confrontations with the mutineers. The turning point came with the ambush of a British army patrol which led to heavy casualties and the evacuation of Crater by the British.[74] By the end of the day 22 British regular soldiers had been killed and Crater was in the hands of NLF and FLOSY guerrillas. The Commissioner of Police was given responsibility for negotiating British re-entry; he thought it prudent to allow an interval before this was attempted. This irritated the Argyll regiment under Colin Mitchell which was eager to return to the town to avenge the deaths of their comrades.[75] In a carefully stage-managed episode Mitchell re-entered Crater on 3 July with pipes playing and flags flying.[76]

Mitchell was determined to restore order in Crater and to root out terrorism but the Argyll regiment's record during the months after their entry was a poor one. Acts of random violence were perpetrated by both sides during the short-lived reoccupation. Senior British military and civilian officials have stressed the self-discipline of British troops in following strict rules of engagement in Aden despite constant provocation.[77] The later testimony of some of the Argyll and Sutherland Highlanders refutes this rosy picture. According to one soldier, instead of shouting *waqaf* meaning halt or stand three times, as prescribed by stop and search procedures, British troops would cheerfully shout 'corned beef' and then instantly gun down bemused civilians.[78] Mitchell admitted that his own view was that 'Any man who appeared in our streets carrying a weapon should be shot dead.'[79] This was confirmed by the journalist Stephen Harper who recorded: 'The Scots never troubled to hide their preference for a terrorist shot dead over a cringing prisoner destined for a few weeks in al Mansour jail with a TV set, and ultimate release as a hero of a revolutionary war.'[80] Mitchell's men went considerably further and engaged in a campaign of revenge for British losses during the mutiny. An anonymous source from the Argylls later recounted a haunting incident to a Scottish Sunday newspaper: 'I was there when a middle-aged Arab was arrested and put in the back of a Land Rover. He was bleeding but was fully conscious and extremely frightened. He was saying in broken English that he was a married man with children and the driver was telling him he would be all right. He was too old to have been a terrorist and there was no evidence of him carrying a weapon. With my own eyes I saw him being given two massive doses of morphine by an ordinary Argyll. When he did not die he was given a third, and the soldier then told the driver: "Give him a bumpy ride to the hospital. He'll be dead by the time you get there." '[81] The direct result of the mutiny and the reoccupation of Crater was therefore to intensify the already strained relations between the inhabitants of Aden and the British army. Its political consequences were the sudden collapse of the federation, the triumph of the NLF over FLOSY and the advance of the date of independence from January 1968 to November 1967.

Last post

The British continued to pursue alternatives to Nasserism in southwest Arabia to the bitter end; the non-Nasserist organisation which did fortuitously emerge in the form of the NLF was of a most peculiar kind but it served British purposes. The refusal of the SAL to join the federal government during the course of 1966 forced the British to plan the future constitution of the country on a very narrow base. In order to overcome this difficulty they persisted in the attempt to lure FLOSY elements disenchanted with Nasser into coalition with the federation. By far the most significant potential FLOSY dissident was al-Asnaj and much effort was put into courting him. Between January and July 1967 a series of secret meetings between al-Asnaj and various British officials were planned. Potential interlocutors included the Labour MP, Colin Jackson, Under-Secretary of State at the Foreign Office, Bill Rodgers and the Minister without Portfolio, Lord Shackleton, but on each occasion al-Asnaj was unwilling or unable to attend.[82] The oddest but most successful of the intermediaries was the maverick Labour MP, Tom Driberg, who met al-Asnaj in Ta'izz on 10 April and Makawi in Khartoum a week later. Officially, these meetings occurred as a result of his private initiative as a Daily Express journalist but it was the Foreign Office which sponsored the mission as part of its plan to detach FLOSY moderates.[83] Despite al-Asnaj's constant prevarication about whether to meet British officials Trevelyan continued to woo independent factions within FLOSY. He recorded on 3 June: 'Nasser is clearly determined to keep them firmly under his control ... we need to concentrate on ... getting to terms with the independent part of FLOSY as represented by Asnag ... Needless to say we must not allow the fact that we are trying to detach Asnag become known.'[84] However, by the time Shackleton eventually met al-Asnaj in Athens on 6 July he appeared an increasingly marginal figure. It was evident that al-Asnaj could do little to save the federal government in the aftermath of the mutiny and he spent most of the conversation complaining that the British were working with his opponents in the NLF. For his part, Shackleton had nothing of substance to offer as British planning for the region's future was in chaos.[85]

Al-Asnaj's influence was by this stage much reduced among NLF and FLOSY cadres operating inside Aden. It was these factions on whom the British began to focus their attention in an attempt to refashion a government, in the midst of the crumbling of the federation. A bizarre meeting of the Federal Supreme Council took place on 5 July at which all the most prominent federal figures quarrelled with one another. Husayn Bayumi, brother of Britain's reliable former confederate, the late Hasan Bayumi, emerged from the meeting as Prime Minister with a mandate to form a caretaker government. By this stage the federal ministers believed that there was no longer any purpose to be served by further British schemes of reconstruction and they treated Husayn Bayumi's appointment as a great joke. His reputation suffered by comparison with his brother's and the Foreign Office were hardly reassured by the Aden High Commission's assessment: 'Although he has in the past been considered to be too temperamental and over-addicted to drink, he has appeared in a much better light since return-ing from New York in December.'[86] The British authorities briefly enter-tained hopes that Bayumi could bring splinter elements of FLOSY and the NLF into a coalition. However, the federal rulers had no confidence in Bayumi; before the end of the month their conspiracies resulted in his removal.[87] British efforts to draw out the opposition groups also failed. Trevelyan was already in 'indirect contact' with the NLF but found they were 'very difficult to get at and their political ideas are negligible.' FLOSY personalities were less elusive and Trevelyan hoped to take advantage of continuing dissension between the local Adenese leadership and their osten-sible masters in Cairo. On 24 July he met potentially dissident FLOSY leaders in London and invited them to join a caretaker government. They were adamant that they would not share power with the NLF and the initi-ative stalled.[88]

Having dispatched Husayn Bayumi the federal rulers returned to their state capitals to await their fate. Although it is difficult to trace the exact circumstances behind the downfall of each, the common factors in the WAP were the refusal of Trevelyan to intervene in order to assist them and the col-lapse of their morale. The implacable opposition of the Wilson government to a permanent defence commitment in southwest Arabia and the mutiny in the army sapped their will and provided an opportunity for tiny NLF and FLOSY cadres to take over the running of the federal states. The disinteg-ration of the federation began in its westernmost regions with the defection of the local security forces in Lahj in mid-August. The mutiny had already demonstrated the extent to which NLF and FLOSY had infiltrated the federal security forces. This was confirmed by the refusal of the South Arabian Army to assist Sultan Fadhl of Lahj with the task of restoring order in his principality. Fadhl was swept out of office by the nationalists and his fall prompted the Na'ib of Dathinah to hand over authority to the SAA.[89] In Dali' the tribes, who had spent years in conflict with the British, declared nominal loyalty either to the NLF or FLOSY. Elsewhere the NLF met little resistance as their militias took control of the central states following small demonstrations in the provincial capitals of Yafi' and Fadli.[90] The eastern-most provinces of the federation were the last to fall but by the end of October it was recorded that NLF flags were flying throughout the Upper 'Awlaqi Shaykhdom. This final victory was partially secured because Muhammad Bubakr capped his long years of opposition to the alliance between the ahl Muhsin and the British with a sudden and opportunistic declaration of support for the NLF.[91] The success of this odd revolution was a consequence of the lassitude of the rulers, the impotence of the British and the tactically astute decision of the NLF to exploit tribal discontent in pursuit of their own ends.

In the EAP the revolutionaries were even fewer in number and the coup that brought them to power was still more dramatic. During the course of 1966 and 1967 the British had expended much energy in attempting to persuade the EAP states to join the federation and had made military assistance for the Hadhrami Bedouin Legion dependent on the rulers' agreement on this point. However, the fragile state of the federation and its uncertain future after independence did not provide any incentive for the other EAP rulers to follow Wahidi into the federation. The new Qu'ayti sultan, Ghalib, believed that membership of the federation might lead to his state becoming infected with the toxic factionalism which characterised WAP politics. Two opposition parties, the South Arabian League and the Arab Socialist Party, did challenge the supremacy of the EAP rulers. However, their numbers were few and Mukalla and Sayyun remained quiet in comparison with Aden. The only matter which greatly exercised the British at this stage was the future of the Hadhrami Bedouin Legion which remained a reliable factor amidst the escalating chaos elsewhere. British military and political officers in Mukalla regarded it as a mercenary force and were adamant that it should continue to be funded by the British Treasury as the only available means of keeping order after independence. The absence of any overt nationalist threat, the desire for economy and the comprehensive ignorance of the region in Whitehall made policy-makers reluctant to countenance additional military assistance. There was a widespread feeling that the EAP was of no significance to British interests but a residual sense of responsibility persuaded Brown to offer continued support to the HBL in his 19 June speech to Parliament.

In the aftermath of the mutiny the EAP states fell victim to Trevelyan's determination to secure a swift exit which meant a complete severance of ties with Qu'ayti and Kathiri. Trevelyan met the EAP rulers at Riyan on 2 August and advised them to visit Geneva to make terms with the UN mission. Sultan Ghalib found Trevelyan 'totally focused on carrying out the mandate that he was given by the Labour government i.e. to withdraw from the region asap with minimum loss and commitment.'[92] The Political Officer responsible for persuading the EAP rulers to go to Geneva later suggested that it was 'frustrating not to say hypocritical, by then to suggest that any course of action was worthwhile, but those were the instructions.'[93] On 19 August Sultan Ghalib and the Kathiri Sultan left for Geneva. In their absence the British residency was withdrawn from Mukalla, leaving behind a power vacuum that the NLF, which in the EAP had its origins in the Arab Socialist Party, rushed to fill. On hearing of these developments Sultan Ghalib insisted on returning to Mukalla, declaring that 'if the NLF wanted a fight they could have one.'[94] However, a fight was the last thing the British wanted at this stage in their withdrawal. The Sultans' efforts to return were obstructed by British officials and they were forced to borrow a cargo boat in order to complete the final leg of their return trip from Geneva. Upon disembarking at his capital, Mukalla, on 11 September Sultan Ghalib was confronted by armed NLF militiamen and forced to turn back.

The EAP Sultans were left with no choice but to retreat to Saudi Arabia, while the British offered support to the HBL in suppressing the tribal disturbances which broke out in the wake of the sudden NLF take-over.[95]

Events in the EAP provide significant evidence of British willingness to accept the creation of an NLF government. This inclination manifested itself in a series of actions that demonstrated at a minimum a degree of favouritism towards the NLF and appear to have approached active collusion. In the midst of the federation's collapse Trevelyan decided to issue a statement offering to negotiate with either FLOSY or the NLF. The ejection of the rulers from their territories by revolutions in each of the federal states meant the federation was no longer viable and, thus left the nationalist parties as the only viable partners in the process of decolonization. Despite this Trevelyan's announcement was greeted with some dismay back in Whitehall where there was still some hope that the UN could play a mediatory role. Trevelyan was dismissive of this idea and returned to London early in September to insist that a public offer of talks with the nationalists should be issued. He warned that this was 'the last chance of getting the NLF to negotiate.' Although publicly holding the door open for negotiations with FLOSY, from August 1967 Trevelyan's aim was to hand over power to the NLF. His advocacy of an NLF government was clearly predicated on his belief that they would be more pragmatic in their relations with Britain after independence and this in turn was a function of their independence from Nasser's control. Although this kind of reasoning had much appeal back in Whitehall, from the perspective of the British government the adamant refusal of the NLF to accept any UN role in the demission of power was problematic.[96] The statement which Trevelyan eventually broadcast on 5 September offered the opposition nationalist parties an opportunity to discuss the handover but was immediately condemned by FLOSY supporters in the SAA. FLOSY leaders were convinced that the machinations of the British and the NLF would lead to their exclusion from power.[97] From an entirely different perspective Saudi officials, who continued to back the SAL, claimed that the High Commission 'had deliberately brought about the present ascendancy of the NLF as a counterweight to FLOSY.' The High Commission's reaction to the Saudi allegations was revealing: they claimed that the NLF were in favour of 'South Arabia for the South Arabians, free from Egyptian influence'; that they were no more radical in their politics than FLOSY; and, most significantly of all, that they would 'rely for support on tribes grounded in Islam [and] are not likely to become Communist.'[98] How much of this was deliberate dissimulation designed to reassure Whitehall is open to question but as events were to prove it was thoroughly misleading. What is clear is that the British on the ground in Aden believed the NLF was both populist and non-Nasserist and were eager to get out as soon as possible and cede authority to them.

Trevelyan had been attempting to get agreement on early withdrawal since the mutiny. On 6 August he proposed that independence should be brought forward to the first ten days of December. This was too precipitate for Brown and Healey who nevertheless wished to retain the option of an accelerated military withdrawal.[99] Brown agreed a provisional date of 10 December but refused to rule out January 1968 and urged that this change be kept secret. Inevitably, the decision leaked.[100] The compromise did not satisfy Trevelyan who continued to lobby for an earlier date. Just two weeks after his initial appeal he again urged ministers to change the timetable because the deteriorating security situation made an early exit essential. He now suggested that they should aim to complete the process of decolonization by November.[101] The crumbling of the federation made Brown more sympathetic to Trevelyan's appeals. On 10 October he provisionally agreed on late November 1967 as the deadline for independence in response to Trevelyan's 'consistent preference for an earlier date.'[102] At the end of the month Brown explained to his colleagues that they should work on the assumption that independence would occur in the second half of November.[103] Crossman claimed that ministers 'couldn't be more pleased' at the early termination of what was an increasingly burdensome commitment.[104] The decision was confirmed by the Cabinet on 30 October and announced to Parliament on 2 November.[105]

The British were accused by Cairo of consistently supporting the NLF and it is evident that they did prefer an NLF government on the grounds that it represented southwest Arabian particularism, while FLOSY were seen as pan-Arabist in theory and Nasser's puppets in practice. There were still obstacles to an NLF take-over, the most significant of which were the determination of Nasser to retain some influence and the existence of strong support for FLOSY within sections of the SAA. The Egyptian government were constant in their efforts to construct a stable coalition between opposition groups but had never been able to incorporate the younger radicals of the NLF into FLOSY. With the prospect of a sudden British withdrawal Nasser exerted himself once again to this purpose and on 1 November it was announced that the NLF and FLOSY had reached 'complete agreement' on the formation of a coalition government following talks in Cairo.[106] As so often in the past, agreements negotiated on the other side of the Red Sea disintegrated in the harsh political climate of Aden. Trevelyan was unimpressed by Nasser's latest manoeuvre and reported that there was a 'prospect of an NLF-Army alliance which might be able to dispose of the remaining FLOSY-PORF fighters'. On 4 November, just days after the signing of the coalition deal in Cairo, fighting broke out between the factions in Aden. As Trevelyan predicted the NLF fighters eliminated the remaining FLOSY cadres with the assistance of the SAA. The key to the NLF victory was their ejection of FLOSY fighters from the border town of Shaykh Uthman in a bloody two-day fight.[107] The township was a strategically significant cockpit: the battle between the opposition groups was for control of the main road that ran through Shaykh Uthman into the centre of Aden. British paratroopers had handed control of the town to the SAA on 24 September.[108]

The British conspicuously absented themselves from Shaykh Uthman during the NLF rout of FLOSY. From Crater Mitchell sensed that 'there were some fairly dubious goings-on' during these final battles and later declared the decision to hand over to the NLF 'utterly disgraceful.'[109] There is no reliable estimate of the number of dead in this final battle but one source suggests 300.[110]

With FLOSY eliminated Trevelyan pressed the need for another public statement; this time it would contain a recognition of the NLF as well as an offer to negotiate.[111] Brown was by this stage extremely sensitive to Parliamentary reactions to events in southwest Arabia and was reluctant to publicly acknowledge the NLF as the successor government for fear of the domestic consequences of what would appear to be another policy reversal. Correspondence between Aden and London grew increasingly fractious over this issue of public recognition of the NLF and the matter was only resolved when on 11 November the NLF took the initiative and declared itself willing to enter negotiations with the British.[112] The Foreign Office was suspicious that the situation was being manipulated by the High Commission but the ejection of the rulers from the interior, the defeat of FLOSY at Shaykh Uthman and the new willingness of the NLF leaders to negotiate created a *fait accompli*: by mid-November there was no alternative to an NLF government. Negotiations with the NLF leaders began in Geneva on 21 November. The goals of the British government were overwhelmingly practical: they wanted guarantees that commercial and diplomatic interests would not be endangered after independence. Their intention was to prolong the negotiations in order to cover the final days of withdrawal.[113] Fortunately, this was easily achieved. The negotiations soon became bogged down in a series of disputes between the British delegation led by Shackleton and Qahtan's NLF team. The previously obscure issue of the future of the Kuria Muria islands, which the British intended to return to the Sultan of Oman, proved a particular source of dissension. Shackleton was unable to offer any concessions on this matter but he did urge his colleagues to accept the extension of aid to the new regime from six months, which was the initial British bargaining position, to a full year.[114] Such was the distress caused to the NLF by the loss of the Kuria Muria islands that Brown agreed to postpone any announcement on this matter and the final agreement offered a package of £12m in aid for the first six months after independence and the possibility of additional funds as a result of future negotiations. This was sufficient to seal a last minute deal with Qahtan on 29 November.[115] He rushed back from Geneva to Aden to be present for the independence celebrations on the morning of 30 November. The last British troops to leave southwest Arabia had been airlifted from Aden's golf course the previous day.[116]

Conclusions

On 30 October 1967 Richard Crossman made an interesting diary entry concerning events in Aden. His view was that the collapse of the federal government 'has forced our speedy withdrawal [which] is nothing but good fortune. It now looks as if we shall get out of Aden without losing a single British soldier, chaos will rule soon after we've gone, and there'll be one major commitment cut – thank God.'[117] The ignorance underlying this comment has secured it a certain degree of notoriety: the regular British army had suffered numerous casualties in Aden and the Protectorates and rather than chaos Aden and the former Protectorates were dominated by a Marxist oriented government after the British exit. Within three years, disputes within the NLF between the pragmatists represented by Qahtan al Sha'bi and the Marxist ideologues led by 'Abd al-Fattah Isma'il had been resolved in the latter's favour. A socialist programme was implemented which lasted until uneasy unification of North and South Yemen at the end of the Cold War.

As southwest Arabia accelerated towards independence, the British government's priorities were a safe military withdrawal and the exclusion of Nasser's allies from the post-independence government. This latter criterion had been a constant in British thinking about the region since the mid-1950s. Crossman's delight is illustrative not merely of a widespread lack of understanding about Arabian affairs but can also be interpreted as expressing, perhaps unconsciously, some of the persistent attitudes which underpinned British policy in Aden and the Protectorates. Crossman was one of a number of pro-Zionist, anti-Nasserist politicians inside the Labour party who regarded Britain's commitment to their last Arabian outpost as a distraction from domestic duties. Brown was a notable exception but the hostility of Labour politicians such as Wilson and Crossman to Nasser produced an element of continuity between Conservative and Labour policies. This commonality was buried underneath rhetorical differences between the parties over the matter of a defence commitment to the federation. The Conservatives had seen the federation as an adequate alternative to Nasserism, Crossman regarded chaos as a viable substitute and, in Aden, Trevelyan was prepared to ignore evidence of the NLF's incipient Marxism in order to keep out the overtly pro-Egyptian elements within FLOSY. Despite their many political and social differences, Trevelyan, like Crossman, could recall the events of the last days of British rule with some pride on the grounds he had achieved a safe withdrawal and that: 'The local boys had made good without the taint of British or Egyptian connivance.'[118]

Notes

1 J. B. Kelly, *Arabia, the Gulf and the West* (London, Weidenfeld and Nicolson, 1980), p. 25.
2 T. R. Mockaitis, *British Counterinsurgency in the Post-Imperial Era* (Manchester, Manchester University Press, 1995), ch. 3.

3 *Parliamentary Debates*, 5th series, vol. 725, cols 234–54.

4 *The Times*, 28 February 1966, p. 11, 4 March 1966, p. 13.

5 *Parliamentary Debates*, 5th series, vol. 725, cols 1748–70; S. Heffer, *Like the Roman: The Life of Enoch Powell* (London, Weidenfeld and Nicolson, 1998), pp. 401–2, 426.

6 *Parliamentary Debates*, 5th Series, vol. 728, col. 217, cols 928–34.

7 Duncan Sandys Papers, DSND 14/1, Trevaskis to Sandys, 12 May 1966.

8 *Parliamentary Debates*, 5th series, vol. 729, col. 285; *The Times*, 17 May pp. 1 and 17, 18 May, p. 8, 19 May, p. 14, 25 May, p.8; H. Wilson, *The Labour Government 1964–1970: A Personal Record* (London, Weidenfeld and Nicolson, 1971), ch. 14; E. Short, *Whip to Wilson* (London, Macdonald, 1989), pp. 267–8.

9 C. Lord and D. Birtles, *The Armed Force of Aden* (Solihull, Helion, 2000), pp. 34–7.

10 PRO: CAB 128/41, CC(66)29th mtg., minute 2, 16 June 1966, CAB 148/25, OPD(66)27th mtg., minute 3, 25 May 1966, CAB 148/27, OPD (66)62, 23 May 1966, PREM 13/705, Callaghan to PM, 25 May 1966, Laskey to Bridges, 26 May 1966.

11 D. Ledger, *Shifting Sands* (London, Peninsular Publishing, 1983), p. 100; J. B. Kelly, *Arabia*, p. 28.

12 G. Brown, *In My Way* (London, Victor Gollancz, 1971), pp. 137–8.

13 R. McNamara, *Britain, Nasser and the Balance of Power in the Middle East 1952–1967* (London, Frank Cass, 2003), pp. 222–3; S. Kear, 'Diplomatic Innovation: Nasser and the Origins of the Interests Section' *Diplomacy and Statecraft* 12 (2001), pp. 71–80.

14 R. McNamara, *Balance of Power*, p. 234.

15 PRO: FCO 8/301, Brenchley minute, 3 January 1967, Thomson minute, 6 January 1967, Brenchley minute, 17 February 1967.

16 PRO: FCO 8/220, FO to Aden, 16 March 1967, Aden (Turnbull) to FO, 17 March 1967, 19 March 1967, Ashworth minute, 20 March 1967, FCO 8/221, Records of Meetings between Thomson and the Federal Supreme Council, 17 March 1967, 18 March 1967.

17 PRO: CAB 128/42, CC(67)13th mtg., minute 3, 16 March 1967, CAB 148/30, OPD(67)11th mtg., minute 1, 10 March 1967, OPD(67)14th mtg., minute 1, 22 March 1967, CAB 148/31, OPD(67)18, 8 March 1967; R. Crossman, *Diaries of a Cabinet Minister, Vol II* (London, Hamish Hamilton and Cape, 1976), pp. 279, 283; B. Castle, *The Castle Diaries 1964–1970* (London, Weidenfeld and Nicolson, 1984), p. 235.

18 PRO: CAB 128/42, CC(67)13th mtg., minute 3, 11 May 1967, CAB 129/129, CP(67)68, 9 May 1967.

19 PRO: FCO 8/184, Shackleton minute, 2 May 1967, FO to Aden, 3 May 1967, Shackleton to FO, 11 May 1967, FCO 8/185, Record of a Meeting between Shackleton and the Federal Security Council, 11 May 1967.

20 PRO: PREM 13/1295, Paymaster-General to Prime Minister, 10 April 1967, PREM 13/1296, Shackleton to Wigg, 3 May 1967, FO note to Palliser, 5 May 1967.

21 M. Thornhill, 'Alternatives to Nasser: Humphrey Trevelyan, Ambassador to Egypt' in S. Kelly and A. Gorst (eds), *Whitehall and the Suez Crisis* (London, Frank Cass, 2000), pp. 14–15; K. Kyle, *Suez: Britain's End of Empire in the Middle East* (2nd ed., London, I. B. Tauris, 2003), pp. 550–1.

22 H. Trevelyan, *Public and Private* (London, Hamish Hamilton, 1980), p. 60.

23 PRO: FCO 8/186, Trevelyan to Brown, 9 June 1967.

24 H. Trevelyan, *The Middle East in Revolution* (London, Macmillan, 1970),

p. 223; PRO: FCO 8/185, Trevelyan to Secretary of State with 'First Impressions' memorandum, 27 May 1967.

25 PRO: CAB 148/30, OPD(67)23rd mtg., 15 June 1967, CAB 148/32, OPD(67)44, 8 June 1967, OPD(67)45, 12 June 1967, FCO 8/185, High Commissioner (Aden) to FO, 8 June 1967, FCO 8/186, FO to High Commissioner (Aden), 15 June 1967, High Commissioner (Aden) to FO, 17 June 1967.

26 *Parliamentary Debates 1966–67*, 5th Series, vol. 748, pp. 1126–43

27 *Parliamentary Debates 1966–67*, 5th Series, vol. 748, pp. 1158, 1178, 1182.

28 Labour Party Archive, PLP minutes 1962–1971, minutes of a party meeting, 28 June 1967.

29 PRO: FCO 8/185, Aden to FO, 7 June 1967.

30 PRO: FO 371/185178, B1052/52, Aden (Turnbull) to Secretary of State, 17 February 1966, B1052/64, McCarthy to Brenchley, 17 February 1966, B1052/68, Ashworth to Elwell, 17 February 1966.

31 M. Crouch, *An Element of Luck* (Radcliffe Press, London, 1993), p. 184.

32 PRO: PREM 13/704, Longford to PM, 25 February 1966 with Wilson minute (ud).

33 PRO: FO 371/185179, B1052/89, Secretary of State to Aden, 21 March 1966.

34 PRO: FO 371/185259, BA 1052/3 Aden (Turnbull) to FO, 12 May 1966, BA 1052/8, FO to Aden, 6 May 1966, BA 1052/13, Aden (Turnbull) to FO, 13 May 1956, FO 371/185230, BA1015/2, McCarthy (Aden) to Goulding, 5 May 1966, BA 1015/3, Aden (Turnbull) to FO, 15 May 1966.

35 PRO: CAB 148/25, OPD(66)24th mtg., minute 5, 13 May 1966, CAB 148/27, OPD(65)55, 10 May 1966, FO 371/185259, BA 1058/1, Aden (Turnbull) to FO, 2 May 1966.

36 PRO: PREM 13/705, Beswick to PM, 24 June 1966, Padley to PM, 24 June 1966, Lee to PM, 24 June 1966, Healey to PM, 5 July 1966, CAB 148/25, OPD(66)32nd mtg., minute 3, 15 July 1966, CAB 148/27, OPD(66)77, 6 July 1966, OPD(66)78, 13 July 1966.

37 K. Chang, 'The United Nations and Decolonization: The Case of Southern Yemen', *International Organization* 26 (1972), pp. 51–3.

38 PRO: FO 371/185262, BA 1054/72, Turnbull (Aden) to Marnham, 11 May 1956.

39 J. Kostiner, *The Struggle for South Yemen* (London, Croom Helm, 1984), pp. 124–5; F. Halliday, *Arabia Without Sultans* (London, Saqi Books, 2002), p. 213.

40 T. Little, *South Arabia* (London, Pall Mall, 1986), pp. 117–19.

41 PRO: CAB 158/63, JIC(66)37, 25 May 1966.

42 PRO: FO 371/185259, BA 1052/10, Note by the Arabian department on Constitutional Advance, 5 May 1966.

43 PRO: FO 371/185230, BA 1015/4, Turnbull to Marnham, 22 April 1966 including record of a meeting with Saleh and Darwish, 20 April 1966.

44 PRO: FO 371/185243, BA 10112/1, Cairo to FO, 6 May 1966, FO to Cairo, 12 May 1966, Cairo to FO, 28 July 1966.

45 PRO: FO 371/185230, BA 1015/11, Brenchley minute, 1 June 1966, BA 1015/14, Aden (Oates) to FO, 23 June 1966, FO 371/185262, McCarthy (Aden) to Weir (FO), 7 July 1956.

46 PRO: FO 371/185231, BA 1015/23, Aden (Oates) to FO, 18 July 1966; IOR: R/20/D/213 Aden Weekly Intelligence Summary, 18 July 1966.

47 PRO: FO 371/185231, BA 1015/31, Aden (Turnbull) to FO, 3 October 1966.

48 PRO: FO 371/185260, BA 1059/39, Young to High Commissioner, 20 October 1966.

49 PRO: FO 371/185260, BA 1052/37, Aden (Turnbull) to FO, 23 October

1966, BA 1059/39, Turnbull to Marnham, 26 October 1966 including Record of Discussion with Saleh, 22 October 1966.

50 D. Ledger, *Sands*, p. 82; PRO: FO 371/185231, BA1015/40, FO to Aden, 3 November 1966, Aden (Turnbull) to FO, 5 November 1966, BA 1015/48, McCarthy to Brenchley, 6 December 1966.

51 PRO: FO 371/185260, BA 1052/44, Marnham and Allen minutes, 17 November 1966.

52 K. Chang, 'United Nations', p. 53.

53 PRO: FO371/185260, BA1052/48, Brown to Turnbull, 8 December 1966.

54 PRO: FO 371/185264, BA 1054/145, Wilton (Aden) to Brenchley, 28 November 1966, with Young memorandum.

55 PRO: PREM 13/1295, Trend to PM, 23 January 1967, Wilson to Brown, 26 January 1967. See also PRO: CAB 158/64, JIC(66)74, 29 December 1966.

56 K. Chang, 'United Nations', p. 55.

57 PRO: FCO 8/315, FO to Aden, 23 March 1967, 25 March 1967, Gore-Booth to Turnbull, 24 March 1967.

58 The daily progress of the mission is recorded in PRO: FCO 8/316, Aden (Turnbull) to FO, 4 April 1967, 5 April 1967, 6 April 1967, 7 April 1967. Recollections of events can be found in D. Ledger, *Sands*, pp. 106–17; T. Little, *South*, pp. 162–4; S. Harper, *Last Sunset* (Collins, London, 1978), pp. 80–8.

59 PRO: FO 371/185233, BA 1016/42, McCarthy to Hillier-Fry with 'A Note on Terrorism in Aden', 14 December 1966.

60 J. Kostiner, *Struggle*, pp. 144–5.

61 J. Paget, *Last Post* (London, Faber and Faber, 1967), pp. 178–82.

62 D. Ledger, *Sands*, pp. 74–80.

63 PRO: CAB 148/31, OPD(67)19, 8 March 1967.

64 IOR: R/20/D/412, High Commissioner (Aden) to Foreign Office, 21 August 1966, 23 August 1966.

65 IOR: R/20/D/155, Deportation Returns for 1966, Aden Police HQ to Secretariat.

66 Private information.

67 K. Connor, *Ghost Force: The Secret History of the SAS* (Weidenfeld and Nicolson, London, 1998), p. 127.

68 S. Harper, *Sunset*, p. 85.

69 Private information.

70 PRO: FCO 8/183, Cooper to Lawrence-Wilson, 27 February 1967.

71 PRO: PREM 13/1296, High Commission (Aden) to FO, 7 June 1967.

72 R. McNamara, *Balance of Power*, pp. 267–70.

73 C. Mitchell, *Having Been a Soldier* (London, Hamish Hamilton, 1969), ch. 1; H. Trevelyan, *Revolution*, pp. 228–34; D. Ledger, *Sands*, ch. 8; S. Harper, *Sunset*, ch. 13.

74 For the contemporary official record see FCO 8/436, Aden to FO, 20 June 1967, Bartlett (HQ, South Arabian Army) to Wild (MoD), 26 June 1967.

75 C. Mitchell, *Soldier*, pp. 14–15.

76 Ibid., pp. 169–87.

77 J. Paget, *Post*, p. 11.

78 *Glasgow Sunday Mail*, 26 April 1981, p. 2.

79 C. Mitchell, *Soldier*, p. 262. See also S. Harper, *Sunset,* p. 101.

80 S. Harper, *Sunset*, p. 114.

81 *Glasgow Sunday Mail*, 10 May 1981, pp. 24–5.

82 PRO: FCO 8/188, Aden department paper on opposition contacts, 22 June 1967, FCO 8/196, FO to Baghdad, 17 February 1967, Asnaj to Jackson, 4 February 1967, McCarthy minute, 28 February 1967, Brown to PM, 7 April

1967, Washington to FO, 14 March 1967, FO to Washington, 22 March 1967, Washington to FO, 25 March 1967, 30 March 1967, 4 April 1967, FCO 8/197, Minister without Portfolio (Aden) to FO, 18 April 1967, FO to Washington, 18 April 1967.

83　PRO: FCO 8/232, FO to Aden, 11 April 1967, Minister without Portfolio (Aden) to FO, 13 April 1967, 14 April 1967, FO to Khartoum, 14 April 1967, Khartoum to FO, 15 April 1967, 20 April 1967, Driberg notes of conversations 10–18 April 1967.

84　PRO: FCO 8/197, Aden to FO, 3 June 1967.

85　PRO: PREM 13/1297, Beirut to FO, 3 July 1967, Hague to FO, 4 July 1967, FCO 8/198, Aden to FO, 5 July 1967, Athens to FO, 6 July 1967, Aden to FO, 9 July 1967.

86　PRO: FCO 8/237, Aden to FO, 6 July 1967, Records of Federal Supreme Council meeting, 5 July 1967, Ashworth to Elwell, 7 July 1967.

87　PRO: FCO 8/237, Aden to FO, 20 July 1967, 25 July 1967, 27 July 1967, 28 July 1967, 31 July 1967, Ashworth to Elwell, 1 August 1967.

88　PRO: FCO 8/198, Aden to FO, 13 July 1967, FO to Aden, 20 July 1967, 25 July 1967.

89　PRO: FCO 8/260, Aden to FO, 13 August 1967, 14 August 1967, 15 August 1967, 16 August 1967.

90　PRO: FCO 8/260, Aden to FO, 25 August 1967, 26 August 1967, 27 August 1967, Memo by Robin Young on the WAP situation (ud).

91　PRO: FCO 8/260, Aden to FO, 27 October 1967, 28 October 1967, 29 October 1967; D. Ledger, *Sands*, pp. 192–3.

92　Sultan Ghalib's written response to author's questions, 24 November 2000.

93　M. Crouch, *Element*, p. 217.

94　PRO: FCO 8/264, Beirut to FO, 4 September 1967.

95　Sultan Ghalib draft memo to Foreign Office, 1970. This detailed document was kindly provided to me by Sultan Ghalib.

96　PRO: FCO 8/264, High Commission (Aden) to FO, 31 August 1967, Hillier-Fry and Brown minutes, 31 August 1967, FO to Aden, 1 September 1967, Aden to FO 1 September 1967, Allen minute, 3 September 1967.

97　S. Harper, *Sunset*, p. 131.

98　PRO: FCO 8/265, Aden to FO, 5 September 1967, Jedda to FO, 7 September 1967, Aden to FO, 11 September 1967.

99　PRO: PREM 13/1297, Aden to FO, 6 August 1967, Brown to Healey, 12 August 1967, Healey to Brown, 12 August 1967, FO to Aden, 17 August 1967.

100　PRO: FCO 8/189, FO to Aden, 17 August 1967; H. Trevelyan, *Revolution*, p. 246.

101　PRO: PREM 13/1297, Aden to FO, 21 August 1967, 22 August 1967.

102　PRO: FCO 8/189, FO to Aden, 10 October 1967, Aden 12 October 1967.

103　PRO: CAB 148/30, OPD(67)34th mtg., minute 2, 27 October 1967.

104　R. Crossman, *Diaries, Vol. 2*, p. 538.

105　PRO: PREM 13/1297, Trend to PM, 26 October 1967, FO to Aden, 31 October 1967, CAB 128/42, CC(67)62nd mtg., minute 2, 30 October 1967, CAB 129/133, CP(67)169, 26 October 1967.

106　H. Trevelyan, *Revolution*, p. 254; PRO: FCO 8/267, Cairo to FO, 1 November 1967, 2 November 1967.

107　E. Downton, *Wars Without End* (Toronto, Stoddart, 1987), pp. 256–7; S. Harper, *Sunset*, pp. 135–6.

108　J. Paget, *Post*, p. 205.

109　C. Mitchell, *Soldier* pp. 225–6.

110　D. Ledger, *Sands* p. 208.

111 H. Trevelyan, *Revolution*, p. 258.
112 PRO: PREM 13/1297, Brown to Wilson with Wilson minute, 13 November 1967, FCO 8/267, Aden to FO, 6 November 1967. 8 November 1967, Allen to Brown, 8 November 1967 with Brown minute, FO to Aden, 8 November 1967, Aden to FO, 9 November 1967, FO to Aden, 9 November 1967, Aden to FO, 11 November 1967.
113 PRO: FCO 8/339, Briefs for Independence Negotiations with McCarthy memo on 'Tactical Handling of the Talks', November 1967.
114 PRO: FCO 8/340, UK Mission (Geneva) to FO, 20 November 1967, 21 November 1967, 22 November 1967, 23 November 1967, 26 November 1967. For a full record of the meetings see FCO 8/342, Minutes of meetings with NLF, various dates.
115 PRO: FCO 8/341, Maitland minute, 24 November 1967, UK Mission (Geneva) to FO, 28 November 1967, Gore-Booth minute, 28 November 1967, FO to UK Mission, 28 November 1967, UK Mission (Geneva) to FO, 29 November 1967.
116 S. Harper, *Sunset*, p. 155.
117 R. Crossman, *Diaries Vol. II*, p. 541.
118 H. Trevelyan, *Revolution*, p. 263.

8 Conclusions

Any account of the transition from colonial government to independence written from the records left by the metropolitan government is certain to be a partial one and the purpose of the preceding narrative is to fill one of many gaps in the modern history of Yemen and to address a conspicuous omission in the historiography of British decolonization. The turbulence of the last years of British rule and the failures of policy-makers in Whitehall and Aden have been stressed but the subsequent history of the region indicates that many of the problems which confronted imperial administrators were quite as troublesome for indigenous governments. Eighteen months after the British withdrawal the NLF initiated the so-called 'corrective movement' in which the pragmatic Qahtan was replaced by a clique of Marxist ideologues including Muhammad 'Ali Haytham and 'Abd al-Fattah Isma'il.[1] In 1970 this group declared the creation of the People's Democratic Republic of Yemen (PDRY). North of the border the conclusion of the Yemen Civil War led to the abolition of the Imamate in 1970 and the inauguration of an era of authoritarian politics and liberal economics in the Yemeni Arab Republic (YAR). The new states set to warring with one another: in 1972 a brief conflict flared up and later in the decade the two governments were implicated in assassination plots directed against their rivals over the frontier. In economic terms the PDRY achieved a measure of social development but remained cripplingly poor while in the YAR a period of economic expansion generated new social divisions.[2] The union of the two Yemens in 1990 reflected both the regional and global victory of capitalism over communism: the free marketeers in the north effectively annexed the socialist government of the south. Southern resentment flared up in 1994 and caused a brief civil war whose conclusion reconfirmed the northern victory. Since the end of that conflict the government of the united Yemen has struggled to introduce social and economic reforms against a background of rising tensions between the nationalist inheritors of the revolution, socialists and Islamic groups. In the aftermath of the 2001 attacks in New York and Washington, in which a number of Yemenis participated, the country began appearing in British and American news bulletins as a breeding ground for Islamic terrorists.[3] Less well publicised were the continuing economic and social problems of the country: Yemen was recently ranked at 148th on the United Nations Human Development Index, placing it amongst the poorest quarter of countries in the world.

Given that events after independence suggest a certain continuity in the political problems of twentieth century Yemen, it is worth making some brief comments on the questions which the Aden episode raises for the study of the end of the British Empire: What was the nature of British policy in the region? Why was Aden one of the last imperial territories to be abandoned? How can we account for the failure of British policy? Where should the study of Britain's informal empire in the Middle East go next?

The nature of British policy

The assumption behind much writing on post-war British foreign and defence policy is that it was formulated in terms of the fairly narrow pursuit of self-interest. In most cases this assumption remains implicit but at least one writer has developed the thesis that the 'realist' approach of British policy-makers was a reaction against inter-war 'idealism'.[4] Although this conclusion runs counter to the arguments made here it does provide a useful starting point to begin to construct an alternative explanation for the evolution of British policy in Aden. In strategic terms it is evident that there was a good deal of continuity in British foreign and colonial policy after 1945: successive governments remained committed to a world role despite the erosion of Britain's material resources during World War II. Reduced circumstances meant that the drama would have to be played out on a smaller stage but there was a commitment to the continuation of the production in some form: after the exit from India the Middle East became the most important venue for the exercise of British imperial instincts. The script changed to allow a greater role for local actors but it was believed that Britain would continue to play its directorial role. The ability to act as a global power was an inheritance that successive Prime Ministers including Churchill, Eden, Macmillan, Douglas-Home and Wilson were reluctant to abandon. The imperial mission of the late Victorian and Edwardian eras survived into the second half of the twentieth century and this is evident in the marked reluctance with which responsibilities were gradually relinquished. For the first post-war generation Britain's identity remained tied up with its global role, and the events of the last two decades from the Falklands war to the invasion of Iraq in 2003 suggest that a part of this globalist instinct has survived into the present.

Such an interpretation of British policy is controversial: the alternative view of decolonization has recently been presented in admirably clear fashion by Frank Heinlein. He argues that 'in general imperial policy was flexible and capable of change. This was due to the fact that the Empire-Commonwealth was always a way to promote British interests, not an end in itself.'[5] This is not at all borne out by the accounts of those officials intimately involved with the end of empire in southwest Arabia. Whatever the flaws in the accounts given by Hickinbotham, Johnston and Trevaskis, it is quite evident that they were interested in far more than the defence of Britain's interests. For the traditionalist Hickinbotham, Britain's mission was to civilise the region, for Johnston, the ties between Aden and Britain were valuable as evidence that Britain had wider horizons than other European powers and, for Trevaskis, Britain's mission was the construction of a modern, orderly state out of chaos. In each case the goals of the men on the spot required that Britain stay on in some form. These aims were tied up with notions of national interest in a complex way but it is difficult to suggest that they were the outcome of some utilitarian calculation of profit and loss. This may be beside the point: national interests are notoriously slippery and Heinlein is addressing the broad sweep of imperial history rather than the relatively minor and, to some degree, exceptional case of Aden and the Protectorates. The problem is that while the interests of middle ranking European states dependent on international trade for survival were broadly similar, the end of their empires were dissimilar: the French under de Gaulle made different choices from the British under Macmillan.

What is most evident from this study is how closely bound together imperialism and decolonization were during the last years of the British Empire. The sudden post-war wave of imperial activism in Africa and Asia has been noted before and points to the fact that decolonization required a more interventionist policy.[6] Independent states had to be built on top of traditional structures and the British sought to exploit their role as architects in order to ensure that the resulting constitutional edifice allowed for easy access by the imperial power. In the case of southwest Arabia the design was to be a federation in which traditional rulers would embrace a programme of social and economic modernisation while retaining a traditional patriarchal system of government and a defence relationship with Britain. Although the comparison was rarely made by policy-makers this was essentially the system which had worked in Malaysia and it was hoped that its extension to the Middle East would guarantee Britain long-term access to base facilities as well as securing access to the military facilities in Aden which were essential if Britain was to maintain credibility as a Middle Eastern power. The instinct to maintain British prestige was shared widely by policy-makers in Whitehall but the architect of British designs for Aden and the Protectorates was Kennedy Trevaskis. He had a coherent plan for an independent southwest Arabia and was eager that the institutions which the British left behind should provide a forum in which those rulers who valued the British connection could dominate. His mention of Cromer's Egypt is, in this context, revealing: Britain retained a position of predominance in Egypt for 80 years without ever making it a formal colony. Clearly, there was a degree of atavism in British thinking about the end of empire which is not always sufficiently acknowledged by those impressed with the idea that policy-makers worked from a carefully prepared balance-sheet of imperial advantages and disadvantages.

Why was the Aden decolonization late?

The telescoping of British imperialism in to such a short period in the late twentieth century makes it difficult to place southwest Arabia in the broader debate about decolonization. The most convincing general explanation for the fairly sudden death of the British Empire is one of mutual disillusionment at both the core and periphery.[7] However, the records of British administrators in Aden and Whitehall evince little desire to permanently terminate their role in the region. By contrast, the disenchantment of the local population is evident from the stream of propaganda issuing from nationalist organisations at the end of the 1950s and perhaps, even more significantly, from the dwindling numbers of local Arabs willing to co-operate with the British. By 1962 the view that Aden was a backwater unaffected by the rising tide of nationalism elsewhere in the Arab world was no longer sustainable. Thus, the episode appears to closely match the template provided by peripheral perspectives on the end of empire whose emphasis on the seminal role of nationalism is exemplified by the impact of Nasserism in southwest Arabia.

The Aden case indicates that there was still a desire to cling to the remains of empire in the metropolis. Even at this short historical distance it takes some effort to recall that in 1955 Britain's future hung very much in the balance. At that time Britain was still the possessor of the largest multi-national empire in the world and, even after the shattering events of Suez the following year, many policy-makers hoped that the country could still act as a global power. Southwest Arabia appeared as a region in which Britain could continue to exercise influence over the long term. It was also seen as a potential base from which to conduct a counter-attack against Nasser. In the second half of the 1950s and early 1960s British statesmen regarded the Egyptian leader as a significant threat to Britain's influence as a world power; and it is this which provides the most convincing explanation of Britain's late decolonization in the region. The slow growth of nationalism prior to 1956 made it seem feasible to use Aden and the Protectorates as a secure haven from which to contain the spread of Nasser's influence: as long as Nasser remained, so would the British.

This interpretation confirms the role of nationalism as the motor of change. Historians working on British decolonization have applied this insight to Africa and this approach could be extended profitably to the Middle East.[8] Contemporaries regarded Nasser as the incarnation of the Arab nationalist spirit and the reasons for this view need to be examined. According to nationalist thinkers the Arab states created in the aftermath of the First World War were artificial creations of the western powers. Yet despite the endless tribulations of the Middle East one of the region's few durable institutions has been the sub-national state and there is every expectation that countries such as Iraq and Syria will reach their centenaries. It was, however, during the 12 years of this study that the replacement of the fragmentary state system with a more united pan-Arab entity appeared most feasible. This was an era in which the conflict between loyalty to one's state or region or *wataniya* was explicitly contrasted with loyalty to the extended nation or *qawmiya*.[9] The British in Arabia, as elsewhere, were quite clear in their preference for *wataniya*; the concept of *qawmiya* played into Nasser's hands. In this sense, Nasser was accurate in his critique of British imperialism: policy-makers in Whitehall and Aden were attempting to impose a recognisably western institution, the state, on a population whose most significant affiliations tended to lie elsewhere.

In tracing the impact of nationalism another common element in the imperial story emerges: the British attempt to substitute informal for formal empire. The Aden case provides a particularly vivid illustration of this because the advocates of formal empire in the metropolis, such as Sandys, came into direct conflict with the proponents of informal empire in the periphery, such as Trevaskis. Policy-makers in Aden were much more sensitive to the rise of nationalism and were convinced that informal means of control would have to act as a substitute for direct British rule. Many in the metropolitan government were reluctant to recognise this but it should be acknowledged that some policy-makers, including Iain Macleod, accepted that the form of British influence would have to change if it was to survive. The lateness of the Aden decolonization can at least be partially ascribed to the initial success of the proponents of the continuation of formal empire in arguing that the retention of British sovereignty in the imperial periphery was essential to the maintenance of the global role.

How and why did British policy fail?

If the goals of the British in southwest Arabia cannot be described adequately in terms of national interest it should nevertheless be recognised that the tactics by which the British sought to retain influence were those which any realist would recognise. From the account given in earlier chapters it is evident that British policy-makers had constant resort to what was variously described as Machiavellianism, keeni-meeni or jiggery pokery. Both Labour and Conservative governments proved dogged in their determination to retain British influence in the Middle East. In one sense, the Aden case was not an absolute failure because the primary goal of keeping out Nasser was achieved. However, the eventual waning of Nasser's influence in South Arabia was more an adventitious consequence of the defeat of the Egyptian army in the June 1967 war than a product of long-standing British efforts to contain his influence on the ground. There is little doubt that the outcome in southwest Arabia was entirely at variance with that for which British governments had planned during the previous decade.

In examining why this occurred hindsight is both a curse and an advantage. Hindsight and detachment are the stock in trade of the historian but they are dangerous when they blind one to the dilemmas faced by policy-makers at the time. The detailed discussion of events between 1955 and 1967 provides clear evidence of the intractability of many of the problems confronting the British. They also point to certain weaknesses in the manner in which British policy developed. Four of these stand out: two might be described as strategic and two as tactical. All were a consequence of over optimism at the extent to which Arabian society could be moulded to suit the ambitions of the imperial metropolis.

The muddled strategic thinking of successive Conservative administrations was illustrated by the Lloyd speech of 1956 which explicitly barred the road to full independence for Aden. This reflected a widespread reluctance to abandon or even much alter Britain's ambitions in the Middle East. Many Conservative politicians hoped the region could be insulated from the wider anti-colonial struggle. While other African and Asian colonies were slipping from British control there was a reluctance to let go of Britain's last outpost in Arabia. Plans for federation and constitutional advance in Aden were greeted sceptically precisely because they were interpreted as stepping-stones to independence. It was not until the summer of 1964 that a timetable for independence was reluctantly accepted by the Cabinet. The consequences of this delay were the frustration of those moderates seeking a gradual loosening of imperial ties and the radicalisation of nationalist sentiment. The frustrations of potential local collaborators were exacerbated in the decade after 1955 by the measures taken by successive Governors and High Commissioners in Aden to bolster the authority of their allies amongst the tribal rulers. The greatest of these provocations was the incorporation of Aden into the federation which was correctly perceived by the workers of Aden as part of wider attempt to subordinate them to the rulers of the hinterland. The merger provoked a final break with even the moderate nationalists of Aden; combined with the accompanying attempts to restrict the franchise and the efforts to undermine the SAL in the Protectorates it established the necessary conditions for the future ascendance of the NLF. The marginalisation of moderate opinion partially reflected broader trends in the Middle East and specific local grievances but it was also encouraged by the failure to grant concessions to nationalist eagerness for independence in a timely manner.

As a partial consequence of Conservative dilatoriness on the independence issue, the Labour government had a difficult inheritance in Aden. Greenwood and Brown have been roundly criticised: the first for attempting to appease the urban nationalists, the second for apparent favouritism to Nasser. Yet some form of compromise with nationalism was essential: Britain could no longer sustain its position by the application of force. Whereas Greenwood was overly sanguine in his belief that the Aden nationalists could become British allies in the process of decolonization, Brown was at least attempting to deal with the source of the problem in treating with Nasser. The greatest error of the Wilson government was its decision not to offer a defence treaty to the federation or to any successor government. There is little reason to doubt the accounts of those who witnessed its impact on the ground in Aden, that the Defence White Paper made the security situation impossible. From February 1966 Britain was seen as increasingly irrelevant, as local actors sought to climb aboard whichever nationalist bandwagon appeared likely to reach the independence finishing line in first place.

At a tactical level the Aden High Commission chose its enemies badly. The Sisyphean task of curbing tribal dissidence in the interior for the purposes of 'tidying up' led to a series of armed encounters across the Protectorates which the British had little hope of resolving. Insurgent tribes were regarded as a nuisance, as were their leaders' demands for a greater say in the affairs of their states. Hickinbotham described the rebels in Dali' as a 'disagreeable bunch of Qat-ridden wasters.'[10] Trevaskis became almost obsessed by the need to destroy Muhammad 'Aydarus's influence in Yafa'. Constant resort to aerial proscription proved ineffective despite the claims of local authorities to the contrary. The campaigns in Upper 'Awlaqi, Dali' and Upper Yafi' added to evidence already available from Oman that policing from the air could not quell tribal revolts. Even though ground campaigns achieved more success it was not feasible to police the whole of the interior in this manner. The problem was exacerbated by the support which the insurgents received from external actors. British outrage at the interference of Soviets, Yemenis and Egyptians in the affairs of Aden and the Protectorates tended to blind them to the impossibility of preventing their foes from exploiting British difficulties. Although the punitive policy pursued towards the Imam briefly succeeded in cutting supplies to tribal rebels the insurgencies continued and in 1962 the fall of the Imamate brought a Republican government to power in the north which was even more effective in exploiting Britain's military dilemma.

The confrontation with the union movement in Aden was perhaps even more ill-judged. The increasing radicalisation of the workforce on the doorstep of the British administration at Steamer Point was a consequence of the confrontational approach of successive Governors and High Commissioners. Even the most liberal of British colonial administrators seemed unable or unwilling to recognise that some form of compromise with this group was necessary. Charles Johnston recalled that he was determined that 'we must not allow this crucial decision of Aden's future to be bedevilled by transient Yemeni labourers who enjoyed no freedom of political expression under the regime then existing in their own country.'[11] It was these attitudes, which ignored the fact that the demographic history of the town was one of transience, that led the British to ban strike action, narrow the franchise and rely upon internment and deportations to maintain order. None of these expedients worked. The Colony was dependent on cheap

Yemeni labour and, with Radio Cairo broadcasting what must have appeared entirely convincing accounts of British perfidy, strong action merely consolidated hostility to the imperial government. Taking an overview of these errors largely confirms the conclusions drawn from the previous analysis of the character and reasons for British withdrawal: the overriding problem was the belief that in an era of decolonization the British could still govern by old-fashioned imperial methods.

The future study of Britain's past role in the Middle East

The pervasive neglect of the Aden episode in imperial history is such that it is possible to write a popular history of Britain's role in the Middle East during the twentieth century, while self-consciously excluding any mention of it.[12] The most important priority is therefore to put Aden back into the narrative of Britain's empire in the Middle East. Although the British government continues to maintain special relations with various Arab governments, most notably Oman, Aden really was Britain's last Arabian outpost in the sense that the government there was run directly from the imperial metropolis until November 1967.

This is the easy part; the more difficult question is how Britain's role can be conceptualised. In the case of Aden the key developments were not changes in the thinking of metropolitan elites back in London but the new political allegiances of the local population, which became manifest in a commitment to nationalism, and the reaction of local British actors who, although constrained by the policy parameters set in Whitehall, nevertheless demonstrated considerable independence and initiative. The famous 'men on the spot' who played such a significant role in the emergence and development of the empire were just as significant in bringing about its end. One might argue that the failure of Luce and Trevaskis to have their proposals for constitutional advance approved by the British government suggests otherwise, but it was the advocacy of the forward policy by them and their predecessors which defined the terms in which Britain's relations with the population of Aden and the Protectorates developed. Proposals for opening up Upper 'Awlaqi, targetting the SAL leadership in Lahj, merging Aden and the Protectorates, attacking the Egyptian forces in Yemen and eventually handing over to the NLF rather than FLOSY were generated in Steamer Point rather than Whitehall. While the imperial proconsuls of earlier eras and other regions have received at least their fair share of attention, additional studies of the men who made and implemented policy on the ground in the Middle East after 1945 may well demonstrate that the British were not governed by a narrow notion of self interest but by a broader conception of Britain's proper role in the world.

From 1955 these local British actors were increasingly concerned with containing the impact of Arab nationalism in general and Nasser's influence in particular. In terms of the local politics of Aden, it is evident that Arab nationalism, in the sense of a commitment to the cultural, social and political unity of the Arab peoples, was imported from Egypt and the Fertile Crescent. However, its foreign origins did not detract from its popularity. The one point on which practically all writers on this period can agree is that Nasser's rhetoric had enormous appeal in southwest Arabia. At least three separate conflicts were sublimated into the broader contest between Britain and Egypt. The first concerned the struggle for autarchy in the protectorates: tribal resentment at British interference led these groups to attach themselves to the anti-imperialist cause. It is doubtful if the Qutaybis in the Radfan had a particularly sophisticated understanding of NLF doctrines but they were quite willing to adopt the rhetoric of the nationalists if it meant the provision of arms. Secondly, those influential families denied British patronage and excluded from power sought to legitimise their own anti-imperialist campaigns. Hence it was to Cairo that the SAL leaders fled when expelled from Lahj. Muhammad 'Aydarus portrayed his struggle with Trevaskis as a front in the wider Arab conflict with Britain. Finally, the Aden labour force regarded Nasser as a valuable ally in their struggle for representation. ATUC and then the PSP challenged British industrial policies and demanded a broadening of the franchise. With their failure, the way was open for the radicals of the NLF and FLOSY to take the struggle onto the streets of Aden.

This account of British policy has provided no more than a sketch of the development of Arab nationalism in southwest Arabia. It served local actors to attach themselves to the Egyptian-led nationalist struggle against the British. In its nascent form it was adopted by the elites of the Protectorates such as Sultan 'Ali of Lahj and Muhammad 'Aydarus of Yafi'. For them, like the Hashemites in the Fertile Crescent, Arab nationalism had an instrumental purpose: tying them to Nasser's coat tails in the aftermath of Suez was a means for them to assert a familial claim to regional authority. It is this mixture of motives which provided the British with an opportunity to reconcile themselves to nationalism which was scorned. For Nasser and his followers there was a fundamental incompatibility between the development of Arab nationalism and a British presence in the Middle East. However, the final outcome of the Aden episode demonstrated that southwest Arabia was not a region particularly susceptible to direction from an external power, whether this was Egypt or Britain.

Differences in perspective between the west and the Arab world remain a significant source of tension today despite the declining fortunes of Arab nationalism. Indeed, some scholars have gone as far as to suggest that there is a fundamental clash of cultures at work in the Middle East. While it would be trite to draw conclusions for the future from events in Aden which took place in the last century, what indications there are suggest the notion of a cultural clash is not a particularly effective analytical tool. It is difficult not to draw parallels between the Arab world's past experience of British rule and present circumstances. Political changes in the Arab world are much too fluid to be interpreted as the consequence of some embedded unchangeable culture. A better starting point may be to examine the consequence of changes in political ideas. Thus, the Zaydi traditions which survived for a millennium in the highlands of Yemen are now in conflict with a different set of Muslim traditions which have been imported from outside the region. The one thing which Nasser's interpretation of nationalism and the new brand of Islamic thinking stress is the hostility of the west to the Arab world. It is therefore worth reflecting on the relationship between conditions in countries such as Yemen and the intellectual environment in which their politics are embedded. Consideration of the current situation is rarely dispassionate and it is in this context that a re-examination of Britain's past relationship with Arab nationalism might be enlightening. For both practical and scholarly reasons, the paradoxical conclusion of a study of British imperialism in southwest Arabia is that it may be time to give less priority to past changes in the imperial metropolis, in favour of a closer examination of the rise of nationalism in the periphery of empire.

Notes

1 F. Halliday, *Arabia Without Sultans* (London, Saqi Books, 2002), pp. 237–9.
2 P. Dresch, *A History of Modern Yemen* (Cambridge, Cambridge University Press, 2000), chs 5–6; R. Bidwell, *The Two Yemens* (Harlow, Longman, 1983).
3 The association of Yemen with terrorism in the western press predates the attacks of 2001 and began first with coverage of kidnappings during the 1990s and continued as a consequence of the attack on the USS *Cole* in Aden harbour in October 2000.
4 D. Sanders, *Losing an Empire, Finding a Role* (Basingstoke, Macmillan, 1990) chs 1 and 9.
5 F. Heinlein, *British Government Policy and Decolonisation 1945–1963* (London, Frank Cass, 2002), p. 308.
6 R. Hyam, 'Africa and the Labour Government 1945–1951', *Journal of Imperial and Commonwealth History* 16 (1988), pp. 148–72; J. Kent, 'Bevin's Imperialism and the Idea of Euro-Africa 1945–1949' in M. Dockrill and J. W. Young (eds), *British Foreign Policy 1945–1956* (Basingstoke, Macmillan, 1989), pp. 47–76.
7 J. Darwin, 'Decolonization and the End of Empire' in R. W. Winks (ed.), *The Oxford History of the British Empire, vol. 5: Historiography*, pp. 550–2.
8 D. A. Low, 'The End of the British Empire in Africa' in D. A. Low, *Eclipse of Empire* (Cambridge, Cambridge University Press, 1993), pp. 226–64.
9 A. Dawisha, Arab Nationalism in the Twentieth Century (Princeton, Princeton University Press, 2003).
10 T. Hickinbotham, *Aden* (London, Constable, 1958), p. 116.
11 C. Johnston, *The View From Steamer Point* (London, Collins, 1964), pp. 119–20.
12 J. Keay, *Sowing the Wind* (London, John Murray, 2003), p. 3.

Bibliography

Primary sources

Archival sources

Public Record Office (Kew)

ADM – Admiralty Office:
ADM 205 – Office of the First Sea Lord: Correspondence and Papers 1937–1965

AIR – Air Ministry:
AIR 8 – Chief of Air Staff's Registered Files 1916–1982
AIR 19 – Private Office Papers 1917–1983
AIR 20 – Unregistered Papers 1874–1983
AIR 23 – Overseas Commands: Reports and Correspondence 1916–1976

CAB – Cabinet Office:
CAB 21 – Registered Files 1916–1973
CAB 128 – Minutes 1945–1974
CAB 129 – Memoranda 1945–1973
CAB 130 – Miscellaneous Committees 1945–1974
CAB 131 – Defence Committee 1946–1963
CAB 133 – Commonwealth and International Conferences and Ministerial Visits 1944–1972
CAB 134 – Miscellaneous Committees and Papers (General Series) 1945–1978
CAB 148 – Defence and Overseas Policy Committee: Minutes and Papers 1964–1974
CAB 158 – Joint Intelligence Sub-Committee memoranda 1947–1968
CAB 159 – Joint Intelligence Sub-Committee minutes 1947–1968

CO – Colonial Office:
CO 967 – Private Office Papers 1873–1966
CO 1015 – Central Africa and Aden Original Correspondence 1950–1962
CO 1025 – Finance Department: Registered Files 1951–1966
CO 1055 – Aden Department: Registered Files 1962–1966

DEFE – Ministry of Defence:
DEFE 4 – Chiefs of Staff Minutes 1947–1972

DEFE 5 – Chiefs of Staff Memoranda 1947–72
DEFE 6 – Joint Planning Staff Reports 1947–1968
DEFE 11 – Chiefs of Staff: Registered Files 1946–1977
DEFE 13 – Private Office; Registered Files 1950–1979
DEFE 24 – Defence Secretariat: Registered Files 1956–1983
DEFE 25 – Chief of Defence Staff: Registered Files 1957–1980
DEFE 32 – Chiefs of Staff Secretary's Standard Files 1946–1983

DO – Commonwealth Relations Office (formerly Dominions Office):
DO 174 – Western and Middle Eastern Department: Registered Files 1957–1966
DO 181 – UN Department: Registered Files 1940–1966

FCO – Foreign and Commonwealth Office:
FCO 8 – Arabian Department: Registered Files 1967–1972
FCO 39 – North and East African Department Registered Files 1967–1972
FCO 73 – Private Office: Various Ministers' and Officials' Papers 1956–74

FO – Foreign Office:
FO 371 – General Correspondence from 1906
FO 800 – Private Office: Papers 1824–1968
FO 953 – Information Policy Department and Regional Information Departments:
  Registered Files 1947–1966

PREM – Prime Minister's Office:
PREM 11 – Prime Minister's Office: Correspondence and Papers 1951–1964
PREM 13 – Prime Minister's Office: Correspondence and Papers 1964–1970

T – Treasury:
T 220 – Imperial and Foreign Division: Registered Files 1914–1961
T 225 – Defence Policy and Material Division: Registered Files 1911–1975
T 296 – Foreign and Commonwealth Division: Registered Files 1960–1963
T 317 – Finance and Overseas Development Division: Registered Files 1960–1972

WO – War Office:
WO 32 – Registered Files 1845–1942
WO 216 – Office of the CIGS: Papers 1935–1964
WO 386 – HQ: Middle East Records 1962–1974

India Office Records (Oriental and India, British Library, St Pancras)
R/20/B – Secretariat of the Government of the Colony of Aden 1937–1962
R/20/C – Records of the Protectorate Secretary 1928–1962
R/20/D – Files of the Aden High Commission 1962–1967

United States National Archives and Records Administration (College Park, Maryland)
RG 59 – State Department Records

John Fitzgerald Kennedy Library (Boston, Massachusetts)
Presidential Papers: National Security Files

Presidential Papers: President's Office Files
Presidential Papers: White House Staff Files (McGeorge Bundy and Walt Rostow)
Oral History Interviews: Robert Komer
Oral History Interviews: Dean Rusk
George Ball Papers
McGeorge Bundy Papers

Lyndon Baines Johnson Library (Austin, Texas)
White House Confidential Files
National Security Files: Country Files
National Security Files: Name Files (Robert Komer)
Oral History Interviews: Lucius Battle
Oral History Interviews: Robert Komer

Bodleian Library, University of Oxford (Department of Special Collections and Western Manuscripts)
Conservative Party Archive
Paul Gore-Booth Papers
Alan Lennox-Boyd Papers
Harold Macmillan Diary and Papers
Walter Monckton Papers

Rhodes House Library, University of Oxford
Kennedy Trevaskis Papers, pts 1 and 2

St. Antony's College, University of Oxford
Harold Ingrams Papers
Richard Holmes Papers

Churchill College, University of Cambridge
Duncan Sandys Papers
Patrick Gordon Walker

University of Manchester
Labour Party Archive

University of Southampton
Peter Thorneycroft Papers
Viscount Mountbatten Papers

Kings College, University of London
Charles Johnston Papers

University of Birmingham
Avon Papers

British Library Newspaper Archive (Colindale)
Glasgow Sunday Mail 1981–1983

London School of Economics, University of London
George Wigg Papers

University of Nottingham
The Times 1951–67

Published documentary collections

British Documents at the End of Empire (London, HMSO):
   Series A, Vol. 2, R. Hyam (ed.), *The Labour Government and the End of Empire 1945–51*, pts 1–4 (1992)
   Series A, Vol. 3, D. Goldsworthy (ed.), *The Conservative Government and the End of Empire 1951–57*, pts 1–3 (1994)
   Series A, Vol. 4, R. Hyam and Wm. R. Louis (eds), *The Conservative Government and the End of Empire 1957–64*, pts 1–2 (2000)
   Series A, Vol. 5, S. R. Ashton and Wm. R. Louis (eds), *East of Suez and the Comonwealth 1964–1971*, pts 1–3 (2004)
   Series B, Vol. 4, J. Kent (ed.), *Egypt and the Defence of the Middle East 1945–56*, pts 1–3 (1998)
Colonial Office Lists (London, HMSO, 1956–66)
Foreign Relations of the United States (Washington, Department of State):
   1955–1957 Vol. 12: Near East Region: Jordan, Yemen (1989)
   1958–1960 Vol. 12: Middle East Region: Iraq, Iran, Yemen (1993)
   1961–1963 Vol. 17: The Near East 1961–2 (1995)
   1961–1963 Vol. 18: The Near East 1962–3 (1995)
   1964–1968 Vol. 21: Near East Region: Arabian Peninsula (2000)
Gorst, A. and Johnman, L. (eds), *The Suez Crisis: A Sourcebook* (London, Routledge, 1997)
Haim, S. (ed.), *Arab Nationalism: An Anthology* (Berkeley, University of California Press, 1976)
Ingrams, D. and Ingrams, L., *Records of Yemen* (Slough, Archive Editions, 1993)
Lucas, W. S. (ed.), *Britain and Suez: The Lion's Last Roar* (Manchester, Manchester University Press, 1996)
Nasser, G. A., *The Philosophy of the Revolution* (English edition, Buffalo, Economica, 1959)
Parliamentary Debates (Hansard) 1945–1967
Parliamentary Papers 1945–67
Porter, A. N. and Goldsworthy, A. J. (eds), *British Imperial Policy and Decolonization 1938–64: Vol. 2: 1951–1964* (Basingstoke, Macmillan, 1989)

Memoirs, diaries and autobiographies

Allfree, P. S., *The Hawks of the Hadhramaut* (London, Robert Hale, 1967)
Lord Avon, *Full Circle* (London, Cassel, 1960)
Lord Belhaven, *The Uneven Road* (London, John Murray, 1955)
Benn, A., *Out of the Wilderness: Diaries 1963–1967* (London, Hutchinson, 1987)
de la Billiere, P., *Looking For Trouble: An Autobiography* (London, HarperCollins, 1994)

Boustead, H., *The Wind of Morning: The Autobiography of Hugh Boustead* (London, Chatto and Windus, 1971)

Brown, G., *In My Way* (London, Victor Gollancz, 1971)

Castle, B., *The Castle Diaries 1964–1970* (London, Weidenfeld and Nicolson, 1984)

Catterall, P., (ed.) (2003), *The Macmillan Diaries: The Cabinet Years 1950–1957* (London, Macmillan, 2003)

Connor, K., *Ghost Force: The Secret History of the SAS* (London, Weidenfeld and Nicolson, 1998)

Copeland, M., *The Game of Nations* (London, Weidenfeld and Nicolson, 1969)

Crossman, R., *Diaries of a Cabinet Minister: Vols 1–3* (London, Hamish Hamilton and Cape, 1976)

Crouch, M., *An Element of Luck: To South Arabia and Beyond* (London, Radcliffe, 1993)

Downton, E., *Wars Without End* (Toronto, Stoddart, 1987)

Falle, S., *My Lucky Life* (Sussex, Book Guild, 1996)

Foster, D., *Landscape with Arabs* (Brighton, Clifton, 1969)

Gandy, C., 'A Mission to Yemen', *British Journal of Middle Eastern Studies*, 25, (1998)

Gore-Booth, P., *With Great Truth and Respect* (London, Constable, 1974)

Groom, N., *Sheba Revealed* (London, Centre of Arab Studies, 2002)

Harper, S., *Last Sunset* (London, Collins, 1978)

Hart, P. T., *Saudi Arabia and the United States: Birth of a Security Partnership* (Bloomington, Indiana University Press, 1998)

Healey, D., *The Time of My Life* (London, Michael Joseph, 1989)

Heath, E., *The Course of My Life* (London, Hodder and Stoughton, 1998)

Hickinbotham, T., *Aden* (London, Constable, 1958)

Holden, D., *Farewell to Arabia* (London, Faber and Faber, 1966)

Lord Home, *The Way the Wind Blows* (London, Collins, 1976)

Ingrams, H., *Arabia and the Isles* (4th ed., London, Kegan Paul International, 1998)

Johnston, C., *The View from Steamer Point* (London, Collins, 1964)

Knox-Mawer, J., *The Sultans Came to Tea* (Gloucester, Alan Sutton, 1984)

Ledger, D., *Shifting Sands: The British in South Arabia* (London, Peninsular Publishing, 1983)

Luce, M., *From Aden to the Gulf: Personal Diaries 1956–1966* (Salisbury, Michael Russell, 1987)

Lunt, J., *The Barren Rocks of Aden* (London, Herbert Jenkins, 1966)

Macmillan, H., *Tides of Fortune 1945–1955* (London, Macmillan, 1969)

Macmillan, H., *Riding the Storm 1956–1959* (London, Macmillan, 1971)

Macmillan, H., *Pointing the Way 1959–1961* (London, Macmillan, 1972)

Macmillan, H., *At The End of the Day 1961–1963* (London, Macmillan, 1973)

Mayhew, C., *Time To Explain* (London, Hutchinson, 1987)

Mitchell, C., *Having Been a Soldier* (London, Hamish Hamilton, 1969)

Paget, J., *Last Post: Aden 1964–1967* (London, Faber and Faber, 1969)

Short, E., *Whip to Wilson* (London, Macdonald, 1989)

Shuckburgh, E., *Descent to Suez: Diaries 1951–1956* (London, Weidenfeld and Nicolson, 1986)

Somerville-Large, P., *Tribes and Tribulations: A Journey in Republican Yemen* (London, Robert Hale, 1967)

Smiley, D., *Arabian Assignment* (London, Leo Cooper, 1975)

Stewart, M., *Life and Labour* (London, Sidgwick and Jackson, 1980)

Thesiger, W., *Desert, Marsh and Mountain* (London, Collins, 1979)

Trevaskis, K., *Shades of Amber: A South Arabian Episode* (London, Hutchinson, 1968)

Trevelyan, H., *Public and Private* (London, Hamish Hamilton, 1980)

Trevelyan, H., *The Middle East in Revolution* (London, Macmillan, 1970)

von Horn, C., *Soldiering for Peace* (London, Cassels, 1966)

Wigg, G., *George Wigg* (London, Michael Joseph, 1972)

Wilson, H., *The Labour Government 1964–1970: A Personal Record* (London, Weidenfeld and Nicolson, 1971)

Secondary sources

Abadi, J., 'Britain's Abandonment of South Arabia: A Reassessment', *Journal of Third World Studies* 12 (1995), pp. 152–80

Abir, M., *Oil, Power and Politics* (London, Frank Cass, 1974)

Aburish, S., *Nasser: The Last Arab* (London, Duckworth, 2004)

Aldrich, R. J., *The Hidden Hand: Britain, America and Cold War Secret Intelligence* (London, John Murray, 2001)

Antonius, G., *The Arab Awakening* (London, Hamish Hamilton, 1945)

Ashton, N. J., *Kennedy, Macmillan and the Cold War* (Basingstoke, Palgrave/Macmillan, 2002)

Ashton, N. J., 'Macmillan and the Middle East' in Aldous, R. and Lee, S. (eds), *Harold Macmillan and Britain's World Role* (Basingstoke, Macmillan, 1996)

Ashton, N. J., *Eisenhower, Macmillan and the Problem of Nasser 1955–59* (Basingstoke, Macmillan, 1996)

Ashton, N. J., 'The Hijacking of a Pact: The Formation of the Baghdad Pact and Anglo-American Tensions in the Middle East, 1955–1958', *Review of International Studies* 19 (1993), pp. 123–37

Balfour-Paul, G., *The End of Empire in the Middle East* (Cambridge, Cambridge University Press, 1991)

Balfour-Paul, G., 'Britain's Informal Empire in the Middle East' in Louis, Wm. R. and Brown, J. M. (eds) (1999), *Oxford History of the British Empire, Vol. 4: The Twentieth Century* (Oxford, Oxford University Press, 1999), pp. 490–514

Barnett, M. N., *Dialogues in Arab Politics* (New York, Columbia University Press, 1998)

Barnett, M. N., 'Sovereignty, Nationalism and Regional Order in the Arab States System', *International Organization*, 49, 3 (1995), pp. 479–510

Bass, W., *Support Any Friend: Kennedy's Middle East and the Making of the US-Israeli Alliance* (Oxford, Oxford University Press, 2003)

Bidwell, R., *The Two Yemens* (Harlow, Longman, 1983)

Blackwell, S. J., 'A Transfer of Power?: Britain, the Anglo-American Relationship and the Cold War in the Middle East' in Hopkins, M. F., Kandiah, M. D. and Staerck, G., *Cold War Britain* (Basingstoke, Palgrave/Macmillan, 2003), pp. 168–79

Blackwell, S. J., 'Pursuing Nasser: The Macmillan Government and the Management of British Policy Towards the Middle East Cold War 1957–1963', *Cold War History*, 14, 3 (2004), pp. 85–103

Bower, T., *The Perfect English Spy: Sir Dick White and the Secret War 1935–1990* (London, Heinemann, 1995)

Boxberger, L., 'Hadhrami Politics 1888–1967' in Freitag, U. and Clarence-Smith, W. (eds), *Hadhrami Traders, Scholars and Statesmen in the Indian Ocean* (Leiden, Brill, 1997)

Boyce, D. G., *Decolonisation and the British Empire* (Basingstoke, Palgrave/Macmillan, 1999)

Brands, H. W., *Into the Labyrinth: The United States and the Middle East 1945–1993* (New York, McGraw-Hill, 1994)

Butler, L. J., *Britain and Empire: Adjusting to a Post-Imperial World* (London, I. B. Tauris, 2002)

Carapico, S., *Civil Society in Yemen* (Cambridge, Cambridge University Press, 1998)

Chamberlain, M. E., *Decolonization: The Fall of the European Empires* (Oxford, Blackwell, 1985)

Catterall, P., 'Foreign and Commonwealth Policy in Opposition: The Labour Party' in Kaiser, W. and Staerck, G. (eds), *British Foreign Policy 1955: Contracting Options* (Palgrave/Macmillan, Basingstoke, 2000), pp. 89–110

Chalala, E., 'Arab Nationalism: A Biblographical Essay' in Farah, T. E. (ed.), *Pan-Arabism and Arab Nationalism* (London, Westview Press, 1987), pp. 18–45

Chang, K., 'The United Nations and Decolonization: The Case of Southern Yemen', *International Organization*, 26, 1 (1972) pp. 37–61

Choueiri, Y., *Arab Nationalism: A History* (Oxford, Blackwell, 2000)

Citino, N. J., *From Arab Nationalism to OPEC: Eisenhower, King Saud and the Making of US-Saudi Relations* (Bloomington, Indiana University Press, 2002)

Clarence-Smith, W. G., 'Hadhramaut and the Hadhrami Diaspora in the Modern Colonial Era' in Freitag, U. and Clarence-Smith, W. (eds), *Hadhrami Traders, Scholars and Statesmen in the Indian Ocean* (Leiden, Brill, 1997)

Cleveland, W. L., 'The Arab Nationalism of George Antonius Reconsidered' in Jankowski, J. and Gershoni, I. (eds), *Rethinking Arab Nationalism in the Middle East* (New York, Columbia University Press, 1997), pp. 65–86

Darby, P., British Defence Policy East of Suez (Oxford, Oxford University Press, 1973)

Darwin, J., *Britain and Decolonisation* (Basingstoke, Macmillan, 1988)

Darwin, J., 'British Decolonisation Since 1945: A Pattern or a Puzzle?', *Journal of Imperial and Commonwealth History*, 12 (1984), pp. 187–209

Darwin, J., 'Decolonization and the End of Empire' in Winks, R. (ed.) (1999), *Oxford History of the British Empire, Vol. 5: Historiography* (Oxford, Oxford University Press, 1999) pp. 541–57

Dawisha, A., *Arab Nationalism in the Twentieth Century: From Triumph to Despair* (Princeton, Princeton University Press, 2003)

Dawn, C. E., 'The Quality of Arab Nationalism' in Hopwood, D. (ed.), *Arab Nation: Arab Nationalism* (Basingstoke, Macmillan, 2000), pp. 41–62

Dessouki, A. E. H., 'Nasser and the Struggle for Independence' in Louis, Wm. R. and Owen, R. (eds), *Suez 1956: The Crisis and its Consequences* (Oxford, Clarendon Press, 1989), pp. 31–43

Devlin, J. F. (1976), *The Ba'th Party* (Stanford, Hoover Institution Press, 1976)

Devlin, J. F., 'The Baath Party: Rise and Metamorphosis', *American Historical Review*, 96 (1991), pp. 1396–407

Dockrill, S., *Britain's Retreat from East of Suez* (Basingstoke, Palgrave/Macmillan, 2002)

Dockrill, S., 'Britain's Power and Influence: Dealing with Three Roles and the

Wilson Government's Defence Debate at Chequers in November 1964', *Diplomacy and Statecraft*, 11 (2000), pp. 211–40

Dorril, S., *MI6: Fifty Years of Special Operations* (London, Fourth Estate, 2000)

Douglas, R., *Liquidation of Empire: The Decline of the British Empire* (Basingstoke, Palgrave/Macmillan, 2002)

Dresch, P., *A History of Modern Yemen* (Cambridge, Cambridge University Press, 2000)

Dresch, P., *Tribes, Government and History in Yemen* (Oxford, Oxford University Press, 1989)

Dutton, D. (1997), *Anthony Eden: A Life and Reputation* (London, Arnold, 1997)

Elliot, M., 'Defeat and Revival: Britain in the Middle East' in Kaiser, W. and Staerck, G. (eds), *British Foreign Policy 1955: Contracting Options* (Palgrave/Macmillan, Basingstoke, 2000), pp. 239–56

Elliot, M., *'Independent Iraq': The Monarchy and British Influence 1941–58* (London, Tauris, 1996)

Fain, W. T., 'Unfortunate Arabia: The United States, Great Britain and Yemen 1955–1963', *Diplomacy and Statecraft*, 12 (2001) pp. 125–52

Fielding, X., *One Man in his Time: The Life of Colonel NLD McLean* (London, Macmillan, 1990)

Fraser, T. G., *The United States and the Middle East* (Basingstoke, Macmillan, 1989)

Freitag, U., 'Hadhramis in International Politics 1750–1967' in Freitag, U. and Clarence-Smith, W. (eds), *Hadhrami Traders, Scholars and Statesmen in the Indian Ocean* (Leiden, Brill, 1997)

Furedi, F., *Colonial Wars and the Politics of Third World Nationalism* (London, I. B. Tauris, 1998)

Gallagher, J., *The Decline, Revival and Fall of the British Empire* (Cambridge, Cambridge University Press, 1982)

Gavin, R. J., *Aden Under British Rule* (London, Hirst, 1975)

Geraghty, T., *Who Dares Wins: The Story of the Special Air Service* (London, Book Club Associates, 1980)

Gerges, F. A., 'The Kennedy Administration and the Egyptian-Saudi Conflict in Yemen', *Middle East Journal*, 49 (1995), pp. 292–311

Gershoni, I., 'Rethinking the Formation of Arab Nationalism in the Middle East 1920–1945' in Jankowski, J. and Gershoni, I. (eds), *Rethinking Nationalism in the Arab Middle East* (New York, Columbia University Press, 1997)

Gorst, A. and Lucas, W. S., 'Operation Straggle and Anglo-American Intervention in Syria', *Intelligence and National Security*, 4 (1989), pp. 576–95

Grove, E., *Vanguard to Trident: British Naval Policy Since World War II* (London, Bodley Head, 1987)

Hahn, P. L., *The United States, Great Britain and Egypt 1945–1956: Strategy and Diplomacy in the Early Cold War* (Chapel Hill, University of North Carolina Press, 1991)

Halliday, F., *Arabia Without Sultans* (London, Saqi Books, 2002)

Halliday, F., 'Formation of Yemeni Nationalism' in Jankowski, J. and Gershoni, I. (eds), *Rethinking Nationalism in the Arab Middle East* (New York, Columbia University Press, 1997), pp. 25–41

Hasou, T. Y., *Struggle for the Arab World: Egypt's Nasser and the Arab World* (London, Routledge, 1985)

Hassouna, H. A., *The League of Arab States and Regional Disputes* (New York, Oceana Publications, 1975)

Heffer, S., *Like the Roman: The Life of Enoch Powell* (London, Wiedenfeld and Nicolson, 1998)

Hoe, A., *David Stirling: The Authorised Biography of the Founder of the SAS* (London, Little Brown, 1992)

Holden Reid, B., 'The Northern Tier and the Baghdad Pact' in Young, J. W. (ed.), *The Foreign Policy of Churchill's Peacetime Administration 1951–1955* (Leicester, Leicester University Press, 1986), pp. 159–80

Holland, R. F., *European Decolonization* (Basingstoke, Macmillan, 1985)

Holland, R. F., 'The Imperial Factor in British Strategies from Attlee to Macmillan 1945–1963', *Journal of Imperial and Commonwealth History*, 12 (1984), pp. 165–86

Hopkins, T., 'Macmillan's Audit of Empire' in Clarke, P. and Trebilcock, C. (eds), *Understanding Decline* (Cambridge, Cambridge University Press, 1997), pp. 234–60

Horne, A., *Macmillan 1894–1956* (London, Macmillan, 1988)

Horne, A., *Macmillan 1957–1986* (London, Macmillan, 1989)

Hyam, R., 'Africa and the Labour Government 1945–1951', *Journal of Imperial and Commonwealth History*, 16 (1988), pp. 148–72

Hyam, R., 'Winds of Change: The Empire and Commonwealth' in Kaiser, W. and Staerck, G. (eds), *British Foreign Policy 1955–64* (Basingstoke, Palgrave/Macmillan, 2000)

Ingrams, H., *The Yemen: Imams, Rulers and Revolutionaries* (London, John Murray, 1963)

Jankowski, J., 'Arab Nationalism in Nasserism and Egyptian State Policy 1952–58' in Jankowki, J. and Gershoni, I. (eds) (1997), *Rethinking Nationalism in the Arab Middle East* (New York, Columbia University Press, 1997), pp. 150–67

Jankowski, J., *Nasser's Egypt, Arab Nationalism and the United Arab Republic* (London, Lynne Rienner, 2002)

Jones, C., *Britain and the Yemen Civil War 1962–1965: Ministers, Mandarins and Mercenaries* (Brighton, Sussex Academic Press, 2004)

Jones, C., 'Among Ministers, Mavericks and Mandarins: Britain, Covert Action and the Yemen Civil War', *Middle Eastern Studies*, 40 (2004), pp. 99–126

Kaufman, B. I., *The Arab Middle East and the United States: Inter-Arab Rivalry and Superpower Diplomacy* (New York, Twayne, 1996)

Kazzika, W. W., *Revolutionary Transformation in the Arab World* (London, Charles Knight, 1975)

Kear, S., 'Diplomatic Innovation: Nasser and the Origins of the Interests Section', *Diplomacy and Statecraft*, 12 (2001), pp. 65–86

Keay, J., *Sowing the Wind: The Seeds of Conflict in the Middle East* (London, John Murray, 2003)

Kedourie, E., 'Pan-Arabism and British Policy' in Kedourie, E., *The Chatham House Version and Other Middle Eastern Studies* (London, Weidenfeld and Nicolson, 1970)

Kelly, J. B., *Arabia, the Gulf and the West* (London, Weidenfeld and Nicolson, 1980)

Kemp, A., *Savage Wars of Peace* (2nd edn. Penguin, London, 2001)

Kent, J., 'Bevin's Imperialism and the Idea of Euro-Africa' in Dockrill, M. and Young, J. W. (eds), *British Foreign Policy 1945–1956* (Basingstoke, Macmillan, 1989), pp. 47–76

Kent, J., 'Britain and the Egyptian Problem' in Cohen, M. and Kolinsky, M. (eds), *Demise of the British Empire in the Middle East* (London, Frank Cass, 1988)

Kent, J., 'The Egyptian Base and the Defence of the Middle East', *Journal of Imperial and Commonwealth History*, 21 (1993), pp. 45–65

Kerr, M., *The Arab Cold War 1958–64* (Oxford, Oxford University Press, 1965)

King, G., *Imperial Outpost: Aden* (London, Oxford University Press, 1964)

Kostiner, J., *The Struggle for South Yemen* (London, Croom Helm, 1984)

Kostiner, J., 'Arab Radical Politics: Al-Qawmiyyun al-Arab and the Marxists in the Turmoil of South Yemen 1963–1967', *Middle Eastern Studies*, 17 (1981), pp. 454–76

Kyle, K., *Suez: Britain's End of Empire in the Middle East* (2nd edn, London, I. B. Tauris, 2003)

Lackner, H., 'The Rise and Fall of the National Liberation Front as a Political Organisation' in Pridham, B. R. (ed.), *Contemporary Yemen: Politics and Historical Background* (London, Croom Helm, 1984), pp. 46–61

Lapping, B., *End of Empire* (London, Granada, 1985)

Lee, D. L., *Flight From the Middle East* (London, Ministry of Defence, 1980)

Leigh Douglas, J., *The Free Yemeni Movement* (Beirut, American University of Beirut, 1987)

Leigh Douglas, J., 'The Free Yemeni Movement 1935–1962' in Pridham, B. R. (ed.), *Contemporary Yemen: Politics and Historical Background* (London, Croom Helm, 1984), pp. 34–45

Lekon, C., *The British and Hadhramaut 1863–1967* (PhD, London, 2000)

Little, T., *South Arabia: Arena of Conflict* (London, Pall Mall, 1968)

Lord, C. and Birtles, D., *The Armed Forces of Aden 1839–1967* (Solihull, Helion, 2000)

Louis, Wm. R., 'Britain and the Crisis of 1958' in Louis, Wm. R. and Owen, R. (eds), *A Revolutionary Year: The Middle East in 1958* (London, I. B. Tauris, 2002), pp. 15–76

Louis, Wm. R., 'The Tragedy of the Anglo-Egyptian Settlement of 1954' in Wm. R. Louis and Owen, R. (eds) (1989), *Suez 1956* (Oxford, Clarendon Press, 1989), pp. 43–72

Louis, Wm. R., 'The Dissolution of the British Empire' in Louis, Wm. R. (ed.) (1999), *Oxford History of the British Empire, Vol. 4: The Twentieth Century* (Oxford, Oxford University Press, 1999), pp. 329–56

Louis, Wm. R., 'Britain and the Middle East' in Brown, C. L. (ed.) (2001), *Diplomacy in the Middle East* (London, I.B. Tauris, 2001)

Louis, Wm. R., 'Churchill and Egypt' in Blake, R. and Louis Wm. R. (eds) (1994), *Churchill* (Oxford, Oxford University Press, 1993)

Louis, Wm. R. and Robinson, R., 'The Imperialism of Decolonization', *Journal of Imperial and Commonwealth History*, 22, 3 (1994), pp. 462–511

Low, D. A., *Eclipse of Empire* (Cambridge, Cambridge University Press, 1991)

Lucas, W. S., 'Alliance and Balance: The Anglo-American Relationship and Egyptian Nationalism', *Diplomacy and Statecraft*, 7 (1996), pp. 631–51

Lucas, W. S., 'The Path to Suez' in Deighton A. (ed.) (1990), *Britain and the First Cold War* (Basingstoke, Macmillan, 1990), pp. 88–112

Lucas, W. S., *Divided We Stand: Britain, the US and the Suez Crisis* (London, Hodder and Stoughton, 1991)

Macro, E., *Yemen and the Western World* (London, Hurst, 1968)

McIntyre, W. D., *British Decolonization 1946–1997* (Basingstoke, Macmillan, 1988)

Macleod, C. A., *The End of British Rule in South Arabia* (PhD thesis, University of Edinburgh, June 2001)

McNamara, R., *Britain, Nasser and the Balance of Power in the Middle East* (London, Frank Cass, 2003)

McNamara, R., 'Britain, Nasser and the Outbreak of the Six Day War', *Journal of Contemporary History*, 35 (2000), pp. 619–39

Mawby, S., 'The Clandestine Defence of Empire: British Special Operation in Yemen 1951–64', *Intelligence and National Security*, 17 (2002), pp. 105–30

Mawby, S., 'Britain's Last Imperial Frontier', *Journal of Imperial and Commonwealth History*, 29 (2001), pp. 75–100

Mockaitis, T. R., *British Counterinsurgency in the Post-Imperial Era* (Manchester, Manchester University Press, 1995)

Monroe, E., *Britain's Moment in the Middle East* (London, Chatto and Windus, 1963)

Morgan, K. O., *Callaghan: A Life* (Oxford, Oxford University Press, 1997)

Murphy, P., *Alan Lennox-Boyd: A Biography* (London, I. B. Tauris, 1999)

Murphy, P., *Party Politics and Decolonization* (Oxford, Clarendon Press, 1995)

Newsinger, J., *British Counter-insurgency: From Palestine to Northern Island* (Basingstoke, Palgrave/Macmillan, 2002)

O' Ballance, E., *The War in the Yemen* (London, Faber and Faber, 1971)

Oren, M. B., 'A Winter of Discontent: Britain's Crisis in Jordan', *International Journal of Middle Eastern Studies*, 22 (1990), pp. 171–84

Ovendale, R., 'Egypt and the Suez Base Agreement' in Young, J. W. (ed.) (1988), *The Foreign Policy of Churchill's Peacetime Administration 1951–1955* (Leicester, Leicester University Press, 1988), pp. 135–55

Ovendale, R., *Britain, the United States and the Transfer of Power in the Middle East*

Pearson, J., *Sir Anthony Eden and the Suez Crisis* (Basingstoke, Palgrave, 2003)

Persson, M., *Great Britain, the United States and the Security of the Middle East* (Lund, Lund University Press, 1998)

Peterson, J. E., *Defending Arabia* (London, Croom Helm, 1986)

Peterson, J. E., *Yemen: The Search for a Modern State* (London, Croom Helm, 1982)

Peterson, T. T., 'Anglo-American Rivalry in the Middle East: The Struggle for the Buraimi Oaisis', *International History Review*, 14 (1993), pp. 71–91

Peterson, T. T., 'Crossing the Rubicon?: Britain's Withdrawal from the Middle East', *International History Review*, 22 (2000)

Pieragostini, K., *Britain, Aden and South Arabia* (London, Macmillan, 1990)

Pimlott, B., *Harold Wilson* (London, HarperCollins, 1992)

Podeh, E., 'The Struggle over Arab Hegemony After the Suez Crisis', *Middle Eastern Studies*, 29 (1993), pp. 91–110

Podeh, E., *The Decline of Arab Unity: The Rise and Fall of the United Arab Republic* (Brighton, Sussex Academic Press, 1999)

Rahman, A. A., *Egyptian Policy in the Arab World: Intervention in Yemen 1962–1967* (Washington, University Press of America, 1983)

Reilly, B., *Aden and the Yemen* (London, HMSO, 1960)

Reynolds, D., *Britannia Overruled: British Policy and World Power in the 20th Century* (Harlow, Longman, 1991)

Reynolds, D., 'Eden the Diplomatist 1931–1956: Suezcide of a Statesman', *History*, 240 (1989), pp. 64–80

Rijwan, N., *Nasserist Ideology: Its Exponents and Critics* (New York, John Wiley, 1974)

Robinson, F., 'The British Empire in the Muslim World' in Louis, Wm. R. and Brown J. M. (eds) (1999), *Oxford History of the British Empire, Vol. 4: The Twentieth Century* (Oxford, Oxford University Press, 1999), pp. 398–420

Rothwell, V., *Anthony Eden: A Political Biography* Manchester, (Manchester University Press, 1992)

Rubin, B., 'Pan-Arab Nationalism: The Ideological Dream as Compelling Force', *Journal of Contemporary History*, 26 (1991)

Rubin, B., 'America and the Egyptian Revolution 1950–57', *Political Science Quarterly*, 97 (1982)

Sanders, D., *Losing an Empire, Finding a Role* (Basingstoke, Macmillan, 1990)

Schmidt, D. A., *Yemen: The Unknown War* (London, Bodley Head, 1968)

Shepherd, R., *Iain MacLeod* (London, Pimlico, 1994)

Sluglett, P., 'Formal and Informal Empire in the Middle East' in Winks, R. (ed.) (1999), *Oxford History of the British Empire, Vol. 5: Historiography* (Oxford, Oxford University Press, 1999), pp. 416–36

Smith, R. and Zametica, J., 'The Cold Warrior Clement Attlee Reconsidered', *International Affairs*, 61 (1985), pp. 237–52

Smith, S., *Britain's Revival and Fall in the Gulf* (London, Routledge Curzon, 2004)

Smith, S., *Kuwait 1950–65: Britain, the al-Sabah and Oil* (Oxford, Oxford University Press 1999)

Smith, S., 'The Making of Neo-Colony: Anglo-Kuwaiti Relations in the Era of Decolonisation', *Middle Eastern Studies*, 37 (2001), pp. 159–72

Smith, S., 'Rulers and Resident: British Relations with the Aden Protectorate 1937–1959', *Middle Eastern Studies*, 31 (1995), pp. 509–23

Smith, S., 'Revolution and Reaction: South Arabia in the Aftermath of the Yemeni Revolution' in Fedorowich, K. and Thomas, M. (eds), *International Diplomacy and Colonial Retreat 1940–1975* (London, Frank Cass, 2000), pp. 193–208

Snell-Mendoza, M., 'In Defence of Oil: Britain's Response to the Iraqi Threat Towards Kuwait', *Contemporary Record*, 10 (1996), pp. 39–61

Spiegel, S. L., *The Other Arab-Israeli Conflict: Making America's Middle East Policy from Truman to Reagan* (Chicago, University of Chicago, 1985)

Springhall, J., *Decolonization Since 1945* (Basingstoke, Palgrave 2001)

Stanford, P., *Lord Longford: A Life* (London, Heinemann, 1994)

Stookey, R. W., *America and the Arab States: An Uneasy Encounter* (New York, John Wiley, 1975)

Stookey, R. W., *Yemen: The Politics of the Yemen Arab Republic* (Boulder, Westview, 1978)

Takeyh, R., *The Origins of the Eisenhower Doctrine: The US, Britain and Nasser's Egypt* (Basingstoke, Macmillan, 2000)

Thornhill, M. T., 'Alternatives to Nasser: Humphrey Trevelyan, Ambassador to Egypt' in Kelly, S. and Gorst, A. (eds), *Whitehall and the Suez Crisis* (London, Frank Cass, 2000), pp. 11–28

Thorpe, D. R., *Eden* (London, Chatto and Windus, 2003)

Thorpe, D. R., *Alec Douglas-Home* (London, Sinclair Stevenson, 1997)

Thorpe, D. R., *Selwyn Lloyd* (London, Jonathon Cape, 1989)

Tibi, B., *Arab Nationalism: A Critical Enquiry* (3rd edn, London, Macmillan, 1997)

Tripp, C., 'Egypt 1945–1952: The Uses of Disorder' in Cohen, M. and Kolinsky, M. (eds), *Demise of the British Empire in the Middle East* (London, Frank Cass, 1988)

Vaughan, J., 'Cloak Without Dagger: How the IRD Fought Britain's Cold War in the Middle East 1948–1956', *Cold War History*, 4, 3 (2004), pp. 56–84

Waterfield, G., *Sultans of Aden* (London, Stacey International, 2002)

White, N. J., *Decolonisation: The British Experience* (London, Longman, 1999)

Wilkinson, J. C., *Arabia's Frontiers: The Story of Britain's Boundary Drawing in the Desert* (London, I. B. Tauris, 1991)

Willis, J., 'British Colonial Policing in Aden 1937–1967', *Arab Studies Journal*, 5 (1997), pp. 57–92

Yapp, M. (1996), *The Near East Since the First World War* (London, Longman, 1991)

Young, J., *Britain and the World in the Twentieth Century* (London, Arnold, 1997)

Young, J., *The Labour Governments 1964–70: Vol. 2 International Policy* (Manchester, Manchester University Press, 2003)

Ziegler, P., *Mountbatten* (London, Fontana, 1985)

Index